TASTES
TO
ASTONISH

TASTES TO ASTONISH

*Recipes That Tease the Palate
and Tantalize the Tongue*

Sandra Granseth
Sharyl Heiken
Rosemary Hutchinson
Liz Woolever

HPBooks

HPBooks
Published by The Berkley Publishing Group
200 Madison Avenue
New York, NY 10016
A member of Penguin Putnam Inc.

Copyright © 1997 by Spectrum Communication Services, Inc.
Book design by Rhea Braunstein
Cover design by Charles Björklund
Cover photograph by Alan Richardson

First edition: September 1997

Published simultaneously in Canada.

The Putnam Berkley World Wide Web site address is http://www.berkley.com

Library of Congress Cataloging-in-Publication Data
Granseth, Sandra.
    Tastes to astonish : recipes that tease the palate and tantalize the tongue / Sandra Granseth . . .
    [et al.].—1st ed.
        p.   cm.
    Includes index.
    ISBN 1-55788-273-8
    1. Cookery.
TX714.G7423 1997   96-54292
641.5—dc21   CIP

Printed in the United States of America

10   9   8   7   6   5   4   3   2   1

We dedicate this book to our families,
who always have believed in us
and given us much love and support

ACKNOWLEDGMENTS

We wish to thank our publisher, John Duff, for giving us the opportunity to write this book; our editor, Jeanette Egan, who thoroughly read every word and answered our questions; and our agent, Jane Dystel, who, with seemingly limitless energy, has given us invaluable advice and assistance.

CONTENTS

INTRODUCTION

Portobello mushrooms, mascarpone cheese, chayote, dried cherries—these and dozens of other foods have gone from exotic names on restaurant menus to commonly available ingredients. As new food markets spring up and the long-established ones expand, all of us have access to the widest range of food products in history. Those of you who enjoy good food as much as we do are searching for recipes that take advantage of this astounding array of ingredients. You're eager to experience bolder flavors and try dishes from unfamiliar ethnic cuisines. You're also looking for new and creative recipes to use when cooking for family or entertaining friends.

In *Tastes to Astonish,* we meet your demand for imaginative cuisine by focusing on sensational ingredient and flavor combinations. We give you exciting recipes woven into a unique style of lively cooking. This book features more than two hundred extraordinary recipes that showcase great-tasting foods. From appetizers to desserts, ingredients are combined in different and delightful ways: portobello mushroom strudel; soup from roasted eggplant and tomatoes; potato and asparagus salad with walnut vinaigrette; fennel and carrots with caviar cream; veal with dried cherries and green peppercorns; chicken with tomatillo and chipotle chile salsa; tomato, basil, and caramelized onion pizza. These and dozens of other fascinating ideas will entice you into the kitchen time and time again.

As you open *Tastes to Astonish,* you will embark on a culinary adventure filled with delectable recipes and interesting personal food anecdotes. Each recipe is broken down into easy-to-follow steps with clearly written directions. In addition to ingredients and techniques that are up-to-the-minute, the book also has helpful buying information and storage tips. Reading and using this cookbook is like having a friend in the kitchen. Our secrets to success will help guarantee that each dish will turn out perfectly for you every time.

Tastes to Astonish captures the essence of increasingly popular bold flavors—the best in "real food." If you're always looking for inspiring cookbooks with great-tasting recipes, this one is the perfect addition to your collection.

SASSY APPETIZERS AND SNACKS

Whatever type of gathering you're planning, you'll find some sensational new ideas for menu starters or between-meal munching in this chapter. Where did the recipes come from? We poked into restaurants, scoured cookbooks, and tasted dozens of dishes at family and neighborhood gatherings. Then, we blended the best of what we found with up-to-the-minute new ingredients and a pinch of our own creativity. What we came up with was this full-flavored array of dips, pâtés, hot appetizers, and cold tidbits that have plenty of pizzazz.

For a dazzling dip, try Roasted Red Pepper Dip with Crudités. We started with roasted red bell peppers and tangy chèvre, then whirled them together with balsamic vinegar, fresh basil, garlic, and a little hot pepper sauce. As a headliner for an appetizer buffet, we recommend Bourbon-Pecan Country Pâté. The combination of this savory pâté served with dill pickle slices and dark rye bread is irresistible. Mesquite-Grilled Beef with Ginger–Red Onion Relish makes an intriguing first course. The smoky flavor of these miniature kabobs blends wonderfully with the refreshing cilantro- and ginger-accented relish. And, remember Fanning-the-Flame Empanadas when everyone comes over to watch the big game on TV. Choose from either the Spicy Picadillo or Peppery Black Bean Fillings.

Whenever you're tired of the same old appetizers and snacks, turn to this chapter for inspiration. You're sure to find an idea or two that's just what you're looking for.

Zesty Jicama Salsa with Crispy Tortilla Chips

Sandra's son, Aaron, likes all kinds of salsas, especially the hot ones. This bright red salsa gets its terrific flavor from jicama and summer-ripe tomatoes, and its fire from jalapeño chiles. The red onion and cilantro also add a touch of pizzazz.

2 to 3 fresh jalapeño chiles
5 medium-size garden-ripe tomatoes, peeled and coarsely chopped (3 cups)
1 cup peeled and finely chopped jicama
¼ cup finely chopped red onion or green onions
2 tablespoons minced fresh cilantro or parsley

2 tablespoons fresh lime juice or lemon juice
1 teaspoon minced garlic
½ teaspoon salt
Crispy Tortilla Chips (see below) or blue tortilla chips

CRISPY TORTILLA CHIPS
10 (7-inch) flour tortillas

Wearing plastic or rubber gloves to protect your skin from the oils in the chiles, halve the chiles lengthwise; discard the stems, seeds, and membranes. Mince the chiles. In a medium-size bowl, combine the jalapeño chiles, tomatoes, jicama, onion, cilantro or parsley, lime or lemon juice, garlic, and salt. Cover and refrigerate at least 1 hour (will keep for up to 3 days).

While the salsa is chilling, prepare the Crispy Tortilla Chips; set aside.

Before serving, bring the salsa to room temperature. Serve the salsa with the homemade or blue tortilla chips.

Makes about 4 cups, about 16 servings.

CRISPY TORTILLA CHIPS
Preheat the oven to 350°F (175°C). Cut each flour tortilla into 8 wedges. Place in a single layer on large ungreased baking sheets. Bake 5 to 8 minutes or until the tortilla wedges are dry and crisp. Serve right away or cool and store in a covered container up to 3 days.

Makes 80 chips.

VARIATION
When garden-ripe tomatoes are not available, use a combination of 1 (14½-oz.) can diced tomatoes, with juice, and 1¼ cups peeled and coarsely chopped fresh tomatoes instead.

Brandied Gorgonzola Cheese Ball

"*Growing up I always looked forward to the blue cheese ball my mother served as an appetizer at family parties,*" *Rosemary recalls.* "*When I started cooking on my own, I developed this more sophisticated version of my childhood favorite. It features a tantalizing mixture of Gorgonzola cheese, fontina cheese, dried fruit bits, sour cream, and brandy.*"

1 (8-ounce) package cream cheese, cut up
1½ cups shredded fontina cheese or Gouda cheese (6 ounces)
½ cup crumbled Gorgonzola cheese (2 ounces)
2 tablespoons butter
½ cup sour cream

2 tablespoons brandy or low-fat (1%) milk
⅔ cup mixed dried fruit bits
12 pickled grape leaves or 1⅓ cups toasted finely chopped pecans or walnuts (see Tip, page 47)
Apple slices dipped in orange juice
Assorted crackers

Let the cream cheese, fontina or Gouda cheese, Gorgonzola cheese, and butter come to room temperature. In a medium-size bowl, combine the cheeses, butter, sour cream, and brandy or milk. Beat with an electric mixer at low speed until combined. Stir in the fruit bits. Cover and refrigerate 1 hour or until the mixture is firm enough to shape.

Meanwhile, if using the grape leaves, separate the leaves. Cover the leaves with cold water. Let stand 30 minutes; drain and pat dry with paper towels.

Divide the chilled cheese mixture into 4 portions. Shape each portion into a ball. Wrap a few of the grape leaves around each cheese ball. Or, place the finely chopped pecans or walnuts on waxed paper and roll the cheese balls in the nuts. Wrap each cheese ball in plastic wrap. Refrigerate at least 2 hours or until firm or overnight.

To serve, unwrap the cheese balls. Peel back the grape leaves, if using. Serve the cheese balls with the apple slices and the crackers.

Makes 4 balls, about 16 servings.

VARIATION

If you can't find Gorgonzola, substitute blue, Roquefort, or Stilton cheeses.

Mesquite-Grilled Beef with Ginger–Red Onion Relish

Start off your next dinner party with style by serving this elegant first course. Grilling these steak-and-pepper kabobs over mesquite adds an enticing smoky flavor.

2 cups mesquite or hickory wood
    chunks or chips
Ginger–Red Onion Relish (see below)
1 pound boneless beef top sirloin
    steak, trimmed of fat and cut into
    1-inch cubes
2 tablespoons cracked black pepper
16 (¾-inch) cubes fresh pineapple

GINGER–RED ONION RELISH
2 tablespoons olive oil
1 large red onion, quartered
    lengthwise and thinly sliced
1 tablespoon minced gingerroot
¼ cup fresh lime juice
1 tablespoon minced fresh cilantro
    or parsley
1 teaspoon sugar
⅛ teaspoon salt
⅛ teaspoon ground black pepper

In a large bowl, cover the wood chunks or chips with water. Let stand at least 1 hour; drain well. Cover 8 (6-inch) bamboo skewers with water. Let stand 30 minutes; drain. Prepare the Ginger–Red Onion Relish; set aside.

For the beef skewers, thread 3 pieces of beef onto each bamboo skewer, leaving ¼ inch space between the pieces. (Leaving a little space between the pieces of meat allows the meat to cook evenly.) Roll the beef in the 2 tablespoons cracked pepper, pressing it into the surface of the meat.

In an uncovered grill, arrange preheated coals in the firebox; test the coals for medium heat (see Tip, page 18). Sprinkle the wood chunks on the hot coals. Place the beef skewers on the grill rack directly over the coals. Grill 12 to 14 minutes or until the beef has reached desired degree of doneness, turning the skewers after half of the cooking time. (Or, place the beef skewers on the unheated rack of a broiler pan. Broil 4 to 5 inches from the heat 5 to 7 minutes or until desired doneness is reached, turning after half of the cooking time.)

To serve, add 2 pineapple cubes to the end of each skewer. Serve the beef-pineapple skewers with the relish.

Makes 8 servings.

GINGER–RED ONION RELISH

In a large skillet, heat the olive oil over medium heat. Add the onion and gingerroot. Reduce heat to medium low and cook, stirring frequently, 20 minutes or until the onion is very soft and golden. Stir in the lime juice, cilantro or parsley, sugar, salt, and black pepper. Simmer 3 to 4 minutes or until most of the liquid has evaporated. Cool to room temperature.

Makes about 1 cup.

After lighting the coals, you can tell that they're ready if they look ash gray during the daytime or glow red after dark. This usually takes 20 to 30 minutes for regular briquettes. Be sure to soak the wood chunks or chips so they will smolder rather than flame when you add them to the hot coals.

Deviled Green Tapénade

Traditional French tapénade is made from oil-cured ripe olives. This contemporary version boasts the bold flavors of green olives, capers, anchovy paste, and Dijon mustard. It's equally tasty spread on crusty French bread as an appetizer or spooned over cold roast beef or grilled lamb as a condiment.

1 cup drained pitted green olives
3 tablespoons olive oil
1 tablespoon minced fresh basil or
   1 teaspoon dried basil leaves
1 tablespoon drained capers
1 tablespoon anchovy paste

1 tablespoon sake or dry sherry
2 teaspoons Dijon mustard
1 teaspoon freshly grated
   orange peel
¼ teaspoon ground black pepper
French bread chunks or breadsticks

In a food processor or blender, combine the green olives, olive oil, basil, capers, anchovy paste, sake or sherry, Dijon mustard, orange peel, and pepper. Cover and process until nearly smooth.

Transfer the tapénade to a serving bowl. Cover and refrigerate at least 1 hour or up to 3 days.

Serve the tapénade with chunks of crusty French bread or breadsticks.

Makes about ¾ cup, 4 to 6 servings.

Tequila Shrimp with Sun-Dried Tomato Aïoli

Succulent shrimp, marinated in a zesty mixture of tequila, lime juice, and cilantro and served with aïoli (garlic-flavored mayonnaise), are showcased in this attractive appetizer. We've found that marinating is easier if you place the shrimp and marinade mixture in a self-sealing plastic bag.

1 pound fresh or thawed frozen large
   shrimp, shelled and deveined
4 cups water
½ teaspoon salt
½ cup tequila
¼ cup finely chopped onion
¼ cup fresh lime juice
2 tablespoons minced fresh cilantro
   or parsley
2 tablespoons olive oil
Sun-Dried Tomato Aïoli (see below)
Cilantro sprig or parsley sprig,
   for garnish

Crushed ice
Lime wedges

SUN-DRIED TOMATO AÏOLI
½ cup sun-dried tomatoes
   (dry packed)
1 cup mayonnaise
1 tablespoon minced fresh cilantro
   or parsley
1 tablespoon low-fat (1%) milk
1 teaspoon minced garlic
⅛ teaspoon salt

Rinse the shrimp. In a large saucepan, bring the water and salt to a boil. Add the shrimp. Return to a boil, reduce heat, and simmer, stirring occasionally, 1 to 3 minutes or until the shrimp are opaque throughout. Drain. Rinse under cold running water; drain again. Place the shrimp in a heavy plastic bag.

For the marinade, combine the tequila, onion, lime juice, minced cilantro or parsley, and olive oil. Pour over the shrimp; seal bag. Marinate in the refrigerator 4 to 6 hours, turning occasionally.

While the shrimp are marinating, prepare the Sun-Dried Tomato Aïoli. Transfer the aïoli to a serving bowl; cover and refrigerate.

To serve, garnish the aïoli with the cilantro or parsley sprig. Set the bowl of aïoli on a small serving platter. Line the platter with the crushed ice. Drain the shrimp, discarding the marinade. Arrange the shrimp and lime wedges on top of the ice.

Makes 8 servings.

SUN-DRIED TOMATO AÏOLI

In a small bowl, cover the sun-dried tomatoes with boiling water. Let stand 5 minutes; drain well. Finely chop the tomatoes. In another small bowl, combine the tomatoes, mayonnaise, cilantro or parsley, milk, garlic, and salt.

Makes about 1½ cups.

◆ TIP

This delicious mayonnaise sauce also is good with cold roast beef, cold grilled chicken, or cold cuts. It's even good on salads; just thin it with a little milk before drizzling the mixture over vegetable salads. The sauce will keep in the refrigerator for up to 5 days.

Roasted Red Pepper Dip with Crudités

The garlic and hot pepper sauce in this elegant, full-flavored dip bring out the natural sweetness of roasted red bell peppers. For an attractive presentation, Sandra serves the dip in a hollowed-out red bell pepper with a selection of her favorite raw vegetables.

2 medium-size red bell peppers
4 ounces chèvre cheese (goat cheese)
1 (3-ounce) package cream cheese, at room temperature
2 tablespoons balsamic vinegar
1 tablespoon minced fresh basil or 1 teaspoon dried basil leaves
1 teaspoon minced garlic
¼ teaspoon hot pepper sauce

Assorted crudités, including jicama, kohlrabi, fennel, carrot, or celery sticks; sugar snap peas; asparagus spears; green onions; fresh mushrooms; cherry tomatoes; radishes; zucchini, yellow summer squash, or cucumber slices or spears; and/or cauliflower or broccoli flowerets
Breadsticks or assorted crackers

Preheat the oven to 425°F (220°C). To roast the bell peppers, line a baking sheet with foil; set aside. Quarter the peppers lengthwise; discard the stems, seeds, and membranes. Cut small slits in the ends of the pepper pieces to make them lie flat. Place the pepper pieces, smooth side up, on the prepared baking sheet. Bake 20 to 25 minutes or until the skins are bubbly and dark brown. Immediately place the peppers in a paper or heavy plastic bag; seal the bag. Let stand 20 to 30 minutes or until the peppers are cool enough to handle. Using a sharp knife, carefully peel the peppers.

In a food processor or blender, combine the roasted peppers, the chèvre cheese, cream cheese, balsamic vinegar, basil, garlic, and hot pepper sauce. Cover and process until nearly smooth. Transfer the dip to a serving bowl. Cover and refrigerate at least 1 hour or up to 3 days.

Serve the dip with the crudités and the breadsticks or crackers.

Makes about 1½ cups, about 8 servings.

VARIATION

This dip is best made with fresh red bell peppers. But in a pinch, use 1 (7-ounce) jar roasted red peppers, drained.

Fanning-the-Flame Empanadas

We've designed these empanadas to work with either of two savory fillings. The Spicy Picadillo Filling is made with pork sausage and seasoned to taste like chorizo, the traditional Mexican hot sausage. The Peppery Black Bean Filling has a mild lime flavor with a hint of hotness.

Spicy Picadillo Filling or Peppery
   Black Bean Filling (see opposite)
3 cups all-purpose flour
½ teaspoon baking powder
¼ teaspoon salt
1 cup (4 ounces) shredded Monterey
   Jack cheese with jalapeño chiles
¾ cup vegetable shortening
1 egg, lightly beaten
½ cup low-fat (1%) milk
1 egg mixed with 1 tablespoon water,
   for glaze
Sour cream

SPICY PICADILLO FILLING
6 ounces ground pork
1 teaspoon minced garlic
⅓ cup peeled and coarsely chopped
   tomato

⅓ cup peeled and chopped tart apple
2 tablespoons raisins
1 tablespoon thinly sliced pimiento-
   stuffed green olives
1 teaspoon paprika
1 teaspoon drained capers
½ teaspoon crushed red pepper
½ teaspoon ground cinnamon
½ teaspoon ground cumin
⅛ teaspoon ground cloves

PEPPERY BLACK BEAN FILLING
1 (15-ounce) can black beans, rinsed
   and drained
2 tablespoons fresh lime juice
½ teaspoon ground coriander
¼ teaspoon hot pepper sauce
⅛ teaspoon ground black pepper

Prepare the Spicy Picadillo Filling or the Peppery Black Bean Filling. Cover and refrigerate at least 1 hour.

Preheat the oven to 425°F (220°C). Line 2 baking sheets with foil; set aside. For the pastry, in a large bowl, combine the flour, baking powder, and salt. Using a pastry cutter or 2 knives, cut in the cheese and shortening until the mixture resembles coarse crumbs. Make a well in the center. In a small bowl, combine the lightly beaten egg and milk; add to the flour mixture. Using a fork, stir until the dry ingredients are moistened.

Turn out onto a lightly floured surface. Gently knead 12 to 15 strokes or only until the dough holds together. Divide the dough in half. Roll out half of the dough to about ⅛-inch thickness. Using a round 3-inch cutter, cut out the dough, dipping the cutter into flour between cuts as needed to prevent sticking. Repeat with the remaining dough, making 40 pastry rounds total.

Place 1 slightly rounded teaspoon of the picadillo or bean filling in the center of each pastry round. Lightly moisten the edge of the pastry with a little water. Gently fold 1 edge of the pastry over the filling to make a semicircle. Using the floured tines of a fork, press the edges of the pastry together to seal. Prick the top of each pastry with the fork several times so steam can escape.

Place the pastries on the prepared baking sheets. Brush the pastries with the egg glaze. Bake 15 to 18 minutes or until golden brown. Serve the empanadas warm with the sour cream.
Makes 40 empanadas.

SPICY PICADILLO FILLING

In a large skillet, cook the ground pork and garlic until the meat is cooked through, breaking up the meat as it cooks. Drain off fat. Stir in the tomato, apple, raisins, green olives, paprika, capers, crushed red pepper, cinnamon, cumin, and cloves. Cover and simmer 20 minutes, stirring occasionally.
Makes about 1¼ cups.

PEPPERY BLACK BEAN FILLING

In a food processor or blender, combine the black beans, lime juice, coriander, hot pepper sauce, and black pepper. Cover and process until nearly smooth.
Makes about 1¼ cups.

Bourbon-Pecan Country Pâté

A delectable combination of ground turkey, pork, and prunes accented with bourbon, brandy, and spices, this old-fashioned pâté is perfect as a first course or as part of an appetizer buffet. Sharyl points out that placing a weight on the pâté and refrigerating it overnight is the secret to a well-shaped loaf that cuts into thin, even slices.

½ cup bourbon
16 pitted prunes
1¼ pounds ground turkey
   or chicken
1¼ pounds ground pork or veal
1 cup finely chopped green onions
½ cup toasted finely chopped pecans
⅓ cup Cognac or other brandy
1 teaspoon ground nutmeg
   or cinnamon

1 teaspoon ground ginger or allspice
¾ teaspoon salt
½ teaspoon ground black pepper
Red-leaf lettuce leaves
Soft-style cream cheese, at room
   temperature, for garnish
Dill pickle slices
Dark rye bread or assorted crackers

In a small saucepan, bring the bourbon just to a boil. Remove from heat. Add the prunes; let stand 15 minutes. Drain the prunes, reserving the bourbon.

Preheat the oven to 350°F (175°C). In a large bowl, combine the reserved bourbon, the turkey or chicken, pork or veal, green onions, pecans, Cognac or other brandy, nutmeg or cinnamon, ginger or allspice, salt, and pepper; mix well. Press half of the meat mixture into a 9 x 5-inch loaf pan. Arrange the prunes in 2 rows down the center of the loaf. Press the remaining meat mixture on top of the prunes. Cover with foil.

Place the loaf pan in a 13 x 9-inch baking pan. Pour boiling water into the baking pan to a depth of 1 inch. Bake 1¼ hours. Remove foil; bake 20 to 25 minutes or until the meat mixture is set and firm to the touch.

Remove from the oven; drain well. Press a sheet of foil against the surface of the meat. Place another 9 x 5- or an 8 x 4-inch loaf pan on top of the hot meat mixture. Press down very firmly to compress the meat mixture. Drain again. Set a heavy weight (such as a large can of fruit) inside the empty loaf pan. Refrigerate the pâté at least 12 hours or overnight.

To serve, line a serving plate with the lettuce leaves. Remove the weight and foil from the pâté. Invert the pâté onto the lettuce; remove the pan. Garnish the pâté by piping the cream cheese around the top. Thinly slice the pâté; serve with the pickles and the rye bread or crackers.

Makes 18 servings.

Crostini with Smoked Trout and Camembert

Whether served as the first course of a special meal or as an accompaniment with your favorite tossed salad, these crisp Italian-style canapés are truly memorable. The tangy tomatoes and crunchy walnuts contrast deliciously with the smoky flavor of the fish and the creamy texture of the Camembert.

1 (4½-ounce) package Camembert
   cheese
1 (3-ounce) package cream cheese
2 tablespoons butter
1 tablespoon low-fat (1%) milk
6 ounces smoked trout, whitefish, or
   salmon, skin and bones removed
   and broken into small pieces

1 (12-ounce) loaf unsliced baguette-
   style French bread
½ (8-ounce) jar sun-dried tomatoes
   (oil packed)
⅓ cup finely chopped walnuts
Small fresh basil leaves or minced
   fresh basil, for garnish

For the spread, let the Camembert cheese, cream cheese, and butter come to room temperature. In a food processor or blender, combine the Camembert cheese, cream cheese, butter, and milk. Cover and process until smooth. Transfer to a small bowl. Stir in the trout, whitefish, or salmon. Cover and refrigerate at least 1 hour or up to 2 days.

For the crostini, preheat the oven to 300°F (150°C). Line 2 baking sheets with foil. Cut the French bread into 40 (¼-inch-thick) slices. Arrange the bread slices in a single layer on the prepared baking sheets. Drain the sun-dried tomatoes, reserving the oil. Lightly brush 1 side of each bread slice with some of the reserved oil. Bake 12 minutes or until golden brown, turning the bread slices over after half of the baking time. Cool.

For the topping, finely chop the sun-dried tomatoes. Cover and refrigerate. Before serving, let the sun-dried tomatoes come to room temperature. In a small bowl, combine the tomatoes and walnuts.

To serve, spread some of the trout mixture on the oiled side of each crostini, leaving a small rim around the outside edge. Spoon a little of the tomato mixture on top of the trout mixture. Garnish with the basil.

Makes 40 servings.

✦ TIP

To make the French bread easier to slice, partially freeze the loaf before cutting it with a serrated knife. If you want to make the crostini ahead, bake the bread slices and let them cool completely, then store them in a covered container or heavy plastic bag up to 3 days.

Caramelized-Onion Tarts with Jarlsberg Cheese Pastry

The slightly sweet Norwegian Jarlsberg cheese in the flaky pastry accents the mellow flavor of the caramelized-onion filling in these sophisticated appetizers. Serve them with champagne or a dry white wine, such as chardonnay, pinot chardonnay, or sauvignon blanc.

1 tablespoon butter
1 medium-size onion, quartered
    lengthwise and thinly sliced
1 teaspoon minced garlic
2 eggs, lightly beaten
⅓ cup half-and-half or whole milk
⅛ teaspoon salt
⅛ teaspoon ground cardamom
    or nutmeg
⅛ teaspoon ground black pepper
Jarlsberg Cheese Pastry (see opposite)
Minced fresh chives, for garnish

JARLSBERG CHEESE PASTRY
1 cup all-purpose flour
1 tablespoon sesame seeds
¼ teaspoon salt
⅓ cup vegetable shortening
⅓ cup (about 1½ ounces) shredded
    Jarlsberg cheese or Swiss cheese
2 to 3 tablespoons ice-cold water

In a large saucepan, melt the butter over medium heat. Add the onion and garlic. Reduce heat to medium-low and cook, stirring occasionally, 20 minutes or until the onion is very soft and golden. In a small bowl, combine the eggs, half-and-half or whole milk, salt, cardamom or nutmeg, and pepper; set aside.

Preheat the oven to 375°F (190°C). Generously grease 24 (1¾-inch) muffin cups; set aside.

Prepare the Jarlsberg Cheese Pastry. Turn out onto a lightly floured surface. Roll out the pastry into a 12-inch circle. Using a round 2¾-inch cutter, cut out the pastry, dipping the cutter into flour between cuts as needed to prevent sticking. Reroll scraps and cut out the pastry as needed to make 24 pastry rounds total.

Gently press the pastry rounds into the prepared muffin cups, pleating the pastry as needed to fit into each cup. Press the edge of the pastry back slightly. Place equal amounts of the onion mixture in the bottom of each pastry shell. Spoon a scant 1 tablespoon of the egg mixture over the onion mixture in each pastry shell. Bake 35 minutes or until the filling is puffed and golden brown and the edges of the pastry are light brown. Cool in the pans on wire racks 5 minutes. Remove the tarts from the pans.

Garnish with the chives. Serve the tarts warm or chilled.

Makes 24 tarts.

JARLSBERG CHEESE PASTRY

In a medium-size bowl, stir together the flour, sesame seeds, and salt. Using a pastry cutter or 2 knives, cut in the shortening and cheese until the mixture resembles coarse crumbs. Sprinkle 1 tablespoon of the water over part of the flour mixture and toss together with a fork.

Push the moistened mixture to one side of the bowl. Repeat, using enough of the remaining water, 1 tablespoon at a time, until all of the flour mixture is moistened. Form the dough into a ball.

+ TIP

Be sure to press each pastry round evenly against the bottom and side of a muffin cup. If the pastry is too thin in any one place, the tart may crack as it bakes, allowing the filling to leak through the pastry.

Caribbean Sweet Cheese and Papaya Dip

There's nothing quite like a ripe papaya. It's creamy, fragrant, and tastes like a luscious blend of peaches and melon. To take advantage of its irresistible tropical flavor, we've whirled it together with ricotta cheese, yogurt, rum, and a little sugar, then folded in some whipped cream. Scoop up the delightfully rich combination with pieces of mango, banana, carambola, or pineapple.

1 large ripe papaya, peeled, seeded, and quartered	½ cup whipping cream
1 cup ricotta cheese	Toasted coconut, for garnish
½ cup plain yogurt	Ti leaves or leaf lettuce leaves
2 tablespoons sugar	Assorted fresh tropical fruit,
2 tablespoons dark rum	including mango slices, banana
1 teaspoon pure vanilla extract	chunks, carambola (star fruit)
	slices, and/or pineapple spears

For the dip, combine the papaya, ricotta cheese, yogurt, sugar, rum, and vanilla in a food processor or blender. Cover and process until smooth. In a medium-size bowl, beat the whipping cream with an electric mixer at high speed just until soft peaks form. Gently fold the papaya mixture into the whipped cream.

Transfer the dip to a serving bowl. Cover and refrigerate at least 1 hour or up to several hours.

To serve, sprinkle the dip with the toasted coconut. Set the bowl of dip on a large serving platter. Line the platter with the ti or lettuce leaves. Arrange the tropical fruit on top of the greens.

Makes about 3¼ cups, 12 to 14 servings.

+ TIP

To keep the banana chunks from turning brown, dip them in lemon juice mixed with a little water before arranging them on the serving platter.

Portobello Mushroom & Spinach Strudel

This appealing version is proof positive that strudel is just as delicious as an appetizer as it is as a dessert. It gets its exquisite flavor from meaty portobello mushrooms, spinach, basil, and feta cheese. Liz cleans these gigantic mushrooms by wiping them with a damp paper towel. "Don't soak them in water," she cautions. "Soaking ruins their texture."

8 ounces fresh portobello
   mushrooms
1 tablespoon butter
1 pound fresh spinach, chopped
   (4 cups)
¼ cup minced fresh basil
1 cup ricotta cheese
¾ cup (3 ounces) crumbled feta
   cheese

2 eggs, lightly beaten
¼ teaspoon ground black pepper
1 (17¼-ounce) package frozen puff
   pastry sheets, thawed 20 minutes
1 tablespoon butter, melted
2 tablespoons dry bread crumbs
1 egg mixed with 1 tablespoon water,
   for glaze

Preheat the oven to 400°F (205°C). Line 2 baking sheets with foil; lightly grease the foil. Set aside.

Cut off the mushroom stems; discard. Coarsely chop the mushroom caps. In a 12-inch nonstick skillet, melt the 1 tablespoon butter over high heat. Add the chopped mushrooms and cook, stirring constantly, 3 to 4 minutes or until tender. Remove the mushrooms. Add the spinach and basil. Reduce heat to medium, cover, and cook, stirring once or twice, 3 to 4 minutes or until the spinach is tender. Drain well.

For the filling, in a medium-size bowl, combine the ricotta cheese, feta cheese, lightly beaten eggs, and pepper. Stir in the mushrooms and spinach; mix well.

Unfold the puff pastry. For the first loaf, place one of the pastry sheets on a prepared baking sheet. Brush the pastry sheet with half of the 1 tablespoon melted butter. Sprinkle half of the bread crumbs in a 3-inch-wide strip down the center of the pastry to within 1 inch of the ends. Spread half of the filling on top of the bread crumbs.

On the long sides, cut the pastry sheet into strips, cutting from the edge of the filling to the edge of the pastry at 1-inch intervals. Starting at one end, alternately fold opposite strips of pastry at an angle across the filling. For the second loaf, repeat with the remaining pastry sheet, melted butter, bread crumbs, and filling.

Brush the loaves with the egg glaze. Bake 35 minutes or until the bottoms of the loaves are brown. Cool on wire racks 5 minutes.

To serve, cut each loaf crosswise into 6 slices, then lengthwise to make 12 pieces.
Makes 24 servings.

◆ TIP

The best portobello mushrooms are those that are firm, plump, and uniformly colored, with no bruises or blemishes.

Brie and Chutney Phyllo Tarts

The tantalizing trio of crispy phyllo, velvety brie, and tongue-tingling chutney makes these delicate tarts hard to pass up. Sandra especially likes them made with spicy yet tangy mango chutney. Shop for it at Asian food markets or larger supermarkets.

1 (4½-ounce) wedge of Brie cheese
    or round of Camembert cheese
¾ cup toasted chopped walnuts
    or pecans
½ cup chutney, finely chopped
1 tablespoon rum or orange juice

4 (18 x 14-inch) sheets frozen phyllo
    dough, thawed
3 tablespoons butter, melted
Fresh strawberries
Apple wedges or pear wedges dipped
    in orange juice

Preheat the oven to 375°F (190°C). Cut the Brie or Camembert cheese into 24 equal pieces. In a small bowl, combine the walnuts or pecans, chutney, and rum or orange juice; set aside.

Lightly brush 1 sheet of phyllo dough with some of the melted butter, keeping the remaining sheets covered with a slightly moistened cloth. Place another sheet of phyllo on top of the first sheet and brush with butter. Repeat with the remaining phyllo and butter. Cut the phyllo stack lengthwise into 4 strips. (Kitchen scissors work well for cutting the phyllo dough.) Cut each strip crosswise into 6 rectangles.

Gently press the rectangles into 24 (1¾-inch) muffin cups, pleating the phyllo dough as needed to fit into each cup. Press the corners of the dough back slightly. Spoon a scant 1 tablespoon of the nut mixture into the center of each phyllo cup. Place 1 piece of cheese on top of the nut mixture in each cup. Bake 10 to 12 minutes or until the phyllo dough is golden brown. Cool in the pans on wire racks 5 minutes. Remove the tarts from the pans.

Serve the tarts warm or at room temperature with the strawberries and apple or pear wedges dipped in orange juice. (Once cut, the apples and pears will brown easily unless they're dipped in the orange juice.)

Makes 24 tarts.

◆ TIP

When thawing the frozen phyllo dough, be sure to keep it wrapped. Once it is unwrapped, the phyllo sheets will quickly dry out and become brittle. As soon as you remove the sheets you need, rewrap the remaining sheets and return them to the freezer.

SUPERB SOUPS AND STEWS

A brimful bowl of steaming soup is hard to beat when you're hungry. And this comforting collection of soups and stews offers you lots of tantalizing choices. To create these dynamite dishes, we grabbed our soup kettles and pulled out all the stops when it came to adding high-impact ingredients.

As you scan the chapter, you'll find Fire-and-Smoke Burgundy Sirloin Stew, Roasted Three-Pepper and Pork Stew, and Lamb Stew with Couscous all make the most of succulent meats and robust seasonings. If chicken is more your style, make Chicken and Orzo Soup with Fennel. These Old World–inspired combinations capitalize on enticing ethnic ingredients. As for fish and seafood, there's everything from Caribbean Soffrito and Shrimp Soup to Curried Fish Bisque. These meal-in-a-pot medleys are exquisitely seasoned to create a bold taste without covering up the delicate fish or seafood. When you're in the mood for meatless, simmer up some East Indian Spiced Red Lentil Soup or Tuscan White Bean and Vegetable Soup. And, for a light meal, serve a sandwich or salad with one of our spirited side-dish soups, such as Fresh Garden Pea and Pasta Soup with Mint Crème Fraîche, or Roasted Eggplant and Tomato Soup.

The next time you say "This is a good day for soup," head for the kitchen and try one of our stick-to-the-ribs soups or stews. We're sure you'll be delighted with the results.

Fire-and-Smoke Burgundy Sirloin Stew

This remarkable stew has the same bold flavors as classic beef burgundy, but adds a new dimension—the slightly sweet flavor that comes from grilling the meat over hickory wood.

1 pound boneless beef top sirloin steak, 1 inch thick and trimmed of fat

3 cups baby-cut carrots (see Tip, page 80)

2 medium-size onions, quartered lengthwise and thinly sliced

1½ cups Burgundy wine

2 tablespoons olive oil or vegetable oil

1 tablespoon minced fresh marjoram or 1 teaspoon dried marjoram leaves

1 tablespoon minced fresh rosemary or 1 teaspoon dried rosemary leaves

¾ teaspoon crushed red pepper

3 cups hickory or mesquite wood chunks or chips

1¾ cups Beef Stock (page 42) or 1 (14½-ounce) can beef broth

2 cups sliced fresh mushrooms

1 (8-ounce) can tomato sauce

¼ cup minced fresh parsley

Place the steak, carrots, and onions in a large heavy plastic bag. For the marinade, combine the burgundy, oil, marjoram, rosemary, and red pepper. Pour the marinade over the meat and vegetables; seal bag. Marinate in the refrigerator 8 to 24 hours, turning occasionally.

In a large bowl, cover the wood chunks or chips with water. Let stand at least 1 hour; drain well.

Remove the meat from the bag, reserving the vegetables and marinade. Pat the meat dry with paper towels. Set the vegetables and marinade aside.

In a large saucepan, combine the reserved vegetables and marinade and the Beef Stock or broth and bring to a boil. Reduce heat, cover, and simmer 20 to 25 minutes or until the vegetables are crisp-tender.

Meanwhile, in an uncovered grill, arrange preheated coals in the firebox; test the coals for medium heat. Sprinkle the wood chunks on the hot coals. Place the meat on the grill rack directly over the coals. Grill 14 minutes, turning the meat after half of the cooking time. (Or, place the meat on the unheated rack of a broiler pan. Broil 4 to 5 inches from the heat 10 minutes, turning after half of the cooking time.) Cool the meat slightly; cut into ¾-inch cubes.

Add the meat pieces, mushrooms, and tomato sauce to the vegetables and broth. Return to a boil. Reduce heat, cover, and simmer 5 minutes or until the meat is heated through.

To serve, ladle the stew into soup bowls. Sprinkle the stew with the parsley.

Makes 6 servings.

◆ TIP

To test the temperature of the preheated coals, place your hand above the coals, or above the drip pan, at the height the food will be cooked. Start counting the seconds, "one thousand one, one thousand two." If you need to remove your hand after 2 seconds, the coals are hot; after 3 seconds, they're medium-hot; after 4 seconds, they're medium; after 5 seconds, they're medium-slow; and after 6 seconds, they're slow.

Chicken and Orzo Soup with Fennel

This aromatic, fresh-tasting dish was inspired by ingredients popular in the cooking of the Mediterranean region—ripe olives, fennel, and orzo. For a satisfying supper, just add some bread-sticks or crusty French bread.

1 bulb fennel	2 tablespoons minced fresh basil or
3¹⁄₂ cups Chicken Stock (page 42)	2 teaspoons dried basil leaves
or 2 (14¹⁄₂-ounce) cans	1 tablespoon minced fresh thyme or
chicken broth	1 teaspoon dried thyme leaves
4 medium-size carrots, sliced	1 teaspoon minced garlic
1³⁄₄ cups chopped tomatoes or 1	¹⁄₄ teaspoon crushed red pepper
(14¹⁄₂-ounce) can diced tomatoes,	3¹⁄₂ cups chopped cooked chicken or
with juice	turkey
³⁄₄ cup dried orzo pasta	1 (2¹⁄₄-ounce) can sliced pitted ripe
³⁄₄ cup fresh orange juice	olives, drained
¹⁄₂ (6-ounce) can tomato paste	¹⁄₄ cup minced fresh parsley
(about ¹⁄₃ cup)	

Remove any tough or bruised outer leaves from the fennel bulb. Trim off the root end and the stems; discard. Thoroughly rinse the trimmed bulb and quarter the bulb lengthwise; remove the core. Chop the fennel. (You should have about 1¹⁄₂ cups.)

In a Dutch oven, combine the chopped fennel, the Chicken Stock or broth, carrots, tomatoes with their juice, orzo pasta, orange juice, tomato paste, basil, thyme, garlic, and red pepper and bring to a boil. Reduce heat, cover, and simmer, stirring occasionally, 15 minutes or until the carrots are tender and the pasta is firm-tender.

Stir in the chicken or turkey and ripe olives. Cook over medium heat, stirring occasionally, 2 to 3 minutes or until heated through.

To serve, ladle the soup into soup bowls. Sprinkle the soup with the parsley.

Makes 6 servings.

◆ TIP

Orzo is a tiny rice-shaped pasta. Sometimes it's called *rosamarina*.

Butternut Squash and Pork Ragoût
with Rich Blue Corn Bread

Pork stew with Southwestern seasonings is the perfect partner for tender corn bread made with blue cornmeal. Sandra makes the combination often and has this tip for getting everything ready: "While the meat simmers, I prepare the corn bread and get it in the oven. Then, I chop the vegetables for the ragoût. This way the ragoût and corn bread are ready at about the same time."

⅓ cup all-purpose flour
1 teaspoon dried marjoram leaves
1 teaspoon ground cumin
¼ teaspoon salt
¼ teaspoon ground black pepper
1 pound lean boneless pork or lamb, trimmed of fat and cut into ¾-inch cubes
1 tablespoon olive oil or vegetable oil
3½ cups Chicken Stock (page 42) or 2 (14½-ounce) cans chicken broth
Rich Blue Corn Bread (see opposite)
2 fresh jalapeño chiles
1¼ pounds butternut squash, peeled and cubed (3 cups)
2 cups pearl onions or frozen small whole onions

1¾ cups chopped tomatoes or 1 (14½-ounce) can tomato wedges, with juice
2 tablespoons fresh lime juice
¼ cup minced fresh cilantro or parsley
¼ cup toasted pine nuts

RICH BLUE CORN BREAD
1 cup all-purpose flour
1 cup blue or yellow cornmeal
¼ cup sugar
1 tablespoon baking powder
½ teaspoon baking soda
½ teaspoon salt
1 cup buttermilk
2 eggs, lightly beaten
¼ cup (½ stick) butter, melted

For the ragoût, in a paper or plastic bag, combine the flour, marjoram, cumin, salt, and pepper. Add the pork or lamb cubes, a few at a time, and shake to coat.

In a Dutch oven, heat the oil over medium-high heat. Add the meat, half at a time, and cook until browned on all sides. Drain off fat. Return all of the meat to the pan. Add the Chicken Stock or broth and bring to a boil. Reduce heat, cover, and simmer 35 minutes.

While the ragoût is simmering, prepare the cornbread.

Wearing plastic or rubber gloves to protect your skin from the oils in the chiles, halve the jalapeño chiles lengthwise; discard the stems, seeds, and membranes. Mince the chiles. Stir the jalapeño chiles, squash, onions, tomatoes with their juice, and lime juice into the broth mixture. Return to a boil. Reduce heat, cover, and simmer 20 to 25 minutes or until the meat is tender and the vegetables are crisp-tender. Stir in the cilantro or parsley.

To serve, ladle the ragoût into soup bowls. Sprinkle with the pine nuts. Serve the ragoût with the corn bread.

Makes 6 servings.

Preheat the oven to 425°F (220°C). Lightly grease an 8-inch-square baking pan; set aside.

In a large bowl, combine the flour, cornmeal, sugar, baking powder, baking soda, and salt. In a medium-size bowl, combine the buttermilk, eggs, and butter. Add to the flour mixture, stirring only until the dry ingredients are moistened.

Pour the batter into the prepared pan. Bake 20 minutes or until the corn bread is golden brown. Let stand in the pan on a wire rack 10 minutes. Cut into squares. Serve warm.

Turkey Kielbasa and Fresh Corn Chowder

We favor turkey kielbasa or another reduced-fat smoked sausage in this hearty chowder. The smoky flavor of the sausage accents the earthy black-eyed peas and slightly sweet corn and parsnips wonderfully.

4 ears of corn or 2 cups frozen
　　whole-kernel corn
1¾ cups Chicken Stock (page 42)
　　or 1 (14½-ounce) can chicken
　　broth
2 medium-size parsnips or potatoes,
　　peeled and cut into ½-inch pieces
1 large onion, chopped
2½ cups whole milk

1 (15-ounce) can black-eyed peas,
　　rinsed and drained
2 tablespoons butter
¼ teaspoon ground red
　　(cayenne) pepper
3 tablespoons all-purpose flour
8 ounces cooked turkey kielbasa,
　　cut into about ½-inch slices

If using the ears of corn, place 1 ear of corn at a time in a shallow pan. Holding the ear at an angle, use a sharp knife to cut down across the tips of the kernels. Using the dull side of the knife, scrape the ear to release the milky juices into the pan. Measure 2 cups of the corn with its juices.

In a large saucepan, combine the fresh or frozen corn, the Chicken Stock or broth, parsnips or potatoes, and onion. Bring to a boil. Reduce heat, cover, and simmer, stirring occasionally, 5 minutes or until the parsnips are nearly tender. Add 2 cups of the milk, the black-eyed peas, butter, and cayenne.

In a small bowl, combine the remaining ½ cup milk and the flour. Stir into the corn mixture. Cook over medium heat, stirring frequently, 5 minutes or until the mixture thickens. Stir in the turkey kielbasa. Cook, stirring frequently, 2 minutes or until heated through.

Makes 6 servings.

✦ TIP

A quick way to combine the cold milk and flour is to shake them together in a tightly sealed jar instead of mixing them in a bowl.

Roasted Three-Pepper and Pork Stew

"My husband loves hot food," says Rosemary, "but I'm a bit timid when it comes to spicy dishes. So sometimes we disagree on how much zip a recipe should have. This inviting pork stew, however, is one we both agree is terrific. The mulato and poblano chiles make it pleasantly hot, while the red bell peppers and sweet potatoes make it delightfully mellow."

2 dried mulato chiles or pasilla chiles
   (see Tip, opposite page)
3½ cups Beef Stock (page 42) or
   2 (14½-ounce) cans beef broth
3 medium-size red bell peppers
2 fresh poblano chiles
2 tablespoons butter
1 pound lean boneless pork or beef,
   trimmed of fat and cut into
   ¾-inch cubes
1½ cups dry red wine, Beef Stock
   (page 42), or beef broth
2 bay leaves

2 tablespoons minced fresh oregano
   or 2 teaspoons dried oregano
   leaves
1½ teaspoons minced garlic
3 medium-size potatoes or parsnips,
   peeled and cut into ½-inch cubes
2 medium-size sweet potatoes,
   peeled and cut into ½-inch cubes
1 medium-size onion, halved
   crosswise and cut into thin wedges
⅔ cup sour cream
¼ cup all-purpose flour

Preheat the oven to 425°F (220°C). To roast the dried mulato or pasilla chiles, line a baking sheet with foil; set aside. Slit open the chiles; discard the stems and seeds. Place the chiles on the prepared baking sheet. Bake 2 minutes.

In a medium-size saucepan, bring the 3½ cups Beef Stock or broth to a boil. Add the roasted mulato chiles; remove from heat. Cover and let stand 30 minutes.

To roast the red bell peppers and poblano chiles, halve them lengthwise; discard the stems, seeds, and membranes. (When working with the poblano chiles, wear plastic or rubber gloves to protect your skin from the oils in the chiles.) Cut small slits in the ends of the pieces to make them lie flat. Place the chile and pepper pieces, smooth side up, on the same prepared baking sheet. Bake 20 to 25 minutes or until the skins are bubbly and dark brown. Immediately place the chiles and peppers in a paper or heavy plastic bag; seal the bag. Let stand 20 to 30 minutes or until the chiles and peppers are cool enough to handle. Using a sharp knife, carefully peel the chiles and peppers. Cut them into 1-inch squares; set aside.

Meanwhile, in a Dutch oven, melt the butter over medium heat. Add the pork or beef, half at a time, and cook until browned on all sides. Drain off fat. Return all of the meat to the pan.

Add the stock with the mulato chiles; the 1½ cups wine, Beef Stock, or broth; the bay leaves; oregano; and garlic and bring to a boil. Reduce heat, cover, and simmer 35 minutes.

Stir in the roasted peppers and poblano chiles, the potatoes or parsnips, sweet potatoes, and onion. Return to a boil. Reduce heat, cover, and simmer 20 to 25 minutes or until the meat is tender and the vegetables are crisp-tender. Discard the bay leaves.

In a small bowl, combine the sour cream and flour. Gradually stir about ⅔ cup of the hot mixture into the sour cream mixture, then return the warmed sour cream to the remaining hot mixture. Cook over medium heat, stirring frequently, until the mixture thickens. Cook, stirring frequently, 1 minute.

Makes 6 to 8 servings.

✦ TIP

The mulato chile is one of several kinds of dried poblano chiles. It has a wide, triangular shape and a distinct smoky flavor. The pasilla is a different variety of chile that is longer and more slender than the mulato and has a less smoky but slightly hotter flavor.

Veal and Wild Rice Soup with Shiitake Mushrooms

The rich flavor of shiitake mushrooms complements the wild rice and veal in this full-bodied dish. When you're slicing the mushrooms, use only the caps and discard the tough stems.

⅓ cup wild rice
4 slices bacon, chopped
12 ounces lean boneless veal or lamb, trimmed of fat and cut into ¾-inch cubes
1 teaspoon minced garlic
1¾ cups Chicken Stock (page 42) or 1 (14½-ounce) can chicken broth
2 stalks celery, sliced

1 cup sliced leek or chopped onion
1 tablespoon minced fresh oregano or 1 teaspoon dried oregano leaves
1½ cups low-fat (1%) milk
¼ cup all-purpose flour
2 cups half-and-half
⅛ teaspoon ground black pepper
1¼ cups sliced fresh shiitake mushrooms or brown mushrooms
¼ cup dry sherry

In a fine wire strainer, rinse the wild rice under cold running water, lifting the rice with your fingers to clean thoroughly; drain.

In a Dutch oven, cook the bacon over medium heat until crisp. Remove the bacon, reserving the drippings. Drain the bacon on paper towels; set aside. Add the veal or lamb and garlic to the reserved drippings and cook until the meat is browned on all sides. Drain off fat.

Add the wild rice, Chicken Stock or broth, celery, leek or onion, and oregano and bring to a boil. Reduce heat, cover, and simmer, stirring occasionally, 40 to 50 minutes or until the wild rice is tender.

In a medium-size bowl, combine the milk and flour. Stir into the meat mixture. Add the half-and-half and pepper. Cook over medium heat, stirring frequently, until the mixture thickens, about 5 minutes. Stir in the mushrooms and sherry. Cook, stirring frequently, 5 minutes longer or until heated through.

To serve, ladle the soup into soup bowls. Sprinkle the soup with the cooked bacon.
Makes 4 servings.

⬥ TIP

To make sure your soups come to the table piping hot, warm the soup bowls. Fill them with hot water and let them stand a few minutes. Then, drain the bowls and fill them with soup.

Lamb Stew with Couscous

Start with lamb, couscous, eggplant, and garbanzo beans; add some chili powder, turmeric, and cinnamon; and what do you get? An impressive North African–inspired meal-in-a-bowl.

1 tablespoon vegetable oil
1 pound lean boneless lamb, trimmed of fat and cut into ¾-inch cubes
1¾ cups Beef Stock (page 42) or 1 (14½-ounce) can beef broth
1 medium-size onion, halved crosswise and cut into thin wedges
1 teaspoon minced garlic
1 small eggplant (about 1 pound), peeled and cut into ¾-inch cubes
1 (15-ounce) can garbanzo beans, drained
1¾ cups chopped tomatoes or 1 (14½-ounce) can diced tomatoes, with juice

2 (5½-ounce) cans spicy vegetable juice
1 (8-ounce) can tomato sauce
1 medium-size zucchini, halved lengthwise and cut into ½-inch-thick slices
1 medium-size green bell pepper, cut into 1-inch pieces
½ cup raisins
1 teaspoon chili powder
1 teaspoon ground turmeric
1 teaspoon ground cinnamon
½ teaspoon salt
Cooked couscous

In a Dutch oven, heat the oil over medium-high heat. Add the lamb, half at a time, and cook until browned on all sides. Drain off fat. Return all of the meat to the pan.

Add the Beef Stock or broth, onion, and garlic and bring to a boil. Reduce heat, cover, and simmer 35 minutes.

Stir in the eggplant, garbanzo beans, tomatoes with their juice, vegetable juice, tomato sauce, zucchini, bell pepper, raisins, chili powder, turmeric, cinnamon, and salt. Return to a boil. Reduce heat, cover, and simmer 15 to 20 minutes or until the meat is tender.

To serve, spoon the couscous into soup bowls. Ladle the stew over the couscous.
Makes 6 servings.

◆ TIP
When shopping for boneless lean lamb, look for roasts from the leg or shoulder area.

Caribbean Soffrito and Shrimp Soup

Soffrito is a traditional Spanish sauce that many Caribbean and Latin American cooks include in their dishes. What makes soffrito distinctive is that it's seasoned with annatto or achiote seeds. In this soup, the seeds add a slightly musky undertone that blends perfectly with the fresh-tasting vegetables and spicy jalapeño chiles. Look for annatto seeds in specialty food stores. Or, in a pinch, substitute paprika.

2 ears of corn or 1 cup frozen whole-kernel corn
4 slices bacon, chopped
¼ teaspoon annatto seeds or 1½ teaspoons paprika
1 large onion, chopped
1 medium-size green bell pepper, chopped
1½ teaspoons minced garlic
2 fresh jalapeño chiles
1¾ cups Chicken Stock (page 42) or 1 (14½-ounce) can chicken broth
1¾ cups chopped tomatoes or 1 (14½-ounce) can diced tomatoes, with juice

1 cup dry white wine
2 bay leaves
1 tablespoon minced fresh oregano or 1 teaspoon dried oregano leaves
½ teaspoon salt
¼ teaspoon ground black pepper
1 pound fresh or thawed frozen medium-size shrimp, shelled and deveined
¼ cup minced fresh cilantro or parsley
2 tablespoons fresh lime juice
About 2 cups cooked rice

If using the fresh ears of corn, place 1 ear of corn at a time in a shallow pan. Holding the ear at an angle, use a sharp knife to cut down across the tips of the kernels. Using the dull side of the knife, scrape the ear to release the milky juices into the pan. Measure 1 cup of the corn with its juices; set aside.

For the soffrito, in a Dutch oven, cook the bacon over medium heat until crisp. Remove the bacon, reserving the drippings. Drain the bacon on paper towels; set aside. Add the annatto seeds or paprika to the reserved drippings and cook, stirring constantly, 1 minute. If using the annatto seeds, strain the drippings mixture through a fine sieve; discard the annatto seeds. Return the drippings to the Dutch oven. (If using the paprika, you don't need to strain the drippings mixture.) Add the onion, bell pepper, and garlic to the drippings and cook, stirring frequently, 5 minutes or until the vegetables are tender.

Wearing plastic or rubber gloves, halve the chiles lengthwise; discard the stems, seeds, and membranes. Mince the chiles. Add the jalapeño chiles, fresh or frozen corn, Chicken Stock or broth, tomatoes with their juice, wine, bay leaves, oregano, salt, and black pepper to the vegetable mixture and bring to a boil. Reduce heat, cover, and simmer 10 minutes.

Meanwhile, rinse the shrimp. Stir the shrimp, cooked bacon, cilantro or parsley, and lime juice into the corn mixture. Return to a boil. Reduce heat, cover, and simmer 3 minutes or just until the shrimp are opaque throughout. Discard the bay leaves.

To serve, spoon the rice into soup bowls. Ladle the soup over the rice.

Makes 4 servings.

✦ TIP

When working with the jalapeño chiles, wear plastic or rubber gloves to protect your skin from the oils in the chiles. Also, wash your hands thoroughly before touching your eyes.

Lamb Shank, Spinach, and Farfalle Soup

Farfalle *is the Italian name for bow-tie pasta. It's also called "little butterflies." The bow ties add an intriguing shape to this rosemary-seasoned soup. When bow ties aren't available, just about any medium-size pasta shape, such as elbow macaroni, wagon wheels, cavatelli, rotini, gemelli, or medium shells, will work.*

1 tablespoon olive oil or vegetable oil
2 lamb shanks (about 2½ pounds total), trimmed of fat
3½ cups Chicken Stock (page 42) or 2 (14½-ounce) cans chicken broth
1¾ cups chopped tomatoes or 1 (14½-ounce) can diced tomatoes, with juice
1 cup dry red wine, Chicken Stock (page 42), or chicken broth

4 stalks celery with leaves, cut up
2 bay leaves
2 cloves garlic, halved
1 tablespoon dried rosemary leaves
¼ teaspoon ground black pepper
4 ounces dried bow-tie pasta (farfalle)
3 cups bite-size pieces spinach or watercress
2 cups sliced fresh mushrooms
Finely shredded Parmesan cheese

In a Dutch oven, heat the oil over medium heat. Add the lamb shanks and cook until browned on all sides. Drain off fat. Add the 3½ cups Chicken Stock or broth; the tomatoes with their juice; the 1 cup wine, Chicken Stock, or broth; the celery; bay leaves; garlic; rosemary; and pepper and bring to a boil. Reduce heat, cover, and simmer 1¼ to 1½ hours or until the meat is tender.

Using a slotted spoon, remove the shanks from the broth mixture; let stand until cool enough to handle. To strain the broth mixture, line a large colander or sieve with 2 layers of 100 percent cotton cheesecloth. Set the colander in a large saucepan. Strain the broth mixture through the colander; discard the vegetables and seasonings. If needed, skim off fat from broth.

Cut the meat off the shank bones. Coarsely chop the meat; discard the bones. Stir the meat and bow-tie pasta into the broth and bring to a boil. Reduce heat, cover, and simmer 8 minutes or until the pasta is firm-tender.

Stir in the spinach or watercress and mushrooms. Cook 1 minute or just until the spinach starts to wilt.

To serve, ladle the soup into soup bowls. Sprinkle the soup with the Parmesan cheese.
Makes 4 or 5 servings.

✦ TIP
Check the bow ties near the end of the suggested 8 minutes cooking time. The pasta is done if a bow tie is tender but still slightly firm when you bite into it.

Curried Fish Bisque

"We got our inspiration for this dish from traditional she-crab soup," says Liz. "But we changed a little of this and that, and before long, we had a new fish stew seasoned with curry and spiked with rum. Then, we tried the recipe with lobster and crab, too. All three versions are scrumptious."

1 tablespoon butter
4 shallots, minced
1 medium-size onion, chopped
1 stalk celery, finely chopped
2 tablespoons curry powder
1 cup half-and-half
¼ cup all-purpose flour
3 cups low-fat (1%) milk
½ teaspoon salt
⅛ teaspoon ground black pepper

⅛ teaspoon ground red (cayenne) pepper
8 ounces fresh or thawed frozen fish fillets, cut into ¾-inch pieces
3 tablespoons dark rum or dry sherry
1 hard-cooked egg yolk, finely chopped
2 tablespoons minced fresh chives or parsley

In a large saucepan, melt the butter over medium heat. Add the shallots, onion, and celery and cook, stirring frequently, 5 to 6 minutes or until the vegetables are tender. Add the curry powder and cook, stirring constantly, 1 minute.

In a small bowl, combine the half-and-half and flour. Stir into the vegetable mixture. Add the milk, salt, black pepper, and cayenne. Cook over medium heat, stirring frequently, 10 minutes or until the mixture thickens. Stir in the fish and rum or sherry and bring to a boil. Reduce heat and simmer 3 to 5 minutes or until the fish is opaque throughout.

To serve, ladle the bisque into soup bowls. Sprinkle the bisque with the hard-cooked egg yolk and chives or parsley.

Makes 4 servings.

VARIATIONS

CURRIED LOBSTER BISQUE
Substitute 8 ounces coarsely chopped cooked lobster meat or 1 (8-ounce) package lobster-flavored fish, cut up, for the fish.

CURRIED CRAB BISQUE
Substitute 8 ounces thawed frozen crabmeat, flaked, or 1 (8-ounce) package crab-flavored fish, cut up, for the fish.

◆ TIP
Shallots are a mild-flavored relative of the onion that grow in heads like garlic. They have thin, reddish-brown skins and are best when firm with no sprouts visible.

Lobster-in-the-Shell Watercress Soup

What could make the combination of lobster and watercress even more elegant? We came up with the answer: adding some saffron and dry vermouth. The herbal flavor of the vermouth and the bittersweet accent of saffron make this decadent soup a cut above the rest. The ingredients are expensive, but the results are worth the splurge.

2 tablespoons olive oil
2 large onions, sliced
2 large carrots, sliced
3 cloves garlic, halved
3½ cups Chicken Stock (page 42)
   or 2 (14½-ounce) cans chicken
   broth
1 (28-ounce) can tomatoes, with
   juice and cut up
1½ cups extra-dry vermouth or
   dry white wine

4 parsley sprigs
2 bay leaves
½ teaspoon salt
½ teaspoon whole black peppercorns
½ cup dried small shell pasta or
   tiny bow-tie pasta
2 thawed frozen rock lobster tails
   (1 to 1½ pounds total)
4 cups bite-size pieces watercress or
   spinach
½ teaspoon thread saffron, crushed

In a Dutch oven, heat the oil over medium-high heat. Add the onions, carrots, and garlic and cook, stirring frequently, 5 to 8 minutes or until the vegetables are tender. Add the Chicken Stock or broth, tomatoes with their juice, vermouth or white wine, parsley sprigs, bay leaves, salt, and peppercorns and bring to a boil. Reduce heat, cover, and simmer 30 minutes.

To strain the broth mixture, line a large colander or sieve with 2 layers of 100 percent cotton cheesecloth. Set the colander in a large saucepan. Strain the broth mixture through the colander; discard the vegetables and seasonings.

Bring the broth to a boil. Add the shell or bow-tie pasta and cook 10 minutes or just until the pasta is firm-tender. Meanwhile, rinse the lobster. Halve the lobster tails lengthwise, then halve crosswise to make 8 portions total. Stir the lobster, watercress or spinach, and saffron into the broth and return to a boil. Reduce heat and simmer, stirring occasionally, 3 to 5 minutes or until the lobster meat is opaque throughout.

Makes 4 servings.

VARIATION

FISH AND WATERCRESS SOUP
Substitute 1 pound fresh or thawed frozen fish fillets, cut into ¾-inch pieces, for the lobster.

◆ TIP
Vermouth is a fortified wine that's been distilled with as many as thirty different herbs and spices. Because it's often used to make martinis, your store may place it next to the gin rather than in the wine section.

East Indian Spiced Red Lentil Soup

We borrowed some of the splendid seasoning tricks of East Indian cooks and accented this rich lentil soup with highly fragrant spices such as cinnamon, mace, ginger, and cumin. We like to use red lentils for lots of color, but brown lentils also are attractive.

1 cup dried red or brown lentils or
    dried yellow or green split peas
2 tablespoons vegetable oil
1 tablespoon butter
2 tablespoons minced gingerroot
1 tablespoon cumin seeds
2 teaspoons minced garlic
2 large onions, chopped
$\frac{1}{2}$ teaspoon salt
$\frac{1}{4}$ teaspoon ground cinnamon or
    cardamom
$\frac{1}{4}$ teaspoon ground red
    (cayenne) pepper

$\frac{1}{8}$ teaspoon ground mace or cloves
7 cups Chicken Stock (page 42) or
    4 (14$\frac{1}{2}$-ounce) cans chicken broth
1$\frac{3}{4}$ cups chopped tomatoes or
    1 (14$\frac{1}{2}$-ounce) can diced tomatoes,
    with juice
$\frac{1}{2}$ cup long-grain white rice
Plain yogurt
Minced fresh cilantro or parsley
Lime wedges

In a mesh strainer, rinse the lentils or split peas under cold running water, lifting the lentils with your fingers to clean thoroughly. Drain and set aside.

In a Dutch oven, heat the oil and butter over medium heat. Add the gingerroot, cumin seeds, and garlic and cook, stirring constantly, 2 minutes. Add the onions, salt, cinnamon or cardamom, cayenne, and mace or cloves. Reduce heat to medium-low and cook, stirring frequently, 20 minutes or until the onions are very soft and golden.

Add the lentils or peas, Chicken Stock or broth, tomatoes with their juice, and rice to the onion mixture and bring to a boil. Reduce heat, cover, and simmer 45 to 60 minutes or until the lentils are tender.

To serve, ladle the soup into soup bowls. Top each serving of soup with a dollop of yogurt and some of the cilantro or parsley. Serve with the lime wedges.

Makes 6 servings.

✦ TIP

Sort through the lentils or split peas as you rinse them, selecting only the plump ones and discarding any shriveled or spotted ones.

Sherried Chipotle–Black Bean Soup

"Using eight chipotle chiles is not for the faint of heart," cautions Sandra. "They add a wonderfully smoky flavor to this soup, which is similar to chili, but they also add lots of heat. Try the soup with six chiles the first time you make it, and then use more the next time, if you dare."

2 cups dried black beans
5¼ cups Beef Stock (page 42) or
   3 (14½-ounce) cans beef broth
6 to 8 dried chipotle chiles
3 bay leaves
1 tablespoon olive oil or
   vegetable oil
1 large yellow, green, or red bell
   pepper, chopped
1 large red or yellow onion, chopped
2 teaspoons minced garlic
2 tablespoons ground cumin
1 tablespoon chili powder
1 tablespoon dried oregano leaves
½ teaspoon salt

1¾ cups chopped tomatoes or
   1 (14½-ounce) can diced tomatoes,
   with juice
3 large carrots, chopped
1¼ cups dry sherry, Beef Stock
   (page 42), or beef broth
¼ cup minced fresh cilantro or
   parsley
2 tablespoons fresh lemon juice or
   white vinegar
Sour cream
1 avocado, pitted, peeled, and
   chopped
Lemon wedges

Sort and rinse the black beans. In a Dutch oven, cover the beans generously with cold water. Cover and let stand overnight. (Or, bring to a boil, reduce heat, and simmer 2 minutes. Remove from heat, cover, and let stand 1 hour.) Drain and rinse the beans.

In the same Dutch oven, combine the drained beans, the 5¼ cups Beef Stock or broth, the chipotle chiles, and bay leaves and bring to a boil. Reduce heat, cover, and simmer 1½ to 1¾ hours or until the beans are tender. Remove the chipotle chiles; discard the bay leaves. Using a fork or potato masher, slightly mash some of the beans against the pan.

Wearing plastic or rubber gloves to protect your skin from the oils in the chiles, halve the chiles lengthwise; discard the stems, seeds, and membranes. Chop the chiles; return to the bean mixture.

In a large skillet, heat the oil over medium heat. Add the bell pepper, onion, and garlic and cook, stirring frequently, 5 minutes or until the onion is tender. Stir in the cumin, chili powder, oregano, and salt. Cook, stirring constantly, 2 minutes.

Stir the onion mixture, tomatoes with their juice, carrots, and 1 cup of the sherry, Beef Stock, or broth into the bean mixture and bring to a boil. Reduce heat, cover, and simmer 20 minutes or until the carrots are crisp-tender. Stir in the remaining ¼ cup sherry, the cilantro or parsley, and lemon juice or vinegar. Cook, stirring occasionally, 3 minutes.

To serve, ladle the soup into soup bowls. Top each serving of soup with a dollop of sour cream and some of the avocado. Serve with the lemon wedges.

Makes 6 servings.

✦ TIP

When sorting the black beans, discard any shriveled or moldy ones. Then, rinse the beans under cold running water, lifting them with your fingers to clean thoroughly; drain. When cooking the beans, test for doneness by removing a bean from the pan. Press the bean between your thumb and forefinger. The bean is done if it feels soft. If there is a hard core, cook the beans a little longer and test again.

Ale 'n' Cheddar Chowder with Dried-Apple Croutons

Onion is a basic building block of many a good soup and this aromatic, creamy cheese soup is no exception. Sharyl has this bit of advice about onions: "When I first started cooking, I learned an average onion equals ½ cup chopped, but over the years, onions seem to have gotten larger. So now, what most cooks would call a medium-size onion actually yields closer to 1 cup of chopped pieces."

Dried Apple Croutons (see opposite)
1 tablespoon olive oil
1 tablespoon butter
1 medium-size onion, finely chopped
1 medium-size carrot, shredded
1 teaspoon minced garlic
1¾ cups Chicken Stock (page 42) or 1 (14½-ounce) can chicken broth
⅓ cup all-purpose flour
½ cup half-and-half or whole milk
½ teaspoon freshly grated lemon peel

⅛ teaspoon ground cinnamon
⅛ teaspoon ground black pepper
2 cups (8 ounces) shredded sharp Cheddar cheese, at room temperature
1 (12-ounce) bottle ale or beer

DRIED APPLE CROUTONS
1 medium-size tart apple
1 cup cold water
1 tablespoon fresh lemon juice
2 tablespoons light brown sugar
½ teaspoon ground cinnamon

Prepare the Dried Apple Croutons; set aside. In a large saucepan, heat the oil and butter over medium-high heat. Add the onion, carrot, and garlic. Reduce heat to medium-low and cook, stirring frequently, 20 minutes or until the onion is very soft and golden.

In a medium-size bowl, combine the Chicken Stock or broth and flour. Stir into the onion mixture. Add the half-and-half or whole milk, lemon peel, cinnamon, and pepper. Cook over medium heat, stirring frequently, 5 minutes or until the mixture thickens.

Gradually stir in the cheese. Reduce heat to low and cook, stirring frequently, until the cheese melts, but do not boil. Stir in the ale or beer. Cook, stirring frequently, until heated through.

To serve, ladle the chowder into soup bowls. Top the chowder with the croutons.

Makes 4 servings.

DRIED APPLE CROUTONS

Preheat the oven to 300°F (150°C). Core the apple. Leaving the skin on, slice the apple into ¼-inch-thick rings. To keep the apple rings from browning, combine the water and lemon juice in a medium-size bowl. Add the apple rings, turning to coat both sides with the lemon mixture. Let stand 5 minutes. Drain well; pat the apple rings dry with paper towels.

Lightly grease a wire rack. Arrange the apple rings in a single layer on the rack. In a small bowl, combine the brown sugar and cinnamon. Sprinkle the sugar mixture evenly over the apple rings. Set the rack on a baking sheet. Bake 30 minutes.

Turn off the oven. Let the apple rings dry in the oven, with the door closed, 1 hour. Remove from the oven.

Makes about 8 croutons. ↘

◆ TIP

Letting the shredded cheese reach room temperature before adding it to the chicken broth mixture helps the cheese to melt more quickly and easily.

Fresh Garden Pea and Pasta Soup with Mint Crème Fraîche

Sharyl suggests, "When spring peas first come into season, start a batch of this mint-flavored crème fraîche. The next day, pick the tender peas from your garden (or purchase them from a nearby farmers' market) and make this exceptional soup. Then, delight dinner guests by topping each serving with some of the tangy crème fraîche."

Mint Crème Fraîche (see opposite) or
   sour cream
2 ounces (1½ cups) medium-size
   plain or spinach dried
   egg noodles
2 tablespoons butter
3 stalks celery, sliced
8 medium-size green onions, sliced
2 pounds fresh green peas, shelled
   (2 cups), or 1 (10-ounce) package
   frozen peas
1¾ cups Chicken Stock (page 42)
   or 1 (14½-ounce) can chicken
   broth

1½ tablespoons minced fresh marjoram
   or 1½ teaspoons dried marjoram
   leaves
½ teaspoon salt
¼ teaspoon ground black pepper
2 cups half-and-half
1 cup low-fat (1%) milk

MINT CRÈME FRAÎCHE
1½ cups whipping cream (not
   ultrapasteurized)
1 tablespoon buttermilk
1 tablespoon minced fresh mint or
   1 teaspoon minced fresh chives

Prepare the Mint Crème Fraîche, if using. For the soup, cook the noodles according to the package directions; drain. Rinse under cold running water and drain again; set aside.

In a large saucepan, melt the butter over medium heat. Add the celery and green onions and cook, stirring frequently, 5 to 6 minutes or until the vegetables are tender. Add the fresh or frozen peas, Chicken Stock or broth, marjoram, salt, and pepper and bring to a boil. Reduce heat, cover, and simmer 15 minutes or until the vegetables are very tender. Cool slightly, but do not drain.

In a food processor or blender, combine half of the pea mixture and half of the cooked noodles. Cover and process until smooth. Transfer to a bowl. Repeat with the remaining pea mixture and cooked noodles. Return all of the mixture to the saucepan. Stir in the half-and-half and milk. Cook over medium heat, stirring frequently, 10 minutes or until heated through.

To serve, ladle the soup into soup bowls. Top each serving of soup with a dollop of crème fraîche or sour cream.

Makes 8 servings.

MINT CRÈME FRAÎCHE

In a small saucepan, heat the whipping cream over low heat until warm [between 90° and 100°F (30° and 40°C)]. Pour the cream into a small bowl. Stir in the buttermilk. Cover and let stand at room temperature 24 to 30 hours or until the mixture thickens, but do not stir. To store, refrigerate up to 1 week. Just before serving, stir in the mint or chives.

Makes 1½ cups.

VARIATIONS

This soup also is wonderful chilled. Just stir in a little extra milk to thin the cold soup to the desired consistency.

To use up the leftover Mint Crème Fraîche, serve it as a salad dressing for a spinach, strawberry, and orange salad (if using either mint or chives) or as a topping for a fruit compote (if using mint).

Spicy Bean, Sweet Potato, and Chayote Stew

For a change of pace, Liz serves this hearty vegetable stew. "Although it contains no meat," says Liz, "it still has plenty of protein from the beans, nuts, and cheese, and a full flavor from the green chiles, basil, and allspice."

1 tablespoon vegetable oil
1 large onion, chopped
1½ teaspoons minced garlic
3 medium-size sweet potatoes, peeled and cut into ½-inch cubes
3 medium-size tart apples, peeled, cored, and coarsely chopped
2 (15½-ounce) cans butter beans, rinsed and drained
3½ cups Chicken Stock (page 42) or 2 (14½-ounce) cans chicken broth
1 (12-ounce) can beer or 1½ cups apple cider
1 (4½-ounce) can diced green chiles, with liquid

2 tablespoons minced fresh basil or 2 teaspoons dried basil leaves
2 to 3 teaspoons hot pepper sauce
1 teaspoon ground allspice or cinnamon
½ teaspoon salt
1 medium-size chayote, peeled, seeded, and cut into ½-inch cubes, or 2 medium-size zucchini, cut into ½-inch cubes
1 cup cashews or peanuts
1½ cups (6 ounces) shredded Muenster, brick, or Swiss cheese

In a Dutch oven, heat the oil over medium heat. Add the onion and garlic and cook, stirring frequently, 5 minutes or until the onion is tender.

Add the sweet potatoes, apples, butter beans, Chicken Stock or broth, beer or apple cider, green chiles with their liquid, basil, hot pepper sauce, allspice or cinnamon, and salt to the onion mixture. Bring to a boil. Reduce heat, cover, and simmer 8 to 10 minutes or until the sweet potatoes are nearly tender.

Stir in the chayote or zucchini and cashews or peanuts and return to a boil. Reduce heat and simmer 5 to 8 minutes or until the chayote is crisp-tender.

To serve, ladle the stew into soup bowls. Sprinkle the stew with the cheese.

Makes 8 servings.

✦ TIP

Pear-shaped chayote has a flavor that's like a mixture of apples and cucumbers. This squashlike fruit, also called mirliton, should be pale green, firm, and free from bruises when you buy it.

Tuscan White Bean and Vegetable Soup

Cannellini beans are popular in many Italian dishes. These white kidney beans come both in dried and canned forms, but in our area, we sometimes have trouble finding them in the stores. When they aren't available, we substitute great Northern or navy beans in this colorful, home-style vegetable soup.

1¼ cups dried cannellini (white kidney) beans, great Northern beans, or navy beans

5¼ cups Beef Stock (page 42) or 3 (14½-ounce) cans beef broth

1 large onion, chopped

2 bay leaves

1 teaspoon minced garlic

1¾ cups chopped Italian plum tomatoes or 1 (14½-ounce) can diced tomatoes, with juice

2 large carrots, sliced

1 large leek, sliced

1 medium-size turnip or potato, peeled and cut into ½-inch pieces

1 cup fresh or frozen cut green beans

2 tablespoons minced fresh thyme or 2 teaspoons dried thyme leaves

½ teaspoon salt

½ teaspoon ground black pepper

1 cup fresh broccoli flowerets or frozen cut broccoli

1 small zucchini, halved lengthwise and sliced crosswise

Finely shredded Parmesan cheese

Sort and rinse the beans. In a Dutch oven, cover the beans generously with cold water. Cover and let stand overnight. (Or, bring to a boil, reduce heat, and simmer 2 minutes. Remove from heat, cover, and let stand 1 hour.) Drain and rinse the beans.

In the same Dutch oven, combine the drained beans, the Beef Stock or broth, onion, bay leaves, and garlic and bring to a boil. Reduce heat, cover, and simmer 1¾ to 2 hours or until the beans are tender. Discard the bay leaves.

Stir the tomatoes with their juice, carrots, leek, turnip or potato, the fresh green beans, if using, the thyme, salt, and pepper into the bean mixture and bring to a boil. Reduce heat, cover, and simmer 15 minutes. Stir in the frozen green beans, if using, the fresh or frozen broccoli, and the zucchini. Return to a boil. Reduce heat, cover, and simmer 5 minutes or until the vegetables are crisp-tender.

To serve, ladle the soup into soup bowls. Sprinkle the soup with the Parmesan cheese.
Makes 6 servings.

✦ TIP

The best leeks have crisp, bright green tops. Avoid those that are larger than 1½ inches in diameter because they can be woody and tasteless.

Roasted Eggplant and Tomato Soup

Roasting the eggplant and tomatoes mellows and intensifies their natural flavors.

1 tablespoon olive oil or
  vegetable oil
1 large red bell pepper, chopped
1 large onion, chopped
1½ teaspoons minced garlic
1 small eggplant (about 1 pound),
  peeled and cut into thick slices
4 medium-size tomatoes, sliced
1¾ cups Chicken Stock (page 42)
  or 1 (14½-ounce) can chicken
  broth

1 (6-ounce) can tomato paste
2 cups low-fat (1%) milk
1 cup half-and-half
1 tablespoon minced fresh basil or
  1 teaspoon dried basil leaves
½ teaspoon salt
½ teaspoon fennel seeds, crushed
¼ teaspoon ground black pepper
Plain yogurt or sour cream

Preheat the oven to 425°F (220°C). In a large saucepan, heat the oil over medium heat. Add the bell pepper, onion, and garlic and cook, stirring frequently, 5 minutes or until the vegetables are tender.

Line a baking sheet with foil; lightly grease the foil. Place the eggplant and tomato slices on the prepared baking sheet. Top the eggplant and tomato slices with the onion mixture. Bake 20 to 25 minutes or until the eggplant is very soft and tender. Cool slightly.

In a food processor or blender, combine half of the eggplant and tomato slices and onion mixture. Cover and process until smooth. Transfer to the saucepan. Repeat with the remaining eggplant and tomato slices and onion mixture. Stir the Chicken Stock or broth and tomato paste into the eggplant mixture and bring to a boil. Reduce heat, cover, and simmer 20 minutes. Strain the eggplant mixture through a sieve; discard the pulp.

In the same saucepan, combine the milk, half-and-half, basil, salt, fennel seeds, and black pepper. Gradually whisk in the eggplant mixture. Cook over low heat, stirring occasionally, until heated through.

To serve, ladle the soup into soup bowls. Top each serving of soup with a dollop of yogurt or sour cream.

Makes 6 servings.

◆ TIP
This full-flavored soup tastes just as delicious cold as it does warm. If you like, stir in a little extra milk to thin the chilled soup.

Tortilla and Banana Pepper Soup

The crunch of tortilla strips, the freshness of banana chiles, the kick of tequila, and the robustness of cilantro make this south-of-the-border–style soup truly a fiesta in a bowl.

6 (6-inch) yellow corn tortillas or
   blue corn tortillas
Vegetable oil
4 fresh yellow banana peppers
1¾ cups Chicken Stock (page 42)
   or 1 (14½-ounce) can chicken
   broth
1¾ cups chopped tomatoes or
   1 (14½-ounce) can diced
   tomatoes, with juice
3 medium-size carrots, thinly sliced
2 (5½-ounce) cans spicy vegetable
   juice

1 (8-ounce) can tomato sauce
1 cup sliced leek or chopped onion
½ cup tequila
1 teaspoon ground cumin
1 small zucchini, thinly sliced
1 cup frozen green peas
¼ cup minced fresh cilantro or
   parsley
1 cup (4 ounces) shredded Monterey
   Jack cheese with jalapeño chiles or
   sharp Cheddar cheese
1 small avocado, pitted, peeled, and
   sliced, for garnish

Halve the tortillas, then cut crosswise into ½-inch-wide strips. In a large heavy saucepan, heat ½ inch of oil over medium-high heat. Add the tortilla strips, half at a time, and cook 45 to 60 seconds or until crisp and lightly browned. Using a slotted spoon, remove the tortilla strips from the hot oil. Drain well on paper towels; set aside.

Wearing plastic or rubber gloves to protect your skin from the oils in the chiles, halve the banana chiles lengthwise; discard the stems, seeds, and membranes. Cut the chiles into 1-inch pieces.

In another large saucepan, combine the banana chiles, Chicken Stock or broth, tomatoes with their juice, carrots, vegetable juice, tomato sauce, leek or onion, tequila, and cumin and bring to a boil. Reduce heat, cover, and simmer 15 minutes. Stir in the zucchini, peas, and cilantro or parsley and return to a boil. Reduce heat, cover, and simmer 5 to 10 minutes or until the vegetables are crisp-tender.

To serve, place the tortilla strips and cheese into soup bowls. Ladle the soup over the tortilla strips and cheese. Garnish the soup with the avocado slices. Serve immediately.

Makes 8 servings.

◆ TIP
To keep the avocado slices looking pretty, dip them in a little lemon juice.

Beef Stock

We've simmered our stock long and slow so it has plenty of rich homemade flavor, yet it is versatile enough to use in all types of recipes.

4 pounds meaty beef, lamb, or veal
    bones (shank crosscuts, short ribs,
    knuckles, or leg bones with
    marrow)
12 cups cold water
2 large onions, cut into wedges
2 large carrots, quartered
2 stalks celery with leaves, cut up

4 outer cabbage leaves or 1 cup sliced
    green onion tops or leek tops
8 parsley sprigs or cilantro sprigs
3 bay leaves
2 teaspoons dried basil leaves or
    thyme leaves
12 whole black peppercorns
1 teaspoon salt

In a 10-quart Dutch oven or stockpot, place the meat bones. Add the water, onions, carrots, celery, cabbage leaves or green onion or leek tops, parsley or cilantro sprigs, bay leaves, basil or thyme, peppercorns, and salt and bring to a boil. Reduce heat, cover, and simmer 3 hours, occasionally skimming off any foam.

Using a slotted spoon, remove the meat bones from the stock. If desired, let the meat bones stand until cool enough to handle, then remove the meat from the bones. Reserve the meat for another use. Discard the bones.

To strain the stock, line a large colander or sieve with 2 layers of 100 percent cotton cheesecloth. Set the colander in a large heatproof bowl or container. Strain the stock through the colander; discard the vegetables and seasonings. If desired, clarify the stock; see Tip, below.

If using the stock while hot, use a large metal spoon to skim off the fat that rises to the surface; discard the fat. (Or, refrigerate the stock 6 to 8 hours, then use a spoon to lift off the fat that solidifies on the surface; discard the fat.)

To store, place the stock and the meat in separate covered containers and refrigerate up to 3 days or freeze up to 6 months. (Be sure to label each container with the type of stock, the amount, and the date of freezing.)

Makes about 11 cups stock.

VARIATION

CHICKEN STOCK
    Substitute 4 pounds bony chicken pieces (backs, necks, or wings) for the meat bones.

✦ TIP

Clarify beef or chicken stock when you want a sparkling clear broth to serve as a first-course appetizer soup or consommé. Clarifying removes the floating particles that are too small to be strained out with cheesecloth and make a soup cloudy.

To clarify stock, strain it and pour it into a Dutch oven. Combine ¼ cup cold water and 1 egg white; pour into the stock. Bring to a boil; remove from heat. Let stand 5 minutes. Strain the stock again through the large colander lined with damp 100 percent cotton cheesecloth.

GREAT GREENS AND SENSATIONAL SALADS

*A*sk a dozen cooks what makes an exceptional salad and you'll get a dozen answers. In this chapter, we share with you some of our favorites. Whether tossed or marinated, hot or cold, savory or sweet, we've made each of these main-dish and side salads an extraordinary dining experience.

You'll find fascinating whole-meal salads, such as Hickory-Smoked Turkey and Shiitake Mushroom Salad with Orange-Balsamic Dressing, which features spinach and radicchio tossed with smoked turkey and a terrific citrus vinaigrette. There are also showpiece side salads, such as New Potato–Asparagus Salad with Walnut Vinaigrette. It's the perfect partner for roasted meats or poached fish. If it's great-tasting grain or pasta salads you're after, sample the likes of Saffron Couscous and Bulgur Salad, which sports a lemon dressing, or Feta Cheese and Fresh Basil Tortellini Salad with a creamy feta-and-Parmesan cheese dressing. For something new in vegetable salads, there's Asparagus, Tomato, and Roasted Beet Salad with Pine Nut Dressing or Marinated Black Bean–Jicama Salad with Chipotle Chile Dressing. And if your taste runs toward the spicy yet sweet, serve Tropical Fruit Salad with Honey-and-Spice Papaya Dressing. It's ideal alongside burgers on a hot summer night.

Remember these refreshing, new combinations the next time you're looking for a sensational salad. They're a great way to expand your salad repertoire.

Fruit-Tossed Spinach Salad with Honey and Sherry Yogurt Dressing

"I always make this salad when I'm looking for a dynamite side dish to serve with roasted or grilled chicken or pork," says Liz.

Honey and Sherry Yogurt Dressing
(see opposite)
2 tablespoons fresh lemon juice
1 medium-size apple, cored and cut
    into chunks
1 medium-size pear, cored and cut
    into chunks
8 cups bite-size pieces spinach
1 stalk celery, sliced
½ cup halved seedless red or green
    grapes

½ cup toasted coarsely chopped
    pecans or walnuts
½ cup alfalfa sprouts

HONEY AND SHERRY YOGURT DRESSING
1 (8-ounce) carton plain yogurt
2 tablespoons honey
2 tablespoons dry sherry or fresh
    orange juice
1 teaspoon freshly grated
    orange peel

Prepare the Honey and Sherry Yogurt Dressing. Cover and refrigerate while preparing the salad.

In a small bowl, combine the lemon juice and a little water. Dip the apple and pear chunks into the lemon juice mixture to coat. Drain well.

In a large bowl, combine the apple, pear, spinach, celery, grapes, pecans or walnuts, and alfalfa sprouts. Toss gently to mix.

To serve, pour the dressing over the spinach mixture. Toss gently to coat.
Makes 6 to 8 side-dish servings.

HONEY AND SHERRY YOGURT DRESSING
In a small bowl, combine the yogurt, honey, sherry or orange juice, and orange peel. Cover and refrigerate up to 1 week.
Makes about 1 cup.

Tropical Fruit Salad with Honey-and-Spice Papaya Dressing

Although we've teamed this spicy, tart-sweet dressing with company-special tropical fruits, it's also delicious with more everyday fruits like cantaloupe, nectarines, pears, apples, and grapes.

Honey-and-Spice Papaya Dressing
   (see opposite)
½ small pineapple (about
   1½ pounds) or 1 (15½-ounce)
   can pineapple chunks, drained
2 carambolas (star fruits) or 2 cups
   halved strawberries
Boston lettuce leaves or Bibb lettuce
   leaves
2 medium-size bananas, cut into
   ½-inch-thick slices
1 medium-size mango, peeled, pitted,
   and cut into bite-size pieces

2 medium-size kiwi fruits, cut into
   ¼-inch-thick slices

HONEY-AND-SPICE PAPAYA DRESSING
1 ripe medium-size papaya
3 tablespoons honey
2 tablespoons fresh lime juice
1 tablespoon vegetable oil
1 teaspoon freshly grated lime peel
¼ teaspoon ground ginger or mace
¼ teaspoon ground cinnamon or
   cardamom
⅛ teaspoon salt

Prepare the Honey-and-Spice Papaya Dressing. Cover and refrigerate while preparing the salad.

Peel, core, and cut the fresh pineapple, if using, into bite-size pieces. Trim off the tops and bottoms of the carambolas, if using, then slice crosswise to show off the star shape. Discard the seeds.

To serve, arrange the lettuce leaves on salad plates. Arrange the fresh or canned pineapple, the carambolas or strawberries, bananas, mango, and kiwi fruits on top of the lettuce. Drizzle the dressing over the fruit.

Makes 6 side-dish servings.

HONEY-AND-SPICE PAPAYA DRESSING

Peel the papaya; cut in half lengthwise. Remove the seeds, reserving 2 tablespoons. Coarsely chop the papaya; measure 1 cup. In a food processor or blender, combine the 1 cup chopped papaya, the 2 tablespoons papaya seeds, the honey, lime juice, vegetable oil, lime peel, ginger or mace, cinnamon or cardamom, and salt. Cover and process until smooth. Cover and refrigerate up to 1 week.

Makes about 1¼ cups.

◆ TIP

When shopping for ripe papayas, look for ones that yield to gentle pressure and have smooth skins that are at least half yellow. Mangoes should be brightly colored, have a fruity fragrance, and be firm but not hard.

Asparagus, Tomato, and Roasted Beet Salad with Pine Nut Dressing

"Marinating asparagus darkens the color a little," says Liz. "But the change is worth all the extra nutty flavor the pieces absorb from the dressing."

Pine Nut Dressing (see opposite)
12 ounces medium-size fresh beets or 1 (16-ounce) can sliced beets, rinsed and drained
1 pound fresh green and/or white asparagus or 1 (10-ounce) package frozen asparagus spears
4 cups bite-size pieces mixed salad greens or mesclun (mixed baby greens)
8 red or yellow baby pear tomatoes, halved, or 4 Italian plum tomatoes, cut into wedges
2 hard-cooked eggs, sliced
¼ cup (1 ounce) crumbled feta cheese or blue cheese

Freshly ground black pepper
Chive flowers and tomatillo wedges, for garnish (optional)

PINE NUT DRESSING
⅔ cup olive oil or vegetable oil
½ cup red wine vinegar
⅓ cup toasted pine nuts (see Tip, opposite page)
¼ cup fresh orange juice
2 tablespoons sugar
1 tablespoon Dijon mustard
⅛ teaspoon freshly ground nutmeg
⅛ teaspoon freshly ground black pepper

Prepare the Pine Nut Dressing; set aside. Preheat the oven to 400°F (205°C). Tear off a 36 x 18-inch piece of heavy foil. Fold in half to make an 18-inch square. Fold up the sides, then use your fist to form a pouch; set aside.

Thoroughly wash the fresh beets, if using, but avoid using a brush because the beets have very thin skins. Trim the beets 1 inch above the stems. Place the beets in the foil pouch. Fold the edges together to seal the pouch securely. Bake 60 to 65 minutes or until the beets are tender.

Carefully open the pouch. Let the beets stand until cool enough to handle, then peel the beets by slipping off the skins. (You want the beets to still be warm so the skins will come off easily.) Slice the beets. Place the sliced cooked or canned beets in a small bowl. Pour ½ cup of the dressing over the beets. Cover and refrigerate at least 4 hours or overnight.

While the beets are baking, wash the fresh asparagus, if using. If desired, use a vegetable peeler to scrape off the scales. Snap off the woody bases at the point where the spears snap easily; discard the bases. Place a steamer basket in a large saucepan. Add water to just below the basket. Bring the water to a boil. Place the fresh or frozen asparagus in the steamer basket. Cover and steam 4 to 8 minutes or until the asparagus is crisp-tender. (Using a fork, break apart the frozen asparagus after 3 minutes of the cooking time.) Place the asparagus in a flat container. Pour ½ cup of the dressing over the asparagus. Cover and refrigerate at least 4 hours or overnight. Transfer the remaining dressing to a small bowl; cover and refrigerate.

To serve, arrange the mixed greens on salad plates. Using a slotted spoon, overlap the beet slices, then arrange the asparagus spears on top of the greens. Arrange the tomatoes and egg slices in separate piles on top of the greens, filling the surfaces of the plates. Stir the remaining ¾ cup dressing well; pour over the salads. Sprinkle the salads with the feta or blue cheese and pepper. Garnish with the chive flowers and tomatillo wedges, if using.

Makes 4 side-dish servings.

PINE NUT DRESSING

In a food processor or blender, combine the oil, vinegar, pine nuts, orange juice, sugar, Dijon mustard, nutmeg, and pepper. Cover and process until smooth.

Makes about 1¾ cups.

✦ TIP

For a toasty flavor, bake the pine nuts in a baking pan in a 350°F (175°C) oven 5 to 10 minutes or until golden brown, stirring occasionally.

New Potato–Asparagus Salad with Walnut Vinaigrette

"The beautiful colors and wonderful textures in this salad are as appealing as its flavor," says Sharyl. "Sprinkle on the walnuts just before serving, and this tasty-and-tangy combination turns out perfect every time."

Walnut Vinaigrette (see opposite)
10 to 12 (about 1 pound) tiny new
    potatoes, quartered
12 ounces fresh asparagus or
    1 (10-ounce) package frozen cut
    asparagus
1 cup cherry tomatoes, halved
3 cups bite-size pieces romaine
    lettuce or red-leaf lettuce
½ cup broken walnuts
Chive blossoms, for garnish
    (optional)

WALNUT VINAIGRETTE
½ cup walnut oil
⅓ cup balsamic vinegar or red wine
    vinegar
¼ cup finely chopped red or yellow
    onion
2 tablespoons water
1 tablespoon honey
1 tablespoon Dijon mustard
¼ teaspoon salt
¼ teaspoon white pepper or black
    pepper

Prepare the Walnut Vinaigrette. Cover and refrigerate while preparing the salad.

In a large saucepan, bring a small amount of lightly salted water to a boil. Add the potatoes. Reduce heat, cover, and simmer 12 to 15 minutes or just until the potatoes are tender; drain well.

Wash the fresh asparagus (if using). If desired, use a vegetable peeler to scrape off the scales. Snap off the woody bases at the point where the spears snap easily; discard the bases. Cut the asparagus into 1½-inch pieces. In a medium-size saucepan, bring a small amount of lightly salted water to a boil. Add the fresh or frozen asparagus. Reduce heat, cover, and simmer 2 to 5 minutes or until the asparagus is crisp-tender; drain well.

In a large bowl, combine the potatoes, asparagus, and cherry tomatoes. Shake the vinaigrette well; pour over the potato mixture. Toss gently to coat. Cover and refrigerate at least 4 hours or overnight.

To serve, arrange the lettuce on salad plates. Spoon the potato mixture on top of the lettuce. Sprinkle with the walnuts. Garnish with the chive blossoms, if using.

Makes 6 side-dish servings.

WALNUT VINAIGRETTE
In a jar with a tight lid, combine the walnut oil, vinegar, onion, water, honey, Dijon mustard, salt, and pepper. Cover and shake well, then refrigerate up to 1 week.

Makes about 1 cup.

VARIATION

Smoked Salmon and New Potato–Asparagus Salad

Add 10 ounces smoked salmon, trout, or whitefish, skin and bones removed and coarsely flaked.

Makes 4 main-dish servings.

✦ TIP

New potatoes can be any variety. They are simply young potatoes with a waxy texture and thin, tender skins. Store new potatoes in the refrigerator if you plan to keep them for more than a day or so.

Marinated Black Bean–Jicama Salad
with Chipotle Chile Dressing

Chipotle chiles are smoked jalapeño chiles. Although they're also sold dried, we chose chipotle chiles packed in tomatoey adobo sauce for this fiery dressing. Because this salad has an imposing, but delightful, smoky flavor, serve it with plain or mildly seasoned beef or lamb.

3 large tomatoes
⅓ cup vegetable oil
⅓ cup fresh lime juice
¼ cup canned chipotle chiles in
    adobo sauce
1 tablespoon sugar
1 (15-ounce) can black beans or
    pinto beans, rinsed and drained

1 cup peeled and cubed jicama or
    1 (8-ounce) can sliced water
    chestnuts, rinsed and drained
1 medium-size yellow, red, or green
    bell pepper, cut into 1-inch pieces
4 green onions, thinly sliced
¼ cup minced fresh cilantro or
    parsley

For the dressing, coarsely chop 1 of the tomatoes. In a food processor or blender, combine the coarsely chopped tomato, the vegetable oil, lime juice, chipotle chiles in adobo sauce, and sugar. Cover and process until smooth.

Cut remaining tomatoes in wedges, remove seeds, and chop. In a large bowl, combine the 2 chopped tomatoes, the beans, jicama or water chestnuts, bell pepper, green onions, and cilantro or parsley. Pour the dressing over the bean mixture. Toss gently to coat. Cover and refrigerate at least 4 hours or overnight.

Makes 6 side-dish servings.

✦ TIP
Jicama is a root vegetable that looks like an oversized turnip with light brown skin. Whole jicama can be stored in the refrigerator up to 3 weeks. Once you cut into it, though, wrap it in plastic wrap and refrigerate it for no longer than a week.

Wilted Sorrel and Mushroom Salad
with Sweet Lemony Ginger Dressing

"The first time I tasted sorrel I was hooked," reminisces Sandra. "I love its lemony, slightly bitter flavor in all kinds of salads, especially in wilted ones like this."

6 cups bite-size pieces sorrel, spinach, or dandelion greens
1½ cups assorted fresh mushrooms (sliced oyster, shiitake, or chanterelle mushrooms; whole small white mushrooms; and/or enoki mushrooms)
½ cup coarsely chopped cashews
⅛ teaspoon ground red (cayenne) pepper or black pepper

2 tablespoons honey
2 tablespoons red wine vinegar or cider vinegar
1 teaspoon freshly grated lemon peel
2 tablespoons butter
4 green onions, thinly sliced
1 tablespoon minced gingerroot
½ teaspoon minced garlic
Violets, pansies, or other edible flowers, for garnish

In a large salad bowl, combine the sorrel, spinach, or dandelion greens; mushrooms; and cashews. Toss gently to mix. Sprinkle with the cayenne or black pepper.

For the dressing, combine the honey, vinegar, and lemon peel in a small bowl; set aside. In a 12-inch skillet, melt the butter over medium heat. Add the green onions, gingerroot, and garlic and cook, stirring frequently, 2 to 3 minutes or until the green onions are tender. Stir in the honey mixture and bring to a boil; remove from heat.

Add the sorrel mixture to the dressing in the skillet. Toss 30 to 60 seconds or just until the sorrel mixture is coated and starts to wilt. Return to the salad bowl. Garnish the salad with the flowers. Serve immediately.

Makes 4 side-dish servings.

✦ TIP
Sorrel has arrow-shaped leaves that range in color from pale to deep green. Look for sorrel with crisp leaves and tender, not woody, stems. Sorrel is also easy to grow in your garden.

Feta Cheese and Fresh Basil Tortellini Salad

This intriguing recipe is a good example of fusion cooking. We've taken Kalamata olives and feta cheese from Greece plus Italian tortellini and Parmesan cheese and created a spectacular salad.

1 (9-ounce) package refrigerated cheese tortellini
2 cups broccoli flowerets
1 small yellow summer squash or zucchini, halved lengthwise and sliced (1 cup)
1 medium-size red, yellow, or green bell pepper, cut into bite-size strips
¼ cup chopped pitted Kalamata olives or sliced pitted ripe olives
⅔ cup sour cream

⅓ cup mayonnaise
¼ cup finely shredded Parmesan cheese
¼ cup (1 ounce) crumbled feta cheese
3 tablespoons low-fat (1%) milk
1 tablespoon minced fresh basil or 1 teaspoon dried basil leaves
¼ teaspoon ground black pepper
⅓ cup coarsely chopped cashews or toasted walnuts

Cook the tortellini according to the package directions; drain. Rinse under cold running water; drain again. In a large bowl, combine the tortellini, broccoli, yellow squash or zucchini, bell pepper, and olives.

For the dressing, combine the sour cream, mayonnaise, Parmesan cheese, feta cheese, milk, basil, and black pepper in a small bowl. Pour the dressing over the pasta mixture. Toss gently to coat. Cover and refrigerate at least 2 hours or overnight.

To serve, stir the cashews or walnuts into the pasta mixture. If needed, stir in a little extra milk to moisten the salad.

Makes 5 or 6 side-dish servings.

◆ TIP

Kalamata olives are full-flavored, brine-cured or marinated black olives that are sometimes slit to allow the marinade to penetrate the fruit. Look for them in Greek or Italian markets.

Saffron Couscous and Bulgur Salad

Sophisticated and sassy all at the same time, this lemony salad features a unique combination of couscous and bulgur plus peppery radicchio and toasty pine nuts.

2 cups water
½ cup bulgur (cracked wheat)
½ teaspoon salt
¼ teaspoon thread saffron, crushed
½ cup couscous
1 cup bite-size pieces radicchio or coarsely shredded red cabbage
1 medium-size green bell pepper, chopped
½ cup toasted pine nuts (see Tip, page 47)

¼ cup olive oil or vegetable oil
¼ cup fresh lemon juice
2 teaspoons sugar
1 teaspoon freshly grated lemon peel
½ teaspoon crushed red pepper
White savoy cabbage leaves or red-leaf lettuce leaves
Thinly sliced green onions, for garnish

In a medium-size saucepan, combine the water, bulgur, ¼ teaspoon of the salt, and the saffron and bring to a boil. Reduce heat, cover, and simmer 10 minutes or until the bulgur is nearly tender. Remove from heat; stir in the couscous. Cover and let stand 5 minutes.

Using a fork, fluff the grain mixture. Transfer to a large bowl; cool slightly. Stir in the radicchio or red cabbage, bell pepper, and pine nuts.

For the dressing, combine the oil, lemon juice, sugar, lemon peel, red pepper, and the remaining ¼ teaspoon salt in a jar with a tight lid. Cover and shake well. Pour the dressing over the grain mixture. Toss gently to coat. Cover and refrigerate at least 4 hours or overnight.

To serve, arrange the savoy cabbage or red-leaf lettuce leaves on salad plates. Spoon the grain mixture on top of the greens. Garnish with the green onions.

Makes 6 side-dish servings.

◆ TIP

Saffron comes in thin threads. To release its distinctive flavor, crush it by rubbing the threads between your fingers.

Chicken, Radicchio, and Peppery Toasted Garlic Bread Salad

Radicchio adds color as well as character to this Italian-inspired salad. The unique presentation—radicchio leaves layered over slices of garlicky toast and topped with cooked chicken, provolone cheese, and a zesty mustard vinaigrette—makes the salad ideal for a company lunch.

2 shallots, minced
¼ cup olive oil
3 tablespoons red wine vinegar
1 teaspoon sugar
1 teaspoon Dijon mustard
¼ cup (½ stick) butter, melted
1 teaspoon lemon pepper
1 teaspoon minced garlic
8 (½-inch) slices Italian bread or sourdough French bread

5 cups bite-size pieces radicchio or finely shredded red cabbage
2 cups chopped cooked chicken or turkey
½ cup (2 ounces) shredded provolone cheese or Gruyère cheese
¼ cup toasted coarsely chopped walnuts

For the vinaigrette, combine the shallots, olive oil, vinegar, sugar, and Dijon mustard in a jar with a tight lid. Cover and shake well. Let stand at least 30 minutes to allow the flavors to blend.

Preheat the broiler. In a small bowl, combine the butter, lemon pepper, and garlic. Lightly brush 1 side of each bread slice with some of the butter mixture. Place the bread slices, buttered side up, on a baking sheet. Broil 4 to 5 inches from the heat 1 to 2 minutes or until the bread is toasted.

To serve, place 2 slices of toasted bread on each of 4 dinner plates. Arrange the radicchio or red cabbage, chicken or turkey, and cheese on top of the toasted bread. Sprinkle with the walnuts. Shake the vinaigrette well; drizzle over the salads.

Makes 4 main-dish servings.

⬦ TIP

Radicchio can be any of several varieties of Italian chicory. Depending on the variety, it can range in color from pink to intense red but usually has a white center core and white ribs. Look for crisp leaves with no bruises or spots. You can store radicchio in the refrigerator for up to a week.

Hickory-Smoked Turkey and Shiitake Mushroom Salad with Orange-Balsamic Dressing

"*We're lucky enough to have a local supermarket that regularly carries smoked turkey,*" explains Rosemary. "*But if smoked turkey or chicken isn't available in your area, you can substitute ham or cooked smoked pork chops.*"

Orange-Balsamic Dressing
   (see opposite)
8 cups bite-size pieces spinach
10 ounces hickory-smoked cooked
   turkey or chicken, cut into
   bite-size pieces
2 cups bite-size pieces radicchio or
   coarsely shredded red cabbage
1 cup sliced fresh shiitake
   mushrooms
1 medium-size yellow, red, or green
   bell pepper, cut into thin bite-size
   strips
2 hard-cooked eggs, chopped

¼ cup coarsely chopped pistachio
   nuts or toasted slivered almonds

ORANGE-BALSAMIC DRESSING
⅓ cup vegetable oil
¼ cup balsamic vinegar or cider
   vinegar
¼ cup fresh orange juice
2 teaspoons minced fresh thyme or
   ½ teaspoon dried thyme leaves
1 teaspoon freshly grated orange peel
¼ teaspoon coarsely ground black
   pepper

Prepare the Orange-Balsamic Dressing. Cover and refrigerate while preparing the salad.

In a large bowl, combine the spinach, turkey or chicken, radicchio or red cabbage, shiitake mushrooms, and bell pepper. Toss gently to mix.

To serve, shake the dressing well; pour over the spinach mixture. Toss gently to coat. Arrange the spinach mixture on dinner plates. Sprinkle with the hard-cooked eggs and pistachio nuts or almonds.

Makes 4 main-dish servings.

ORANGE-BALSAMIC DRESSING

In a jar with a tight lid, combine the oil, vinegar, orange juice, thyme, orange peel, and black pepper. Cover and shake well, then refrigerate up to 1 week.

Makes about 1 cup.

✦ TIP

Balsamic vinegar is a sophisticated vinegar made from sweet white grape juice and aged in wooden barrels. It has a deep brown color and a mildly sweet flavor. It's available in a wide range of prices in many supermarkets and food specialty stores.

Beef Brochette and Portobello Mushroom Salad with Sun-Dried Tomato Vinaigrette

Revive jaded appetites with this hearty main-dish salad. The tongue-tingling dried tomato dressing brings out the best in the skewered beef or lamb, aromatic chèvre, and meaty portobello mushrooms.

1 pound boneless beef top sirloin
    steak or lean boneless lamb,
    ¾ inch thick and trimmed of fat
Sun-Dried Tomato Vinaigrette
    (see opposite)
4 ounces herbed or plain chèvre
    cheese (goat cheese)
8 ounces fresh portobello
    mushrooms
Olive oil
Red-leaf lettuce leaves
1 (15-ounce) can garbanzo beans,
    chilled, rinsed, and drained
4 small tomatoes, cut into wedges

SUN-DRIED TOMATO VINAIGRETTE
½ cup vinegar
⅓ cup olive oil
¼ cup finely chopped sun-dried
    tomatoes (oil packed)
2 tablespoons oil from sun-dried
    tomatoes
2 tablespoons water
1 tablespoon minced fresh oregano
    or 1 teaspoon dried oregano leaves
2 teaspoons sugar
1 teaspoon minced garlic
½ teaspoon ground cumin
½ teaspoon ground coriander
½ teaspoon paprika
¼ teaspoon crushed red pepper

Rinse the beef or lamb and pat dry with paper towels. Partially freeze the meat, then thinly slice across the grain into bite-size strips. Place the meat in a large heavy plastic bag.

Prepare the Sun-Dried Tomato Vinaigrette. Pour ½ cup of the vinaigrette over the meat; seal bag. Marinate in the refrigerator at least 6 hours or overnight, turning occasionally. Cover and refrigerate the remaining vinaigrette.

Meanwhile, shape the chèvre into 12 balls. Place the cheese balls in a single layer in a flat container; cover and refrigerate.

Shortly before assembling the salads, cover 8 (6-inch) bamboo skewers with water. Let stand 30 minutes; drain. Preheat the broiler.

Cut off the mushroom stems; discard. Using a damp paper towel, wipe the mushroom caps clean. Cut the mushroom caps into ½-inch-thick slices. Place the mushroom slices on the un-heated rack of a broiler pan. Brush with a little olive oil. Broil 4 to 5 inches from the heat 9 to 10 minutes or until the mushrooms are lightly charred and tender, turning the mushrooms after half of the cooking time. Transfer the mushrooms to a sheet of foil; wrap in the foil and keep warm.

For the meat skewers, drain the meat, discarding the vinaigrette. Thread the meat in ac-cordion fashion on the bamboo skewers, leaving ¼ inch space between the pieces. (Leaving a little space between the pieces of meat allows the meat to cook evenly.) Place the skewers on the rack of the broiler pan. Broil 4 to 5 inches from the heat 5 to 7 minutes or until the meat is of desired doneness, turning the meat skewers after half of the cooking time.

To serve, arrange the lettuce leaves on dinner plates. Arrange the cheese balls, garbanzo beans, and tomato wedges in separate piles on top of the lettuce, filling half of the surface of each plate.

Arrange the mushroom slices on top of the lettuce on the remaining half of the plates. Place the meat skewers on top of the mushroom slices. Shake the remaining vinaigrette well; pour over the salads.

Makes 4 main-dish servings.

SUN-DRIED TOMATO VINAIGRETTE

In a jar with a tight lid, combine the vinegar, olive oil, sun-dried tomatoes, oil from the sun-dried tomatoes, water, oregano, sugar, garlic, cumin, coriander, paprika, and crushed red pepper. Cover and shake well, then refrigerate up to 1 week.

Makes about 1 cup.

✦ TIP

To make slicing the meat easy, place it in the freezer 45 to 55 minutes or until partially frozen. Then, hold a knife at a slight angle to the cutting surface and slice the meat across the grain, making very thin slices (about 1/16 inch thick) 2 to 3 inches long.

Southwestern-Style Grilled Pork Salad
with Creamy Salsa Dressing

When you're in the mood to grill, treat your family to this tantalizing tequila-and-lime–marinated pork salad topped with a creamy salsa dressing. It includes many popular Tex-Mex ingredients, such as cilantro, chili powder, tomatoes, jicama, avocado, and olives.

1 (1-pound) boneless pork loin roast, trimmed of fat
1/3 cup tequila
1/3 cup fresh lime juice or lemon juice
2 tablespoons minced fresh cilantro or parsley
1 tablespoon minced fresh oregano or 1 teaspoon dried oregano leaves
1 tablespoon freshly grated lime peel or lemon peel
1 1/2 teaspoons chili powder
1 1/2 teaspoons minced garlic
Creamy Salsa Dressing (see opposite)
8 cups bite-size pieces romaine lettuce or mixed salad greens

1 cup cherry tomatoes, halved
1 cup peeled and coarsely chopped jicama or 1 (8-ounce) can sliced water chestnuts, rinsed and drained
1 ripe large avocado, pitted, peeled, and cut into bite-size pieces
1/2 medium-size red onion, thinly sliced and separated into rings
1/4 cup sliced pitted ripe olives
Tortilla chips

CREAMY SALSA DRESSING
1/3 cup mayonnaise
1/3 cup plain yogurt
1/3 cup bottled salsa

Cut the pork crosswise into 1/2-inch-thick slices. Place the meat in a heavy plastic bag. For the marinade, combine the tequila, lime or lemon juice, cilantro or parsley, oregano, lime or lemon peel, chili powder, and garlic. Pour over the meat; seal bag. Marinate in the refrigerator at least 6 hours or overnight, turning occasionally. Meanwhile, prepare the Creamy Salsa Dressing. Cover and refrigerate.

In an uncovered grill, arrange preheated coals in the firebox; test for medium-hot heat (see Tip, page 18). Drain the meat, discarding the marinade. Place the meat on the grill rack directly over the coals. Grill 10 to 12 minutes or until the meat is cooked through and the juices run clear when meat is pierced with a fork, turning after half of the cooking time. (Or, place the meat on the unheated rack of a broiler pan. Broil 4 to 5 inches from the heat 8 to 10 minutes or until the meat is cooked through and the juices run clear, turning after half of the cooking time.) Thinly cut the meat slices into bite-size strips.

In a large bowl, combine the meat strips, romaine lettuce or mixed greens, cherry tomatoes, jicama or water chestnuts, avocado, red onion, and olives. Toss gently to mix. Pour the dressing over the romaine mixture; toss gently to coat. Serve the salads with the tortilla chips.

Makes 4 main-dish servings.

CREAMY SALSA DRESSING

In a small bowl, stir together the mayonnaise, yogurt, and salsa. Cover and refrigerate up to 1 week.

Makes about 1 cup.

◆ TIP

If the avocados you buy are still quite firm, place them in a paper bag, close the bag, and let the avocados stand at room temperature for a day or so until they yield to a slight squeeze.

Arugula Salad with Warm Tuna and Creamy Braised Garlic Vinaigrette

Here's a tip from Sandra: "In the summer when tomatoes are at their peak, slice them and serve them with the mellow garlic dressing from this main-dish salad. It's an easy side dish that's so good!"

Creamy Braised Garlic Vinaigrette
   (see opposite)

4 medium-size tomatoes, peeled
   and cut into wedges

12 ounces fresh tuna, salmon,
   swordfish, or halibut steaks, cut
   1 inch thick

2 tablespoons fresh lemon juice

8 cups bite-size pieces arugula,
   sorrel, or spinach

1 cup shredded daikon or
   red radishes

1 cup cubed Muenster, creamy
   Havarti, or Monterey Jack cheese
   (4 ounces)

2 hard-cooked eggs, sliced

CREAMY BRAISED GARLIC VINAIGRETTE

2 teaspoons butter

5 large cloves garlic

3 large green onions, thinly sliced

$\frac{1}{3}$ cup olive oil or vegetable oil

$\frac{1}{3}$ cup red wine vinegar

2 tablespoons mayonnaise

1 tablespoon minced fresh basil or
   1 teaspoon dried basil leaves

$\frac{1}{4}$ teaspoon salt

$\frac{1}{8}$ teaspoon ground black pepper

Prepare the Creamy Braised Garlic Vinaigrette. Place the tomatoes in a medium-size bowl. Shake the vinaigrette well; pour over the tomatoes. Toss gently to coat. Cover and refrigerate at least 4 hours or overnight, stirring occasionally.

Preheat the broiler. Rinse the fish and pat dry with paper towels. Place the fish on the un-heated greased rack of a broiler pan. Brush the lemon juice on both sides of the fish. Broil 4 to 5 inches from the heat 12 to 16 minutes or until the fish is opaque throughout, turning after half of the cooking time. Cut the fish into bite-size pieces, being careful to remove all bones.

While the fish is broiling, arrange the arugula, sorrel, or spinach on dinner plates. Arrange the fish pieces, daikon or red radishes, and cheese on top of the greens. Using a slotted spoon, remove the tomatoes from the vinaigrette and arrange the tomatoes on top of the salads. Top with the egg slices. Drizzle the vinaigrette over the salads. Serve immediately.

Makes 4 main-dish servings.

CREAMY BRAISED GARLIC VINAIGRETTE

To braise the garlic, melt the butter over medium-high heat in a small saucepan. Add the garlic. Reduce heat to low, cover, and cook, stirring frequently, 15 minutes or until the garlic is soft and golden. Remove from heat. Using the tines of a fork, mash the garlic until it is well combined with the butter.

In a jar with a tight lid, combine the braised garlic mixture, the green onions, oil, vinegar, mayonnaise, basil, salt, and pepper. Cover and shake well, then refrigerate up to 1 week.

Makes about ¾ cup.

✦ TIP

Arugula is a leafy green that's also called "rocket." It has a pungent mustardlike flavor that's delicious as a counterpoint to milder greens. Look for small leaves with bright green color (larger leaves have a stronger flavor).

Scallop and Fennel Salad with Creamy Tarragon Vinaigrette

"Growing up, my Italian-born grandmother often cooked with a vegetable she called 'finocchio,'" recalls Rosemary. *"It wasn't until I went away to college that I discovered that the American name for it is 'fennel.' Its mild anise flavor provides an enchanting accent to the scallops, oranges, and creamy tarragon dressing in this salad."*

Creamy Tarragon Vinaigrette
(see opposite)
1½ pounds fresh or thawed frozen
sea scallops
2 small bulbs fennel with tops
12 cups mesclun (mixed baby greens)
or 8 cups bite-size pieces romaine
lettuce and 4 cups bite-size pieces
curly endive, chicory, or escarole
4 oranges, peeled and sectioned
Vegetable oil
3 large shallots, thinly sliced and
separated into rings

CREAMY TARRAGON VINAIGRETTE
⅔ cup white wine vinegar or
rice vinegar
⅓ cup sugar
2 large shallots, quartered
2 tablespoons minced fresh tarragon
or 2 teaspoons dried tarragon
leaves
2 teaspoons dry mustard
¼ teaspoon salt
¼ teaspoon ground red (cayenne)
pepper
½ cup olive oil or vegetable oil

Prepare the Creamy Tarragon Vinaigrette. Cover and refrigerate while preparing the salad.

Rinse the scallops and pat dry with paper towels. Remove any tough or bruised outer leaves from the fennel bulbs. Trim off the root ends; discard. Pull off the feathery tops from the stems; finely chop the tops. Trim off the stems; discard. Thoroughly rinse the trimmed bulbs and quarter each bulb lengthwise; remove the core. Cut the bulbs crosswise into thin slices; toss with the fennel tops.

Arrange the mesclun or romaine lettuce and endive, chicory, or escarole on dinner plates. Arrange the fennel and orange sections on top of the greens.

In a wok or large heavy saucepan, heat 1 to 1½ inches of vegetable oil over medium-high heat to 375°F (190°C). Add the shallot rings, half at a time, and cook 30 to 60 seconds or until the shallots are crisp and golden brown. Using a wire strainer or slotted spoon, remove the shallots from the hot oil. Drain well on paper towels.

Add the scallops to the hot oil, a few at a time, and cook 1 to 1½ minutes or until the scallops are opaque throughout. Using a wire strainer or slotted spoon, remove the scallops from the hot oil. Drain well on paper towels.

Arrange the fried scallops and shallots on top of the greens mixture. Drizzle the dressing over the salads. Serve immediately.

Makes 6 main-dish servings.

CREAMY TARRAGON VINAIGRETTE

In a food processor or blender, combine the vinegar, sugar, shallots, tarragon, mustard, salt, and cayenne. Cover and process until smooth. With the processor or blender running, add the ½ cup olive or vegetable oil in a thin, steady stream and process 2 minutes or until the mixture thickens. Cover and refrigerate (will keep for up to 1 week).

Makes about 1½ cups.

◆ TIP

If the scallops are very large, cut them in half so they are bite-size.

Baked Chèvre and Garden Salad

Marinated rounds of crumb-coated baked chèvre give an exquisite tart flavor to the vegetables in this tossed salad.

8 ounces chèvre cheese (goat cheese)
¼ cup walnut oil or olive oil
1 tablespoon minced fresh marjoram or 1 teaspoon dried marjoram leaves
¼ teaspoon hot pepper sauce
8 cups bite-size pieces mixed salad greens
1 cup alfalfa sprouts
½ medium-size red onion, thinly sliced and separated into rings
½ cup thinly sliced zucchini, yellow summer squash, or cucumber
½ cup sliced radishes

1 (15-ounce) can great Northern beans, rinsed and drained
¾ cup toasted soft bread crumbs
1 tablespoon toasted sesame seeds
¼ cup fresh lime juice or lemon juice
1 tablespoon Dijon mustard
1 teaspoon sugar
1 teaspoon minced garlic
Violas or other edible flowers, for garnish
4 small pita bread rounds, split horizontally, cut into wedges, and toasted

Slice or shape the cheese into 8 (½-inch-thick) rounds (see Tip, opposite page). In a shallow dish, arrange the cheese rounds in a single layer. For the marinade, combine the oil, marjoram, and hot pepper sauce. Pour over the cheese rounds; turn the cheese over to coat with the marinade. Let stand 30 minutes, occasionally spooning the marinade over the cheese. (Or, cover and marinate in the refrigerator at least 4 hours or overnight, occasionally spooning the marinade over the cheese.)

In a large bowl, combine the mixed greens; alfalfa sprouts; red onion; zucchini, yellow squash, or cucumber; and radishes. Toss gently to mix. Arrange the greens mixture on dinner plates. Arrange the beans on top of the greens mixture.

Preheat the oven to 425°F (220°C). Lightly grease a baking sheet; set aside. In a shallow bowl, combine the bread crumbs and sesame seeds. Remove the cheese rounds from the marinade, reserving the marinade. Pat the bread crumb mixture onto both sides of the cheese rounds. Place the cheese rounds on the prepared baking sheet. Bake 5 to 6 minutes or until the cheese is softened, slightly bubbly, and golden brown.

While the cheese bakes, prepare the dressing: In a jar with a tight lid, combine the marinade, the lime or lemon juice, Dijon mustard, sugar, and garlic. Cover and shake well.

Using a metal spatula, carefully place the hot, soft cheese rounds on top of the greens mixture. Shake the dressing well; drizzle over the greens mixture and cheese rounds. Garnish the salads with the flowers. Serve immediately with the toasted pita wedges.

Makes 4 main-dish servings.

◆ TIP

There are several types of chèvre cheese available. If the kind you purchase is soft and creamy, you'll need to shape it into rounds with your hands. If the chèvre is firm-textured, simply slice it.

Thai-Style Beef Salad

"*After eating at a variety of Thai restaurants, we created this salad to try to capture some of those wonderful authentic flavors,*" *says Sandra.* "*We started with traditional seasonings, such as mint, cilantro, lemongrass, lime juice, and fish sauce, and let our imaginations take us from there.*"

3 fresh green serrano chiles
¼ cup vegetable oil
¼ cup water
¼ cup fish sauce (nam pla) or
   soy sauce
¼ cup fresh lime juice
3 tablespoons sugar
3 cloves garlic
2 medium-size cucumbers
1 small red or yellow onion, thinly
   sliced and separated into rings

8 cups bite-size pieces mixed salad
   greens
¼ cup minced fresh mint
¼ cup minced fresh cilantro
2 stalks lemongrass, finely chopped
   (1 tablespoon)
12 ounces lean cooked beef, cut into
   thin strips
¼ cup coarsely chopped dry-roasted
   peanuts

Wearing plastic or rubber gloves to protect your skin from the oils in the chiles, halve the chiles lengthwise; discard the stems, seeds, and membranes.

For the dressing, combine the serrano chiles, oil, water, fish sauce or soy sauce, lime juice, sugar, and garlic in a food processor or blender. Cover and process until nearly smooth; set aside.

Peel the cucumbers. Halve the cucumbers lengthwise; scoop out and discard the seeds. Thinly slice or coarsely shred the cucumbers. In a medium-size bowl, combine the sliced or shredded cucumbers and the onion rings. Pour the dressing over the cucumber mixture; toss gently to coat. Cover and refrigerate at least 2 hours or up to 3 days, stirring occasionally.

To serve, arrange the mixed greens on dinner plates. Sprinkle the mint, cilantro, and lemongrass on top of the greens. Arrange the beef strips on top of the herbs. Using a slotted spoon, place the cucumber mixture on top of the beef. Pour some of the dressing from the cucumber mixture over the salads. Sprinkle with the peanuts.

Makes 4 main-dish servings.

VARIATION

If you can't find lemongrass, substitute ½ teaspoon freshly grated lemon peel for the 1 tablespoon lemongrass.

VIBRANT VEGETABLES

Vegetables have come a long way. No longer are they something your mother insists that you eat. With today's new ingredients, imaginative seasonings, and innovative cooking methods, they've become a gustatory adventure. And, with the remarkable recipes in this chapter, we'll show you just how marvelous vegetables can be.

Consider Oven-Roasted Asparagus with Pine Nut Dressing, for example. Not only does this sophisticated recipe have an awesome pine nut and cilantro seasoning, it's easy on the cook. If Asian flavors tempt you, try Broccoli Stir-Fry in Oyster Sauce. This side-dish-in-a-wok combines black mushrooms, shallots, and broccoli with a savory oyster sauce, ginger, and garlic combination. When you need an elegant accent, Grand Marnier–Glazed Carrots and Spiced Grapes is the perfect solution. Ruby red grapes spiced with balsamic vinegar, cinnamon, and nutmeg are tossed with julienne carrots and a Grand Marnier sauce. For a newfangled twist on an old-fashioned favorite, enjoy Sautéed Corn Pudding. This velvety custard is loaded with browned-in-butter fresh corn, nutmeg, and hot pepper sauce. And when it comes to mashed potatoes, there's Whipped Potatoes with Chipotle Chiles, which features a mix of sweet potatoes and Yukon Golds blended with sour cream and potent Southwestern-style chiles.

These cream-of-the-crop vegetables have played a delicious part in some of our most memorable meals. Try several soon and see if they don't add an extra flavor boost to some of yours.

Oven-Roasted Asparagus with Pine Nut Dressing

"Baking is an easy way to cook asparagus," suggests Sharyl. "You can use an ordinary baking dish and don't have to find a pan the right size for steaming the spears. Also, the asparagus retains its rich green color and fresh-from-the-garden flavor."

1 pound fresh asparagus	2 tablespoons butter, cut into pieces
2 tablespoons fresh orange juice	2 teaspoons minced fresh thyme or
1/3 cup toasted pine nuts (see Tip,	1/2 teaspoon dried thyme leaves
page 47)	1/8 teaspoon ground nutmeg
2 tablespoons minced fresh cilantro	1/8 teaspoon ground black pepper

Preheat the oven to 350°F (175°C). Wash the asparagus. If desired, use a vegetable peeler to scrape off the scales from the asparagus. Snap off the woody bases at the point where the spears snap easily; discard the bases.

Place the asparagus spears in a 12 x 7½-inch baking dish. Pour the orange juice around the asparagus. Add the pine nuts, cilantro, butter, thyme, nutmeg, and pepper. Cover with foil and bake 25 minutes or until the asparagus is crisp-tender.

Makes 4 servings.

+ TIP

For best flavor, buy asparagus the same day you plan to use it. (However, you can store it up to 4 days, if necessary.) When you get home, stand the stalks upright in a tall container with a small amount of water in the bottom. Or, wrap the ends of the stalks in a damp paper towel and seal the asparagus in a plastic bag. Store in the refrigerator.

Roasted Beets with Apples and Honey-Ginger Butter

We baked rather than boiled the beets for this rosy side dish so they would retain as much of their color and flavor as possible. The mellow ginger butter brings out the best in both the beets and the apples, while the walnuts add crunch.

1½ pounds small fresh beets, about 1½ inches in diameter
½ cup water
3 tablespoons tarragon vinegar
1 tablespoon olive oil
¼ cup (½ stick) butter

2 tablespoons honey
2 tart apples, peeled, cored, and thinly sliced
1 tablespoon minced gingerroot
½ cup toasted broken walnuts

Preheat the oven to 375°F (190°C). Thoroughly wash the fresh beets, but avoid using a brush because the beets have very thin skins. Trim the beets 1 inch above the stems. Place the beets in a 12 x 7½-inch baking dish.

In a small bowl, combine the water, vinegar, and olive oil. Pour over the beets. Cover with foil and bake 35 to 40 minutes or until the beets are tender. (A small knife or toothpick should slip in and out easily.) Discard the cooking liquid. Let the beets stand until cool enough to handle, then peel the beets by slipping off the skins. (You want the beets to still be warm so the skins will come off easily.) Slice the beets ¼ inch thick; set aside.

In a large skillet, heat the butter and honey over medium heat. Add the apples and gingerroot. Reduce heat to medium-low and cook, stirring occasionally, 3 minutes or just until the apples are tender. Add the beets and cook, stirring occasionally, 2 minutes longer or until heated through. Sprinkle with the walnuts.

Makes 4 servings.

VARIATION

When time is short, substitute 2 (16-ounce) cans sliced beets, rinsed and drained, for the fresh beets. Just add the canned beets to the apple mixture and heat through.

Broccoli Stir-Fry in Oyster Sauce

Oyster sauce adds a bold, tart yet sweet flavor to this broccoli and mushroom combination. Make this stir-fry soon to go along with roast beef, pork, or poultry.

8 dried black mushrooms	1/2 teaspoon crushed red pepper
1/3 cup chicken broth	1 tablespoon vegetable oil
1/3 cup water	1/4 cup finely chopped shallots
1/4 cup oyster sauce	2 teaspoons minced gingerroot
2 1/2 teaspoons cornstarch	1 teaspoon minced garlic
1 teaspoon sugar	6 cups broccoli flowerets

In a small bowl, cover the dried mushrooms with hot water. Let stand 30 minutes. Rinse under warm running water; squeeze out excess moisture. Remove and discard the stems. Thinly slice the mushroom caps.

For the sauce, stir together the chicken broth, water, oyster sauce, cornstarch, sugar, and crushed red pepper in a small bowl; set aside.

In a wok or large nonstick skillet, heat the oil over medium-high heat. (If needed, add more oil during cooking.) Add the shallots, gingerroot, and garlic and stir-fry 1 minute. Add the broccoli and mushrooms and stir-fry 3 to 4 minutes or until the broccoli is crisp-tender. Push the vegetables against the side of the wok.

Stir the sauce; add to the center of the wok. Cook, stirring constantly, 1 to 2 minutes or until the sauce thickens. Stir the vegetables into the sauce until coated. Cook, stirring constantly, 1 minute longer or until the vegetables are heated through. Serve immediately.

Makes 4 servings.

✦ TIP

Look for broccoli stalks with heads that are a rich green color. Avoid those with very light green heads or small yellow flowers. You can store fresh broccoli in a plastic bag in the refrigerator up to 4 days.

Grand Marnier–Glazed Carrots and Spiced Grapes

This sophisticated fruit and vegetable medley will add an elegant touch to even the simplest meat dishes. We especially like it with Pesto-Stuffed Chicken Breasts au Poivre (page 92).

2 cups seedless red grapes, halved
2 tablespoons light brown sugar
1 tablespoon balsamic vinegar
¼ teaspoon ground cinnamon
⅛ teaspoon ground nutmeg
8 medium-size carrots

3 tablespoons Grand Marnier
  liqueur or brandy
1 teaspoon cornstarch
2 tablespoons butter
2 tablespoons minced fresh parsley

In a medium-size bowl, combine the grapes, brown sugar, balsamic vinegar, cinnamon, and nutmeg. Toss gently to coat. Let stand at room temperature 30 minutes, tossing occasionally.

Meanwhile, thoroughly wash the carrots; trim off the ends. Peel or scrub the carrots. Cut the carrots into thin 2½-inch-long sticks. (To make the thin sticks, cut the carrots into thirds cross-wise, then in half lengthwise. Continue cutting the carrots lengthwise to create long, thin sticks.)

To steam the carrots, place a steamer basket in a Dutch oven. Add water to just below the basket. Bring the water to a boil over high heat. Place the carrot sticks in the steamer basket. Cover and steam 6 to 8 minutes or until the carrots are crisp-tender. Remove from heat.

Drain the grapes, reserving the liquid. In a small bowl, stir together the reserved grape liquid, the Grand Marnier or brandy, and cornstarch.

In a large skillet, melt the butter over medium heat. Add the grapes, tossing gently to coat with the butter. Stir the cornstarch mixture into the grapes in the skillet. Cook, stirring constantly, until the mixture thickens. Stir in the carrots. Cook, stirring constantly, 1 to 2 minutes or until the grapes are heated through.

To serve, transfer the carrot mixture to a serving bowl. Sprinkle with the parsley.

Makes 4 servings.

+ TIP

When steaming, be sure to add only enough water to the pan so that the water level is just below, but doesn't touch, the steamer basket.

Braised Celery and Celeriac Provençal

Celeriac or celery root is an irregularly shaped vegetable that's brown on the outside and white on the inside. It has a mild flavor that's somewhere between celery and parsley. Here, we've cooked and combined it with celery, onion, carrot, and tomatoes, and then added some white wine, orange peel, and nutmeg for good measure.

4 stalks celery	½ cup dry white wine
2 small celeriacs (about 1 pound total)	1 teaspoon freshly grated orange peel
3 tablespoons butter	½ teaspoon freshly ground black pepper
1 large carrot, chopped	¼ teaspoon salt
1 medium-size onion, halved lengthwise and thinly sliced	⅛ teaspoon ground nutmeg
1 teaspoon minced garlic	1 tablespoon minced fresh parsley
2 medium-size tomatoes, cut into thin wedges	1 tablespoon fresh lemon juice
	Celery leaves, for garnish

Thoroughly wash the celery. If desired, use a vegetable peeler to remove as many strings as possible from the celery. Halve the stalks lengthwise, then slice diagonally into ¾-inch pieces. In a medium-size saucepan, bring a small amount of water to a boil over high heat. Add the celery. Return to a boil and cook 1 minute. Drain well.

Peel the celeriacs. Quarter the celeriacs lengthwise, then cut crosswise into slices. In a large saucepan, melt the butter over medium heat. Add the celeriacs, carrot, onion, and garlic and cook, stirring frequently, 5 minutes or until the vegetables are crisp-tender. Add the celery and tomatoes and cook 3 minutes.

Stir in the wine, orange peel, pepper, salt, and nutmeg. Bring to a boil. Reduce heat, cover, and simmer 5 minutes or until the celery is tender. Uncover and cook 3 to 5 minutes or until the mixture is of desired consistency. Stir in the parsley and lemon juice.

To serve, transfer the vegetable mixture to a serving bowl. Garnish with the celery leaves. Serve the vegetable mixture in small individual dishes.

Makes 4 servings.

● TIP

Choose small celeriacs (celery roots) that are firm with as few roots and knobs as possible. Larger ones tend to be woody and tough. Store celeriac in a plastic bag in the refrigerator up to a week.

Spicy Stuffed Chayote

"Chayote's pear shape and mild applelike flavor make it ideal for stuffing," says Liz. "In this recipe, we heaped chayote halves with a zesty filling of toasted soft bread crumbs, powerful jalapeño chiles, cilantro, garlic, and ground red pepper, then topped them with Monterey Jack cheese."

2 chayotes (12 to 14 ounces each)
¼ cup (½ stick) butter
1½ cups soft bread crumbs
1 or 2 fresh jalapeño chiles
2 stalks celery, chopped
½ cup thinly sliced green onions
1 tablespoon minced garlic
2 tablespoons minced fresh cilantro
   or parsley

½ teaspoon salt
¼ teaspoon ground red (cayenne)
   pepper
¼ teaspoon ground black pepper
½ cup (2 ounces) shredded
   Monterey Jack cheese or sharp
   cheddar cheese

In a large saucepan, cover the chayotes with lightly salted water and bring to a boil. Reduce heat, cover, and simmer 35 to 40 minutes or until the chayotes are tender. (A wooden skewer should slip in and out easily.) Drain. In a large bowl, cover the chayotes with ice water. When cool enough to handle, peel the chayotes. Cut each chayote in half lengthwise and remove the single flat seed. Using a spoon, scoop out the pulp, leaving ½-inch-thick shells. Chop the pulp. Squeeze the chopped pulp between paper towels to remove excess moisture; set aside.

Preheat the oven to 350°F (175°C). For the stuffing, melt 2 tablespoons of the butter in a large skillet over medium heat. Add the bread crumbs and cook, stirring frequently, 3 minutes or until the bread crumbs are golden brown and crisp. Transfer the crumbs to a medium-size bowl.

Wearing plastic or rubber gloves to protect your skin from the oils in the chile(s), halve the chile(s) lengthwise; discard the stem(s), seeds, and membranes. Mince the chile(s).

In the same skillet, melt the remaining 2 tablespoons butter over medium heat. Add the chile(s), celery, green onions, and garlic and cook, stirring frequently, 5 to 6 minutes or until the vegetables are tender. Add the vegetables to the bread crumbs. Stir in the chayote pulp, cilantro or parsley, salt, cayenne, and black pepper.

Spoon the stuffing into the chayote shells. Place the shells in a 12 x 7½-inch baking dish. Bake 25 to 30 minutes or until the stuffing is heated through. Sprinkle with the cheese. Bake 5 minutes or until the cheese is melted.

Makes 4 servings.

✦ TIP

To make soft bread crumbs quickly, just whirl torn pieces of bread in a blender or food processor. You'll get about ¾ cup crumbs from each slice of bread.

Sautéed Corn Pudding

This savory custard, brimming with corn and seasoned with nutmeg, hot pepper sauce, and cayenne, is a delicious change of pace from ordinary vegetables. We found sautéing the corn with a little butter and garlic gives it a tantalizing "browned" flavor.

3 ears of corn or 1½ cups frozen
   whole-kernel corn
2 tablespoons butter
1 medium-size onion, finely chopped
1 tablespoon minced garlic
4 eggs, lightly beaten
1½ cups half-and-half

½ teaspoon sugar
¼ teaspoon salt
¼ teaspoon ground nutmeg
⅛ to ¼ teaspoon hot pepper sauce
⅛ teaspoon ground red (cayenne)
   pepper
Minced fresh chives, for garnish

If using the fresh ears of corn, place 1 ear of corn at a time in a shallow pan. Holding the ear at an angle, use a sharp knife to cut down across the tips of the kernels. Using the dull side of the knife, scrape the ear to release the milky juices into the pan. Measure 1½ cups of the corn with its juices.

Preheat the oven to 325°F (165°C). In a large skillet, melt the butter over medium heat. Add the onion and garlic and cook, stirring frequently, 5 minutes or until the onion is tender. Stir in the fresh or frozen corn. Cook, stirring occasionally, 10 minutes or until the corn is crisp-tender.

Meanwhile, lightly grease 6 (6-ounce) individual ramekins or casserole dishes; set aside. In a medium-size bowl, stir together the eggs, half-and-half, sugar, salt, nutmeg, hot pepper sauce, and cayenne. Stir in the cooked corn mixture.

Pour about ½ cup of the corn custard mixture into each prepared ramekin. Place the ramekins in a large shallow baking pan. Pour boiling water into the baking pan to a depth of 1 inch. Bake 18 to 20 minutes or until a knife inserted off-center comes out clean.

To serve, garnish the corn puddings with the chives.

Makes 6 servings.

◆ TIP

The safest way to pour boiling water into the baking pan is to arrange the ramekins in the pan and place the pan on the oven rack. Then, pour the boiling water around the ramekins. This way, you avoid carrying a baking pan full of hot water.

Fennel and Carrots with Caviar Cream

While the caviar favored by connoisseurs (salted sturgeon roe) is costly, the roe from other fish, such as lumpfish, whitefish, and salmon, is much more affordable and very tasty—at least for the caviar novice. In this company-special vegetable, we've used salmon or red caviar to give the cream sauce a rosy tint.

2 medium-size bulbs fennel with tops	2 tablespoons fresh lemon juice
4 medium-size carrots	1/8 teaspoon ground black pepper
3 tablespoons unsalted butter	1/2 cup whipping cream
2 large shallots, finely chopped	1 tablespoon salmon or red caviar
1/2 cup dry white wine	

Remove any tough or bruised outer leaves from the fennel bulbs. Trim off the root ends; discard. Pull off the feathery tops from the stems. Finely chop the tops; reserve 2 tablespoons of the tops. Trim off the stems; discard. Thoroughly rinse the trimmed bulbs and halve each bulb lengthwise; remove the core. Cut the bulbs crosswise into 1/4-inch-thick slices.

Thoroughly wash the carrots; trim off the ends. Peel or scrub the carrots and cut them into thin 2½-inch-long sticks. (To make the thin sticks, cut the carrots into thirds crosswise, then in half lengthwise. Continue cutting the carrots lengthwise to create long, thin sticks.)

In a large saucepan, bring a small amount of water to a boil over high heat. Add the fennel slices and carrots. Reduce heat, cover, and simmer 7 to 9 minutes or until the vegetables are crisp-tender. Drain well. Transfer the fennel and carrots to a serving bowl; keep warm.

Meanwhile, for the sauce, melt the butter in a medium-size heavy saucepan, over medium heat. Add the shallots and cook, stirring frequently, 3 to 5 minutes or until the shallots are tender. Stir in the wine, lemon juice, and pepper and bring to a boil over high heat. Reduce heat to medium-high and cook 5 to 8 minutes or until the wine mixture is reduced to about 1/3 cup. Remove from heat.

Slowly add the whipping cream to the wine mixture, stirring constantly. Cook over medium heat, stirring occasionally, until the mixture slightly thickens. Stir in the caviar; heat through.

To serve, spoon the sauce over the fennel and carrots. Sprinkle with the reserved fennel tops. **Makes 4 servings.**

+ TIP

Fresh fennel is most commonly sold from September to April. Look for firm bulbs that have no cracks, bruises, or brown spots. The leaves should be bright green. You can refrigerate fennel up to 4 days in a plastic bag.

Mixed Mushrooms and Red Onion with Porcini Mushroom Oil Marinade

Three different types of mushrooms plus red onion wedges and bell pepper strips give this broiled vegetable medley an enticing blend of colors, tastes, and textures. The porcini mushroom oil– and sherry vinegar–accented marinade offers a hint of sophistication and a lot of flavor interest. (Photo on cover.)

4 cups (about 12 ounces) assorted fresh mushrooms, quartered (large brown and white mushrooms or medium-size chanterelle mushrooms)

1 large red bell pepper, cut into bite-size strips

1 small red onion, cut into wedges

½ cup dry white wine

¼ cup porcini mushroom oil or walnut oil

3 tablespoons sherry vinegar or red wine vinegar

2 teaspoons minced roasted garlic

1 teaspoon sea salt or ½ teaspoon kosher salt

½ teaspoon dry mustard

⅛ teaspoon ground red (cayenne) pepper

Watercress sprigs, for garnish

Place the mushrooms, bell pepper, and onion in a heavy plastic bag.

For the marinade, combine the white wine, oil, vinegar, garlic, salt, dry mustard, and cayenne. Pour over the vegetables; seal bag. Marinate in the refrigerator 3 to 5 hours, turning occasionally.

Preheat the broiler. Drain the vegetables, reserving the marinade. Place vegetables on an unheated broiler rack. Broil 4 to 5 inches from the heat 10 to 12 minutes or until the onion wedges are lightly charred and tender, turning the vegetables after half the cooking time and brushing with more marinade.

To serve, arrange the vegetables on 4 small plates. Garnish with watercress.

Makes 4 servings.

Red Onion with Pears, Green Peppercorns, and Blue Cheese

Wonderfully sharp blue cheese sprinkled over delicate pears and mellow red onion makes a memorable taste sensation.

3 tablespoons butter
1 large red onion, quartered
   lengthwise and thinly sliced
1 tablespoon minced fresh thyme or
   1 teaspoon dried thyme leaves
2 medium-size Bartlett or Bosc pears,
   cored, sliced, and halved crosswise

1 (1.94-ounce) can green
   peppercorns, drained and crushed
   (2 tablespoons)
¼ cup (1 ounce) crumbled
   blue cheese

In a large skillet, melt 2 tablespoons of the butter over medium heat. Add the onion and thyme and cook, stirring frequently, 5 minutes or until the onion is tender. Push the onion mixture against the side of the skillet.

Add the remaining 1 tablespoon butter to the center of the skillet; melt the butter over medium heat. Add the pears to the center of the skillet, tossing gently to coat with the butter. Cook 1 minute. Gently stir the crushed peppercorns and the onion mixture into the pears. Cook, stirring occasionally, 2 minutes or just until the pears are tender.

To serve, transfer the onion mixture and pears to a serving bowl. Sprinkle with the blue cheese.

Makes 4 servings.

❖ TIP

Bartlett pears, sold in summer and fall, and Bosc pears, available in winter and spring, are the best for this recipe because they are sturdy enough to stand up to cooking in a skillet.

Braised Springtime Peas and Pods in Crème Fraîche

Extra-sweet sugar snap peas are usually eaten pods and all. They differ from Chinese pea pods (snow peas) in that the pods are more rounded and they have fully developed peas inside. They add a tasty texture contrast to regular peas in this recipe.

Crème Fraîche (see opposite) or
   sour cream
12 ounces fresh sugar snap peas or
   pea pods or 1 (6-ounce) package
   frozen pea pods
4 to 6 lettuce leaves
2 cups shelled fresh green peas or
   1 (10-ounce) package frozen
   green peas
8 medium-size green onions, thinly
   sliced

1 tablespoon minced fresh tarragon
   or 1 teaspoon dried tarragon leaves
1 teaspoon sugar
¼ teaspoon salt
⅛ teaspoon ground black pepper
2 tablespoons minced fresh parsley

CRÈME FRAÎCHE
¾ cup whipping cream
   (not ultrapasteurized)
1 tablespoon buttermilk

Prepare the Crème Fraîche, if using. Wash the fresh snap peas or pea pods. To remove the strings from the pods, use your fingers or a paring knife to pull off the tip of each pod without breaking the string, then gently pull the string down the length of the pod; discard the string.

Moisten the lettuce leaves, leaving a few drops of water clinging to the leaves. In a large skillet, line the bottom with the lettuce leaves. Top with the fresh or frozen snap peas or pea pods, the fresh or frozen peas, and the green onions. Sprinkle with the tarragon, sugar, salt, and pepper.

Cover tightly and cook over low heat 18 to 20 minutes or until the peas are crisp-tender. Drain well; discard the lettuce. Toss the pea mixture with the crème fraîche or sour cream and the parsley. If needed, stir in a little milk to thin the mixture.

Makes 6 servings.

CRÈME FRAÎCHE

In a small saucepan, heat the whipping cream over low heat until warm (between 90 and 100°F, 30 and 40°C). Pour the cream into a small bowl. Stir in the buttermilk. Cover and let stand at room temperature 24 to 30 hours or until the mixture thickens, but do not stir. To store, refrigerate up to 1 week.

Makes ¾ cup.

Whipped Potatoes with Chipotle Chiles

"Forget plain sweet potatoes!" exclaims Sandra. "This mixture of whipped Yukon Gold potatoes and sweet potatoes is truly extraordinary. The chipotle chiles in adobo sauce give the potatoes plenty of smoky bite, while the sour cream makes them creamy and rich."

3 large Yukon Gold potatoes or
   other potatoes (6 to 8 ounces each)
2 large sweet potatoes or yams
   (6 to 8 ounces each)
¼ cup sour cream
2 tablespoons butter

2 canned chipotle chiles in adobo
   sauce, finely chopped
½ teaspoon salt
¼ teaspoon ground black pepper
1 tablespoon minced fresh chives

Peel and cube the potatoes and sweet potatoes or yams. In a medium-size saucepan, bring a small amount of lightly salted water to a boil over high heat. Add the potatoes and sweet potatoes. Reduce heat, cover, and simmer 20 to 25 minutes or until the potatoes and sweet potatoes are tender. Drain well.

In a large bowl, place the potatoes and sweet potatoes. Beat with an electric mixer at low speed until the potatoes and sweet potatoes are nearly smooth. Add the sour cream, butter, chipotle chiles, salt, and pepper. Beat until the potato mixture is light and fluffy. (Don't over-beat the whipped potatoes; a lump or two left in the potatoes is just fine.)

To serve, transfer the potato mixture to a serving bowl. Sprinkle with the chives.
Makes 6 servings.

✦ TIP

Yukon Gold potatoes are just one of several varieties that are creamy yellow with a slight buttery flavor. They're especially good for mashing or whipping. Other gold potatoes include Finnish Yellow and Yellow Rose.

Garlicky Potato, Fennel, and Carrot au Gratin

"This showy version of potatoes au gratin is perfect for company," declares Rosemary. "I make it ahead and then just tuck it in the oven about 40 minutes before mealtime. Because there's little last-minute preparation, I have more time to spend with my guests."

4 large baking potatoes
 (6 to 8 ounces each)
1 large bulb fennel
2 cups baby-cut carrots (see Tip, below)
2 leeks, sliced
2 bay leaves
2 tablespoons butter
1 tablespoon minced garlic
2 tablespoons all-purpose flour

½ teaspoon salt
¼ teaspoon ground white pepper
 or black pepper
2 cups low-fat (1%) milk
1 cup (4 ounces) shredded Jarlsberg
 cheese, Swiss cheese, or Gruyère
 cheese
½ cup seasoned dry bread crumbs
2 tablespoons butter, melted

Peel and thinly slice the potatoes. Remove any tough or bruised outer leaves from the fennel bulb. Trim off the root end and the stems; discard. Thoroughly rinse the trimmed bulb and halve the bulb lengthwise; remove the core. Cut the bulb crosswise into thin slices.

In a Dutch oven, bring a small amount of lightly salted water to a boil over high heat. Add the potatoes, fennel, carrots, leeks, and bay leaves and return to a boil. Reduce heat, cover, and simmer 6 to 8 minutes or just until the vegetables are crisp-tender. Drain well; discard the bay leaves.

For the sauce, in a medium-size saucepan, melt the 2 tablespoons butter over medium heat. Add the garlic and cook, stirring frequently, 2 minutes. Stir in the flour, salt, and white or black pepper. Add the milk gradually, stirring until blended. Cook, stirring constantly, until the mixture thickens. Cook, stirring constantly, 1 minute. Remove from heat. Stir in ½ cup of the cheese until the sauce is smooth.

Lightly grease a 13 x 9-inch baking dish. Place the vegetables in the prepared dish. Pour the sauce over the vegetables. For the topping, in a small bowl, stir together the bread crumbs and the 2 tablespoons melted butter. Sprinkle the topping over the vegetable mixture. (At this point, you can cover and refrigerate the vegetable mixture up to 2 hours.)

Preheat the oven to 350°F (175°C). Bake the casserole 25 minutes (if chilled, bake 35 minutes) or until the vegetable mixture is heated through and bubbly. Sprinkle with the remaining ½ cup cheese. Bake 5 minutes or until the cheese is melted.

Makes 8 servings.

◆ TIP
   Baby-cut carrots are miniature carrot logs cut from full-size carrots. They're sold in plastic bags in most grocery stores.

Sweet Potato Torta with Tomatoes and Mozzarella

Torta *in both Italian and Spanish means "cake." This sweet potato "cake" is seasoned with oregano and garlic, and layered with tomatoes, onion, and lots of mozzarella cheese.*

2 tablespoons olive oil
1 large onion, halved lengthwise
    and thinly sliced
1 tablespoon minced fresh oregano
    or 1 teaspoon dried oregano
    leaves
1 teaspoon minced garlic
½ teaspoon salt
¼ teaspoon ground black pepper

3 large sweet potatoes, yams, or
    baking potatoes (6 to 8 ounces
    each), thinly sliced
1½ cups (6 ounces) shredded
    mozzarella cheese
1¾ cups coarsely chopped tomatoes
    or 1 (14½-ounce) can diced
    tomatoes, drained
¼ cup minced fresh parsley

Preheat the oven to 425°F (220°C). Lightly grease a 9-inch-square baking pan; set aside.

In a large skillet, heat the olive oil over medium heat. Add the onion, oregano, garlic, salt, and pepper and cook, stirring frequently, 5 minutes or until the onion is tender. Spread the onion mixture in the prepared pan.

Layer ⅓ of the sweet potatoes, yams, or baking potatoes; ½ cup of the mozzarella cheese; and half of the tomatoes on top of the onion mixture. Repeat the layers, then top with a final layer of sweet potatoes.

Cover and bake 50 to 55 minutes or until the sweet potatoes are tender. Sprinkle with the remaining ½ cup cheese. Bake, uncovered, 5 minutes or until the cheese is melted. Sprinkle with the parsley.

Makes 4 servings.

Baked Basil Tomatoes with Lobster Mushrooms and White Cheddar

Braised garlic and meaty reddish-orange lobster mushrooms make a flavorful filling for luscious ripe tomatoes. Nestle these eye-catching vegetable cups on the plate with Tongues-of-Fire Beans with Rice (page 185).

1 (½-ounce) package dried lobster mushrooms or chanterelle mushrooms
2 tablespoons olive oil
6 large cloves garlic, peeled
¼ cup minced fresh basil

4 large garden-ripe tomatoes
⅛ teaspoon salt
½ cup shredded white Cheddar cheese, Muenster cheese, or Swiss cheese (2 ounces)
1 tablespoon minced fresh parsley

In a small bowl, cover the dried mushrooms with hot water. Let stand 30 minutes. Rinse under warm running water; squeeze out excess moisture. Finely chop the mushrooms; set aside.

Preheat the oven to 375°F (190°C). To braise the garlic, heat 1 tablespoon of the oil in a small saucepan over medium-high heat. Add the garlic; reduce heat to low. Cover and cook, stirring frequently, 15 minutes or until the garlic is soft and golden. Remove from heat. Using the tines of a fork, mash the garlic until it is well combined with the oil. For the filling, stir the chopped mushrooms and the basil into the garlic mixture; set aside.

Thoroughly wash the tomatoes; drain well. Cut a ¼-inch slice off the stem end of each tomato. Using a spoon, remove and discard the pulp from inside the tomatoes. Drain the tomato shells. Sprinkle the shells with the salt. Spoon the filling into the tomato shells.

Pour the remaining 1 tablespoon oil into a 2-quart casserole dish. Set the tomatoes in the dish. Bake 20 to 25 minutes or until the tomatoes are soft and the filling is heated through.

To serve, transfer the tomatoes to a serving platter. Sprinkle the tomatoes with the cheese and then with the parsley.

Makes 4 servings.

Provençal Summertime Vegetable Tian

"My grandmother grew Swiss chard in her garden every year," remembers Sharyl. "She usually served it cooked and seasoned with a splash of vinegar. Over the years, I've found other delicious ways to enjoy it, like this layered-vegetable casserole."

12 ounces Swiss chard
4 tablespoons olive oil
1 large onion, halved lengthwise and thinly sliced
1 tablespoon minced garlic
½ teaspoon salt
¼ teaspoon ground black pepper
1 medium-size Japanese eggplant, cut diagonally into ½-inch-thick slices, or ½ small eggplant, peeled and cut into 1-inch cubes

1 medium-size yellow summer squash or zucchini, halved lengthwise and cut diagonally into ½-inch-thick slices
4 Italian plum tomatoes, cut into ½-inch pieces
¼ cup minced fresh cilantro or parsley
2 tablespoons minced fresh basil or 2 teaspoons dried basil leaves
½ cup (2 ounces) shredded Gruyère cheese or Swiss cheese

Thoroughly wash the Swiss chard under cold running water; drain well. Cut off the stalks at the base of the leaves. Cut the stalks into 1-inch pieces. Cut out the heavy center vein in the leaves; discard. Stack the leaves and cut into thin shreds.

Preheat the oven to 375°F (190°C). In a large skillet, heat 2 tablespoons of the oil over medium heat. Add the onion, garlic, salt, and pepper and cook, stirring frequently, 5 minutes or until the onion is tender. Add the Swiss chard leaves and cook, stirring constantly, 1 minute or just until the leaves start to wilt. Spread the onion mixture in a 9-inch-square baking pan.

Layer the Swiss chard stalks, eggplant, yellow squash or zucchini, and tomatoes on top of the onion mixture. Sprinkle with the cilantro or parsley and basil. Drizzle with the remaining 2 tablespoons oil. Cover and bake 35 minutes. Sprinkle with the cheese. Bake, uncovered, 5 minutes or until the cheese is melted.

Makes 6 servings.

+ TIP

The word *tian* is French for a mixed vegetable dish that's baked in a casserole dish and topped with cheese or bread crumbs.

TANTALIZING POULTRY

*P*oultry is puzzling. On one hand, it represents the best in old-fashioned cooking. Almost all of us remember a favorite chicken, turkey, or game bird dish from our childhood. Yet on the other hand, visit the most trendy restaurant and what's on the menu? You've got it—poultry. As you glance through our tempting selection of recipes, you'll see that same paradox. We've mixed time-honored seasonings and techniques in original, new ways. It's a can't-miss combination!

Whether it's chicken, turkey, Cornish hen, pheasant, or duck you fancy, you'll find it prepared with flair in this chapter. For Lemon and Sage Roast Chicken with Vegetables a whole bird is oven roasted with artichoke hearts, baby-cut carrots, and onions for simply outstanding results. If your first choice is fried chicken, try American Country Chicken with Whisky Cream Sauce. The Scotch-based sauce is outrageously creamy and rich. When it comes to chicken rolls, Herb- and Cheese-Stuffed Chicken Rolls with Orange Butter Sauce gives you the flavors of Muenster cheese, Romano cheese, basil, and rosemary all in one mouthwatering package. Roast Spiced Turkey Breast with Cranberry Couscous takes advantage of the versatile turkey breast portion. It's ideal for a holiday dinner party. Cornish hens take center stage in Tarragon and Mustard-Broiled Cornish Hens. The herbed topper broils to crispy perfection. And, glorious Smoked Pheasant with Onion and Caper Sauce and Country French Duck with Calvados Sauce show off the full-bodied flavor of these classic game birds.

Take your pick of these first-rate poultry recipes. You'll find them enticing, flavor-packed, and sure-to-please.

Four Cheese– and
Chanterelle Mushroom–Stuffed Chicken

"I first learned about putting stuffing under the chicken skin in a gourmet cooking class my husband and I took twenty years ago," says Sharyl. *"This easy-to-do technique turns chicken and stuffing into a company-special dish."*

1 (½-ounce) package dried
    chanterelle mushrooms
⅔ cup ricotta cheese
½ cup (2 ounces) shredded
    mozzarella cheese (2 ounces)
½ cup (2 ounces) shredded
    Muenster cheese, fontina cheese,
    or Gouda cheese (2 ounces)
¼ cup freshly grated Romano
    cheese or Parmesan cheese
¼ cup minced fresh parsley

2 tablespoons seasoned dry bread
    crumbs
2 tablespoons finely chopped shallots
1 tablespoon minced fresh oregano
    or 1 teaspoon dried oregano leaves
1 (3¼- to 3½-pound) whole frying
    chicken, giblets removed
1 tablespoon olive oil
Watercress sprigs and fresh oregano
    sprigs, for garnish

In a small bowl, cover the dried mushrooms with hot water. Let stand 30 minutes. Rinse under warm running water; squeeze out excess moisture. Finely chop the mushrooms.

For the stuffing, combine the chopped mushrooms, all the cheeses, parsley, bread crumbs, shallots, and oregano in a medium-size bowl; set aside.

Preheat the oven to 375°F (190°C). Rinse the chicken and pat dry with paper towels. Using poultry shears, cut closely on one side of the backbone along the entire length of the chicken. Repeat on the other side. (Or, with the chicken breast side up, insert a long knife into the body cavity close to one side of the backbone. Press down hard with a rocking motion to cut through. Repeat on the other side.) Discard the backbone.

Place the chicken, skin side up; open the chicken out as much as possible so the drumstick tips point out. Cover the breast with plastic wrap. Using the flat side of a meat mallet, strike the breast firmly in the center. (This breaks the bones so the chicken lies flat.) Starting at the neck, on one side of the breast, slip your fingers between the skin and meat. Carefully work your fingers toward the tail end, loosening the skin as you work. Once your entire hand is under the skin, free the skin around the thigh and leg area up to, but not around, the tip of the drumstick. Repeat on the other side of the breast.

Lift the skin at the neck and push some of the stuffing under the skin. Stuff the drumstick-thigh area, then the breast. Press gently on the skin to smooth the stuffing into an even layer.

To truss the chicken, pull the neck skin over the opening and secure it to the back with a small skewer. On each side of the chicken, make a 1-inch slit in the skin, halfway between the thigh and breast and about 1 inch from the tail, making the slit parallel to the breast. Push the end of each drumstick through the nearest slit. Twist the wing tips behind the back. Smooth the stuffing to follow the curve of the chicken.

Place the chicken, breast side up, on a rack in a shallow roasting pan. Brush with the olive oil. Insert a meat thermometer into the center of an inside thigh muscle. Do not allow the thermometer to touch bone.

Roast 1¼ to 1½ hours or until the juices run clear when the chicken is pierced with a fork and the internal temperature reaches 180 to 185°F (80 to 85°C). Cover with foil after 30 minutes of roasting.

Remove the chicken from the oven. Let stand 10 minutes before carving the chicken. To carve, cut gently through the skin and stuffing down the center of the breast. Split each half by cutting between the thigh and breast. Garnish the chicken with the watercress and oregano sprigs.

Makes 4 servings.

✦ TIP

If you prefer, you can use this same stuffing between the skin and meat of 6 bone-in chicken breast halves (about 2¼ pounds total). Bake the chicken in a 425°F (220°C) oven 30 to 35 minutes.

Broccoli-Stuffed Chicken with Mornay Sauce

This show-off chicken entree is the kind that brings lots of "oohs" and "aahs" when you serve it to company.

3 tablespoons butter
1 cup finely chopped broccoli
½ cup finely chopped red bell pepper
½ cup sliced green onions
1 tablespoon minced garlic
7 slices firm bread, cut into cubes
   and dried (5 cups)
4 ounces prosciutto or cooked ham,
   chopped
⅓ cup pine nuts or slivered almonds
1 tablespoon minced fresh basil or
   1 teaspoon dried basil leaves
1 tablespoon minced fresh oregano
   or 1 teaspoon dried oregano leaves
½ teaspoon ground black pepper
1 cup chicken broth
1 (3¼- to 3½-pound) whole frying
   chicken, giblets removed

MORNAY SAUCE
3 tablespoons butter
2 tablespoons finely chopped shallots
2 tablespoons all-purpose flour
¼ teaspoon salt
¼ teaspoon ground nutmeg
⅛ teaspoon ground black pepper
1⅓ cups half-and-half
⅓ cup dry white wine
¼ cup (1 ounce) shredded Gruyère
   cheese or Swiss cheese
2 tablespoons freshly grated
   Parmesan cheese
1 egg yolk, lightly beaten

In a medium-size saucepan, melt butter over medium-high heat. Add the broccoli, bell pepper, green onions, and garlic and cook, stirring frequently, 5 minutes or until the vegetables are tender. Remove from heat and cool slightly.

For the stuffing, combine the bread cubes, prosciutto or ham, pine nuts or almonds, basil, oregano, and black pepper in a large bowl. Stir in the broccoli mixture. Gradually add the chicken broth, tossing gently to moisten.

Preheat the oven to 375°F (190°C). Rinse the chicken and pat dry with paper towels. Lightly spoon some of the stuffing into the neck cavity. Pull the neck skin over the opening and secure it to the back with a small skewer. Lightly spoon more of the stuffing into the body cavity. (Spoon the remaining stuffing into a lightly greased 1½-quart casserole dish; cover and refrigerate.) Tie the drumsticks together with cotton string. Twist the wing tips behind the back. Place the chicken, breast side up, on a rack in a shallow roasting pan. Insert a meat thermometer into the center of an inside thigh muscle. Do not allow the thermometer to touch bone.

Roast 1¼ to 1½ hours or until the juices run clear when the chicken is pierced with a fork, the drumsticks move easily in their sockets, and the internal temperature reaches 180 to 185°F (80 to 85°C). Place the covered casserole of stuffing in the oven alongside the chicken during the last 30 minutes of roasting. Baste the chicken occasionally with the pan drippings, except during the last 5 minutes of roasting.

Remove the chicken and casserole of stuffing from the oven; cover the chicken with foil. Let stand 10 minutes before carving the chicken.

Meanwhile, prepare the Mornay Sauce. Serve the sauce with the chicken and stuffing.

Makes 6 servings.

MORNAY SAUCE

In a medium-size saucepan, melt butter over medium heat. Add the shallots and cook, stirring frequently, 3 to 5 minutes or until the shallots are tender. Stir in the flour, salt, nutmeg, and black pepper. Add the half-and-half. Cook, stirring constantly, until the mixture thickens. Cook, stirring constantly, 1 minute.

Stir in the wine. Stir in the Gruyère or Swiss cheese and Parmesan cheese until the cheese is melted. Gradually stir about ½ cup of the hot mixture into the egg yolk, then return yolk to the remaining hot mixture. Cook, stirring constantly, until the mixture thickens.

Makes 1¾ cups.

✦ TIP

Cream-colored pine nuts also are sold under the names *pignoli* and *piñon* nuts. Store them in the refrigerator for no more than 2 months or in the freezer for up to 6 months.

Lemon and Sage Roast Chicken with Vegetables

"One Sunday as I was getting ready to roast chicken and vegetables for dinner, I realized I was out of potatoes," remembers Sandra. "I raided my freezer and found a package of artichoke hearts, so I improvised. That's when this recipe was born. The results were so delightful, I make this new version of an old classic often."

1 (3¼- to 3½-pound) whole frying chicken, giblets removed
3 lemons
2 bay leaves
1 tablespoon dried sage leaves
1 teaspoon minced garlic
½ teaspoon salt
½ teaspoon ground black pepper

1 (9-ounce) package frozen artichoke hearts
4 cups baby-cut carrots (see Tip, page 80)
3 medium-size onions, cut into wedges
¼ cup (½ stick) butter, melted
2 tablespoons balsamic vinegar

Preheat the oven to 375°F (190°C). Rinse the chicken and pat dry with paper towels. Squeeze the juice of 1 of the lemons over the chicken. Place the squeezed lemon and the bay leaves in the body cavity. In a small bowl, combine the sage, garlic, salt, and pepper. Rub half of the mixture over the surface of the chicken.

To truss the chicken, pull the neck skin over the opening and secure it to the back with a small skewer. Tie the drumsticks together with cotton string. Twist the wing tips behind the back. Place the chicken, breast side up, on a rack in a shallow roasting pan. Insert a meat thermometer into the center of an inside thigh muscle. Do not allow the thermometer to touch bone.

To separate the frozen artichokes, place them in a colander and rinse under warm running water; drain. Arrange the artichokes, carrots, and onions in the bottom of the roasting pan. Squeeze the juice of the remaining 2 lemons into the remaining sage mixture. Stir in the melted butter and balsamic vinegar. Brush some of the lemon mixture over the chicken and vegetables.

Roast 1 to 1¼ hours or until the juices run clear when the chicken is pierced with a fork, the drumsticks move easily in their sockets, and the internal temperature reaches 180 to 185°F (80 to 85°C). Baste the chicken and vegetables occasionally with the remaining lemon mixture, and then with the pan drippings, except during the last 5 minutes of roasting.

Remove the chicken and vegetables from the oven; cover loosely with foil. Let stand 10 minutes before carving the chicken.

Makes 6 servings.

● TIP

If your regular meat thermometer is too big and heavy to stand upright in the chicken's thigh, use an instant-read thermometer to check on the chicken's doneness.

Port-Marinated Chicken with Honeyed Figs

"Figs were one of my childhood favorites. I remember being thrilled when I discovered a package of figs as the 'candy' in my Christmas stocking," recalls Sharyl. "The mingling of the fig, port wine, and honey flavors in this easy chicken dish make it exceptional."

4 bone-in chicken breast halves
   (about 1½ pounds total)
1¼ cups port or sweet red wine
⅓ cup raspberry vinegar
2 tablespoons olive oil
1 tablespoon minced fresh thyme
   or 1 teaspoon dried thyme leaves

1 teaspoon minced garlic
½ cup honey
1 teaspoon freshly grated orange peel
1 (9-ounce) package dried Black
   Mission figs
Orange twists, for garnish

Rinse the chicken pieces and pat dry with paper towels. Place the chicken in a heavy plastic bag. For the marinade, combine ¾ cup of the port or sweet red wine, the raspberry vinegar, olive oil, thyme, and garlic. Pour over the chicken; seal bag. Marinate in the refrigerator 4 to 24 hours, turning occasionally.

Preheat the oven to 425°F (220°C). Lightly grease a shallow baking pan. Remove the chicken from the bag, reserving the marinade. Place the chicken, skin side up, in the prepared baking pan. Brush with some of the marinade; discard the remaining marinade. Bake 25 to 30 minutes or until the chicken is tender and the juices run clear when the chicken is pierced with a fork.

Meanwhile, in a 1½-quart casserole dish, combine the remaining ½ cup port, the honey, and orange peel. Stir in the figs. Cover and bake 25 minutes.

To serve, transfer the chicken pieces to a serving platter. Using a slotted spoon, arrange the figs around the chicken. Spoon the honey mixture over the chicken and figs. Garnish with the orange twists.

Makes 4 servings.

◆ TIP

Mission figs have dark purple skins and a very fruity flavor. Look for them in the dried-fruit section of the supermarket or at food specialty stores.

Pesto-Stuffed Chicken Breasts au Poivre

"It's hard to believe that a recipe with only five ingredients can be so sophisticated and satisfying. I especially like the flavor that mixed peppercorns (a combination of different colors of whole peppercorns and sometimes other whole spices) add to the chicken," proclaims Rosemary.

⅓ cup purchased pesto
3 tablespoons finely chopped
   pine nuts
4 bone-in chicken breast halves
   (about 1½ pounds total)

1 tablespoon mixed whole
   peppercorns
Fresh basil sprigs, for garnish

Preheat the oven to 425°F (220°C). Lightly grease a shallow baking pan. In a small bowl, combine the pesto and pine nuts; set aside. Rinse the chicken pieces and pat dry with paper towels. Using your fingers, gently separate the skin from the meat along the rib edge of each chicken piece, leaving the skin attached at the breast bone. Spread a generous tablespoon of the pesto mixture between the skin and meat of each chicken piece.

Coarsely crack the peppercorns. Sprinkle the peppercorns over the chicken pieces. Using your fingers, gently press the peppercorns into the surface of the chicken.

Place the chicken, skin side up, in the prepared baking pan. Bake 25 to 30 minutes or until the chicken is tender and the juices run clear when the chicken is pierced with a fork. Garnish with the basil sprigs.

Makes 4 servings.

◆ TIP
A good way to crack the mixed whole peppercorns is to place them in a small self-sealing plastic bag and crush them with the flat side of a meat mallet.

American Country Chicken with Whisky Cream Sauce

An enchanting mushroom cream sauce turns a home-style classic—fried crumb-coated chicken—into a truly elegant entree.

4 boneless skinless chicken breast
   halves (about 1 pound total)
1/3 cup whole-wheat flour or
   all-purpose flour
1 tablespoon minced fresh thyme or
   1 teaspoon dried thyme leaves
1 teaspoon paprika
1/4 teaspoon plus 1/8 teaspoon salt
1/4 teaspoon plus 1/8 teaspoon black
   pepper
1/4 cup low-fat (1%) milk

2 tablespoons vegetable oil
1 large onion, halved lengthwise and
   thinly sliced
1 cup halved fresh mushrooms
1 stalk celery, thinly sliced
1 teaspoon minced garlic
1/2 cup Scotch whisky or bourbon
3/4 cup whipping cream
2 tablespoons minced fresh parsley
Cooked noodles

Rinse the chicken pieces and pat dry with paper towels. In a shallow dish or plastic bag, combine the flour, thyme, paprika, the 1/4 teaspoon salt, and the 1/4 teaspoon pepper. Pour the milk into a small bowl. Dip each chicken piece in the milk, then coat with the flour mixture.

In a large skillet, heat the oil over medium heat. Add the chicken pieces and cook 5 minutes or until browned on both sides. Reduce heat to medium-low. Cook 5 to 7 minutes longer or until the chicken is cooked through, turning occasionally. Remove the chicken from skillet; cover with foil and keep warm.

For the sauce, add the onion, mushrooms, celery, and garlic to the skillet and cook over medium heat, stirring frequently, 5 to 6 minutes or until the vegetables are tender. Add the Scotch whisky or bourbon, the remaining 1/8 teaspoon salt, and the remaining 1/8 teaspoon pepper. Bring to a boil, reduce heat, and simmer, stirring occasionally, 8 minutes or until most of the liquid has evaporated. Stir in the whipping cream. Cook, stirring constantly, 5 minutes or until the mixture thickens. Stir in the parsley.

To serve, place the cooked noodles on a serving platter. Arrange the chicken on top of the noodles. Spoon the sauce over the chicken and noodles.

Makes 4 servings.

Tomatillo and Chipotle–Marinated Chicken

The Tomato-Chipotle Salsa is unlike any you'll find in a jar. The tomatillos give it a hint of tart apple flavor and the chipotle chiles add an enticing smoky bite. Not only is the salsa delicious with chicken, it's first-rate as a dipping sauce for tortilla chips, too.

Tomatillo-Chipotle Salsa (see below)
6 boneless skinless chicken breast
   halves (about 1½ pounds total)
¼ cup tequila
Cooked rice
Fresh cilantro sprigs, for garnish

TOMATILLO-CHIPOTLE SALSA
6 medium-size tomatillos (about
   12 ounces total)

2 medium-size tomatoes, quartered
1 small onion, quartered
⅓ cup canned chipotle chiles in
   adobo sauce
¼ cup loosely packed fresh cilantro
   leaves
4 cloves garlic, peeled
¼ teaspoon salt
¼ teaspoon ground black pepper

Prepare the Tomatillo-Chipotle Salsa. Rinse the chicken pieces and pat dry with paper towels. Place the chicken in a heavy plastic bag.

For the marinade, combine 1 cup of the salsa and the tequila. Pour marinade over the chicken; seal bag. Marinate in the refrigerator 6 to 24 hours, turning occasionally. Cover and refrigerate the remaining salsa.

Shortly before broiling the chicken, let the salsa come to room temperature. Preheat the broiler. Remove the chicken from the bag, reserving the marinade. Place the chicken pieces, boned side up, on the unheated rack of a broiler pan. Spoon some of the marinade over the chicken. Broil 5 to 6 inches from the heat 9 to 11 minutes or until the chicken is cooked through, turning and spooning some of the marinade over the chicken after half of the cooking time. Discard the remaining marinade.

To serve, place the cooked rice on a serving platter. Arrange the chicken on top of the rice. Drizzle the salsa over the chicken and rice. Garnish with the cilantro sprigs.

Makes 6 servings.

TOMATILLO-CHIPOTLE SALSA
Remove the husks from the tomatillos; rinse and quarter the tomatillos. In a food processor or blender, combine the tomatillos, tomatoes, onion, chipotle chiles in adobo sauce, cilantro leaves, garlic, salt, and pepper. Cover and process until smooth. Transfer the mixture to a medium-size saucepan and bring to a boil. Reduce heat, cover, and simmer 10 minutes. Transfer to a medium-size bowl; cool slightly. Cover and refrigerate 6 to 24 hours. For best flavor, let the salsa come to room temperature before serving.

Makes 3½ cups.

◆ TIP
To keep broiled chicken, steaks, or chops moist, turn the pieces with tongs as they cook. Piercing them with a fork lets some of the juices escape.

Chicken and Fennel in Fresh Tarragon–Wine Sauce

The licoricelike flavor and fragrance of both fennel and tarragon combine magnificently in this summer-fresh chicken dish. For an extra flavor boost, team it with tomato- or pepper-flavored linguine or fettuccine instead of plain noodles.

2 medium-size bulbs fennel with tops
2 medium-size carrots
4 boneless skinless chicken breast halves (about 1 pound total)
2 tablespoons olive oil or vegetable oil
1 cup frozen small whole onions
1 cup halved fresh mushrooms
1 cup dry white wine
½ cup chicken broth
1 bay leaf

2 teaspoons minced fresh tarragon or ½ teaspoon dried tarragon leaves
1 teaspoon sugar
¼ teaspoon salt
¼ teaspoon ground black pepper
2 tablespoons all-purpose flour
2 tablespoons butter, room temperature
Cooked noodles

Remove any tough or bruised outer leaves from the fennel bulbs. Trim off the root ends; discard. Pull off the feathery tops from the stems. Finely chop the tops; reserve 2 tablespoons of the tops. Trim off the stems; discard. Thoroughly rinse the trimmed bulbs and halve each bulb lengthwise; remove the core. Cut the bulbs crosswise into ¼-inch-thick slices.

Thoroughly wash the carrots; trim off the ends. Peel or scrub the carrots. Cut the carrots into thin 2½-inch-long sticks. (To make the thin sticks, cut the carrots in thirds crosswise, then in half lengthwise. Continue cutting the carrots lengthwise to create long, thin sticks.)

Rinse the chicken pieces and pat dry with paper towels. In a large skillet, heat the oil over medium-high heat. Add the chicken and cook 3 minutes or until browned on both sides. Remove the chicken from skillet.

Add the fennel slices, the reserved fennel tops, the carrots, onions, mushrooms, wine, chicken broth, bay leaf, tarragon, sugar, salt, and pepper to the skillet and bring to a boil. Return the chicken to the skillet. Reduce heat, cover, and simmer 7 to 9 minutes or until the chicken is cooked through and the vegetables are tender. Transfer the chicken and vegetables to a serving platter; cover and keep warm. Discard the bay leaf.

For the sauce, combine the flour and butter in a small bowl. Stir the butter mixture into the wine mixture in the skillet. Cook, stirring constantly, until the mixture thickens. Cook, stirring constantly, 1 minute.

To serve, spoon the sauce over the chicken and vegetables. Serve with the cooked noodles. **Makes 4 servings.**

◆ TIP

If you have some of the feathery fennel tops left over, chop them to sprinkle over foods as you would minced fresh parsley or chives.

Grilled Brochettes of Curried Chicken

Be sure to cook up lots of rice to go along with these high-powered curry kabobs. You'll need it to soothe your taste buds.

1 medium-size onion, cut into
    8 wedges
3 tablespoons butter
1 tablespoon curry powder
1 teaspoon minced gingerroot
1 teaspoon minced garlic
2 tablespoons lemon juice
2 tablespoons water
½ teaspoon salt
¼ teaspoon ground red (cayenne)
    pepper

4 boneless skinless chicken breast
    halves (about 1 pound total)
1 large red bell pepper, cut into
    1-inch squares
1 large green bell pepper, cut into
    1-inch squares
16 (1-inch) cubes mango or pineapple
Fresh cilantro sprigs or parsley
    sprigs, for garnish
Cooked rice

Cover 8 (10-inch) bamboo skewers with water. Let stand 30 minutes; drain. In a small saucepan, bring a small amount of water to a boil. Add the onion wedges, reduce heat, and simmer 4 minutes. Drain; set aside.

Meanwhile, in another small saucepan, melt the butter over medium-high heat. Add the curry powder, gingerroot, and garlic and cook, stirring constantly, 1 minute. Remove from heat. Stir in the lemon juice, 2 tablespoons water, salt, and cayenne; set aside.

Rinse the chicken and pat dry with paper towels. Cut the chicken into thin bite-size strips. For the skewers, thread the chicken, in accordion fashion, with the onion wedges, red and green pepper squares, and mango or pineapple cubes on the bamboo skewers, leaving ¼ inch space between the pieces. (Leaving a little space between the pieces allows them to cook evenly.) Brush the curry mixture on all sides of the skewers.

In an uncovered grill, arrange preheated coals in the firebox; test the coals for medium heat (see Tip, page 18). Place the skewers on the grill rack directly over the coals. Grill 10 to 12 minutes or until the chicken is cooked through, turning the skewers after half of the cooking time. (Or, place the skewers on the unheated rack of a broiler pan. Broil 5 to 6 inches from the heat for 10 minutes or until the chicken is cooked through, turning after half of the cooking time.)

To serve, arrange 2 skewers on each dinner plate. Garnish with the cilantro or parsley sprigs. Serve with the cooked rice.

Makes 4 servings.

✦ TIP
    Soaking the bamboo skewers before you thread the kabobs keeps the skewers from catching fire as you grill.

Herb- and Cheese-Stuffed Chicken Rolls
with Orange Butter Sauce

Liz says, "Baked stuffed chicken rolls are a Christmas Eve tradition at our house. One year I had to work all day, so my husband chose a chicken-roll recipe from a cookbook and prepared them as a surprise. They tasted wonderful! Over the years, we've tinkered with the recipe to come up with this version. It uses several cheeses our family loves, as well as some of our favorite herbs."

6 boneless skinless chicken breast halves (about 1½ pounds total)
1 cup (4 ounces) shredded Muenster cheese
¾ cup ricotta cheese
⅓ cup plus 3 tablespoons freshly grated Romano cheese or Parmesan cheese
5 teaspoons minced fresh basil or 1½ teaspoons dried basil leaves
4 teaspoons minced fresh rosemary or 1¼ teaspoons dried rosemary leaves
1 teaspoon minced garlic
¼ teaspoon ground black pepper
1 egg, lightly beaten
1 tablespoon water
½ cup dry bread crumbs
6 tablespoons butter, melted
½ cup fresh orange juice
Cooked noodles

Preheat the oven to 350°F (175°C). Rinse the chicken pieces and pat dry with paper towels. Place 1 piece of chicken, boned side up, between sheets of plastic wrap. Using the flat side of a meat mallet, pound lightly from the center to the edges to form a rectangle about ¼ inch thick. Remove the plastic wrap. Repeat with the remaining chicken pieces.

For the filling, combine the Muenster cheese, ricotta cheese, ⅓ cup of the Romano or Parmesan cheese, 1 tablespoon of the fresh or 1 teaspoon of the dried basil, 1 tablespoon of the fresh or 1 teaspoon of the dried rosemary, the garlic, and pepper in a medium-sized bowl. Spoon the filling onto the chicken pieces. Fold in the sides of each chicken piece and roll up. Secure each roll by inserting a wooden pick across the top.

In a shallow dish, combine the egg and water. Dip the chicken rolls into the egg mixture, then roll in the bread crumbs to coat. Place the chicken rolls, seam side down, in a 13 x 9-inch baking dish. Drizzle with 2 tablespoons of the melted butter. Bake 35 to 40 minutes or until the chicken is cooked through.

Meanwhile, for the sauce, combine the remaining 4 tablespoons butter, the orange juice, the remaining 2 teaspoons fresh or ½ teaspoon dried basil, and the remaining 1 teaspoon fresh or ¼ teaspoon dried rosemary in a small saucepan over medium heat. Heat through.

To serve, place the cooked noodles on a serving platter. Discard the wooden picks from the chicken rolls; arrange the chicken on top of the noodles. Drizzle the sauce over the chicken and noodles. Sprinkle with the remaining 3 tablespoons Romano or Parmesan cheese.

Makes 6 servings.

Szechwan Chicken with Cashews

"Although my family loves to eat at Chinese restaurants, I still like to make an authentic stir-fry at home now and then," says Sandra. "I always use thighs instead of chicken breast in this recipe because the richer flavor of the dark meat marries well with the robust seasonings."

6 boneless skinless chicken thighs
   (about 1¼ pounds total)
1 egg white, lightly beaten
2 tablespoons plus 1 teaspoon
   soy sauce
1 tablespoon cornstarch
⅛ teaspoon white pepper
2 tablespoons dry sherry
2 tablespoons rice vinegar or vinegar
1 tablespoon sugar
2 teaspoons hot chili paste
2 tablespoons vegetable oil
1 large green or red bell pepper,
   cut into 1-inch squares

1 medium-size onion, halved
   crosswise and cut into thin wedges
1 teaspoon minced gingerroot
1 teaspoon minced garlic
1 (8-ounce) can bamboo shoots,
   drained
1 cup unsalted dry-roasted cashews
   or peanuts
2 tablespoons thinly sliced
   green onion
1 teaspoon sesame oil

Rinse the chicken thighs and pat dry with paper towels. Cut the chicken thighs into 1-inch cubes. For the marinade, combine the egg white, 1 teaspoon of the soy sauce, 1 teaspoon of the cornstarch, and the white pepper in a medium-size bowl. Stir in the cubed chicken. Cover and refrigerate 2 hours.

Meanwhile, for the sauce, combine the remaining 2 tablespoons soy sauce, the sherry, vinegar, sugar, the remaining 2 teaspoons cornstarch, and the chili paste in a small bowl; set aside.

In a wok or large nonstick skillet, heat 1 tablespoon of the vegetable oil over medium-high heat. Add bell pepper squares, onion wedges, gingerroot, and garlic and stir-fry 2 minutes or until the vegetables are crisp-tender. Remove the vegetables from the wok.

Add the remaining 1 tablespoon vegetable oil to the hot wok. (If needed, add more oil during cooking.) Add the chicken mixture and stir-fry 5 minutes or until the chicken is cooked through. Push the chicken against the side of the wok.

Stir the sauce; add to the center of the wok. Cook, stirring constantly, 1 to 2 minutes or until the sauce thickens. Stir the chicken into the sauce until coated. Return the vegetables to the wok; stir in the bamboo shoots. Cook, stirring constantly, 1 minute or until the vegetables are heated through. Stir in the cashews or peanuts, green onion, and sesame oil. Serve immediately.

Makes 4 servings.

Look for both chili paste and sesame oil at an ethnic food market or in the Asian food section of your supermarket. Chili paste is a combination of chiles, vinegar, and seasonings and packs a fiery wallop. Sesame oil is available in both light and dark varieties. For this recipe, we recommend the deep-colored roasted sesame oil. It has a much richer flavor and fragrance than the lighter oils and is designed to be used in small amounts.

Tarragon and Mustard–Broiled Cornish Hens

Guests will be so impressed with these extraordinary hens they'll think you went to a lot of work. Actually, this dish is easy to make.

2 (1¼- to 1½-pound) Cornish game hens, split in half lengthwise	1 tablespoon minced fresh tarragon or 1 teaspoon dried tarragon leaves
1 tablespoon olive oil or cooking oil	½ teaspoon minced garlic
⅔ cup mayonnaise	⅛ teaspoon hot pepper sauce
2 tablespoons finely chopped shallots	
2 tablespoons Dijon mustard	

Preheat the broiler. Lightly grease the unheated rack of a broiler pan; set aside. Rinse the Cornish hens and pat dry with paper towels. Place the hens, skin side down, on the prepared rack of the broiler pan. Brush the hens with the oil. Broil 5 to 6 inches from the heat 20 minutes.

Meanwhile, in a small bowl, stir together the mayonnaise, shallots, Dijon mustard, tarragon, garlic, and hot pepper sauce.

Using tongs, turn the hens, skin side up. Broil 10 minutes. Brush the hens liberally with the mayonnaise mixture. Broil 4 to 6 minutes or until the hens are tender and the juices run clear when the hens are pierced with a fork.

Makes 4 servings.

VARIATION

To make this recipe lower in fat and calories, remove the skin from the Cornish hens before broiling and use fat-free mayonnaise in place of regular mayonnaise.

Rich and Savory Artichoke-Leek Chicken Pot Pie with Herb Pastry

"Chicken pot pie fits my definition of comfort food. The kind I liked as a child had peas and carrots, tiny cubes of chicken in a creamy white sauce, and a melt-in-your-mouth flaky pie crust," says Sharyl. "Today, this more elaborate version fits my 'grown-up' tastes perfectly. It's a recipe with a lot of steps, but the delicious result is worth the extra effort."

Herb Pastry (see opposite)
1 tablespoon butter
4 medium-size leeks, thinly sliced
1 teaspoon minced garlic
1¾ cups Chicken Stock (page 42) or 1 (14½-ounce) can chicken broth
¾ cup extra-dry vermouth or dry white wine
2 tablespoons minced fresh summer savory or 2 teaspoons dried summer savory leaves
½ teaspoon salt
¼ teaspoon ground white pepper or black pepper
2 egg yolks, lightly beaten
1 cup whipping cream
¼ cup all-purpose flour
4 cups quartered fresh mushrooms
3 cups cubed cooked chicken or turkey

2 small yellow summer squash or zucchini, halved lengthwise and thinly sliced (2 cups)
1 (9-ounce) package frozen artichoke hearts, thawed and halved
1 egg mixed with 1 tablespoon water, for glaze

HERB PASTRY
1⅓ cups all-purpose flour
1 cup whole-wheat flour
½ teaspoon salt
½ cup vegetable shortening
¼ cup (½ stick) cold unsalted butter, cut into 1-tablespoon-size pieces
1 egg yolk, lightly beaten
⅓ cup ice-cold water
1 tablespoon minced fresh parsley
1 teaspoon minced fresh thyme or ¼ teaspoon dried thyme leaves

Prepare the Herb Pastry. Cover and refrigerate while preparing the filling.

Preheat the oven to 450°F (230°C). For the filling, melt the 1 tablespoon butter over medium-high heat in a Dutch oven. Add the leeks and garlic and cook, stirring frequently, 5 minutes or until the leeks are tender. Add the Chicken Stock or broth, vermouth or white wine, summer savory, salt, and pepper and bring to a boil. Reduce heat, cover, and simmer 5 minutes.

Meanwhile, in a medium-size bowl, combine the 2 egg yolks, the whipping cream, and flour. Gradually stir about 1 cup of the hot mixture into the egg yolk mixture, then return yolks to the remaining hot mixture. Cook, stirring constantly, until the mixture thickens. Stir in the mushrooms, chicken or turkey, yellow squash or zucchini, and artichokes. (The mixture will become more saucy after baking.) Divide the filling among 6 (14- to 16-ounce) au gratin dishes or individual casseroles.

On a lightly floured surface, roll out half of the dough at a time until ⅛ to ¼ inch thick (keep the remaining dough chilled). Using one of the au gratin dishes or casseroles as a guide, cut out 6 circles or ovals measuring 1 inch larger than the top of the dish. Make slits or tiny cutouts in the pastry circles or ovals to let steam escape.

Place a pastry circle on top of each dish. Fold under the extra pastry; flute the pastry to the edge of the dish. (To flute the pastry, press the dough with the thumb of one hand against the thumb and forefinger of the other hand.) Brush the pastry with the egg glaze. (If desired, place the tiny cutouts on top of the pastry and brush the cutouts with the egg glaze.)

Bake 12 to 14 minutes or until the edges of the pastry are brown and the centers are golden brown.

Makes 6 servings.

Herb Pastry

In a medium-size bowl, stir together the all-purpose flour, whole-wheat flour, and salt. Using a pastry cutter or 2 knives, cut in the shortening and butter until the mixture resembles coarse crumbs. Make a well in the center. In a small bowl, combine the egg yolk, the water, parsley, and thyme; add to the flour mixture. Using a fork, stir until the dry ingredients are moistened.

Divide the dough in half; form each half into a ball. Wrap each ball in plastic wrap and chill in the freezer 20 minutes or in the refrigerator 1½ hours before rolling.

✦ TIP

An easy way to make decorative cutouts in the top pie crust is to use small hors d'oeuvre cutters.

Baked Chicken with Amaretto and Cherry Orange Sauce

The versatile almond- and fruit-flavored sauce brings out the best in chicken. We've used it on chicken hindquarters, but it's equally good on chicken breasts.

6 chicken legs (thigh-drumstick pieces) (about 3½ pounds total)
2 tablespoons butter, melted
⅔ cup fresh orange juice
3 tablespoons light brown sugar
2 tablespoons fresh lemon juice
4 teaspoons cornstarch

1 teaspoon freshly grated orange peel
1 tablespoon butter
½ cup sliced almonds
2 cups fresh or thawed frozen pitted tart red pie cherries
2 tablespoons amaretto or brandy

Preheat the oven to 375°F (190°C). If desired, remove the skin from the chicken legs. Rinse the chicken and pat dry with paper towels. Arrange the chicken legs, cut side down, in a 15 x 10-inch jelly roll pan, making sure the pieces do not touch. Brush the chicken with the 2 tablespoons melted butter. Bake 50 to 55 minutes or until the chicken is tender and the juices run clear when the chicken is pierced with a fork.

While the chicken is baking, prepare the sauce. In a small bowl, combine the orange juice, brown sugar, lemon juice, cornstarch, and orange peel; set aside. In a medium-size saucepan, melt the 1 tablespoon butter over medium-high heat. Add the almonds and cook, stirring frequently, 2 to 3 minutes or until the almonds are golden brown.

Add the orange juice mixture and the cherries to the almonds in the saucepan. Cook, stirring frequently, until the mixture thickens. Cook, stirring constantly, 2 minutes longer. Stir in the amaretto or brandy. Heat through.

To serve, spoon the sauce over the chicken.

Makes 6 servings.

❖ TIP
Line the baking pan with foil before you start and you won't have a sticky pan to scrub.

Roast Spiced Turkey Breast with Cranberry Couscous

"*My husband, Brian, first introduced me to couscous. He learned to like it while he was in west Africa with the Peace Corps," explains Liz. "Before long, I was using couscous frequently in place of rice or noodles because it was so quick to cook. Over the years, I've dressed it up many different ways, but one of my favorites is this cranberry version.*"

1 ($2\frac{1}{2}$- to $3\frac{1}{2}$-pound) bone-in
    turkey breast portion
1 tablespoon vegetable oil
$\frac{1}{2}$ teaspoon ground allspice
$\frac{1}{2}$ teaspoon ground coriander
$\frac{1}{2}$ teaspoon ground ginger
$\frac{1}{2}$ teaspoon ground cumin
$\frac{1}{2}$ teaspoon ground mace
$\frac{1}{2}$ teaspoon freshly ground black
    pepper

$1\frac{3}{4}$ cups Chicken Stock (page 42)
    or 1 ($14\frac{1}{2}$-ounce) can chicken broth
$\frac{1}{2}$ cup fresh orange juice
1 tablespoon butter
1 (10-ounce) package couscous
1 cup dried cranberries or currants
$1\frac{1}{2}$ teaspoons freshly grated
    orange peel

Preheat the oven to 325°F (165°C). Remove the skin from the turkey portion. Rinse the turkey and pat dry with paper towels. Place the turkey, bone side down, on a rack in a shallow roasting pan. In a small bowl, combine the oil, allspice, coriander, ginger, cumin, mace, and pepper. Rub the spice mixture onto the surface of the turkey.

Insert a meat thermometer into the thickest part of the breast. Do not allow the thermometer to touch bone. Cover the turkey loosely with foil. Roast $2\frac{1}{2}$ to 3 hours or until the juices run clear when the turkey is pierced with a fork and the internal temperature reaches 170°F (75°C). Brush the turkey occasionally with the pan drippings, except during the last 5 minutes of roasting. Remove the foil after 2 hours of roasting. Remove the turkey from the oven. Let stand 10 minutes before carving the turkey.

Meanwhile, for the cranberry couscous, bring the Chicken Stock or broth, orange juice, and butter to a boil in a large saucepan. Stir in the couscous, cover, and remove from heat. Let stand 5 minutes. Stir in the cranberries or currants and orange peel. Serve the cranberry couscous with the turkey.

Makes 6 to 8 servings.

✦ TIP

Look for couscous in the grain aisle of your supermarket. It's a semolina product made in the shape of tiny beads.

Broiled Turkey Tenderloins with Tomato, Pistachio, and Vodka Sauce

Ever wonder why pistachio nuts are sometimes dyed red? We did, so we checked into it. Originally, the nuts were dyed to hide blemished shells. Today, the shells don't need dyeing, but growers dye some of the crop anyway because consumers expect pistachio nuts to be red. You may find both dyed and natural-colored nuts at your supermarket. This dish is prettier if you use the plain ones.

2 tablespoons olive oil
1 medium-size yellow or green bell pepper, cut into bite-size strips
½ cup thinly sliced green onions
1 teaspoon minced garlic
1¾ cups chopped tomatoes or 1 (14½-ounce) can diced tomatoes, with juice
1 (6-ounce) can tomato paste
½ cup vodka or fresh orange juice
½ cup plus 3 tablespoons fresh orange juice
1 teaspoon sugar
1 teaspoon freshly grated orange peel
½ teaspoon fennel seeds, crushed
½ teaspoon ground red (cayenne) pepper
⅓ cup shelled pistachio nuts or slivered almonds
2 turkey breast tenderloins or 4 boneless skinless chicken breast halves (about 1 pound total)
Cooked rotini pasta or wagon wheel pasta
Orange wedges, for garnish

For the sauce, in a medium-size saucepan, heat the olive oil over medium-high heat. Add the bell pepper strips, green onions, and garlic and cook, stirring frequently, 5 minutes or until the vegetables are tender.

Stir in the tomatoes with their juice, tomato paste, vodka or orange juice, the ½ cup orange juice, the sugar, orange peel, fennel seeds, and cayenne and bring to a boil. Reduce heat and simmer 10 minutes or until the mixture is of desired consistency. Stir in the pistachio nuts or almonds.

Meanwhile, preheat the broiler. Rinse the turkey or chicken and pat dry with paper towels. Dip the turkey in the remaining 3 tablespoons orange juice. Place the turkey on the unheated rack of a broiler pan, tucking under the thin edges. Broil 5 to 6 inches from the heat 9 to 12 minutes or until the turkey is cooked through, turning the turkey and brushing with the orange juice after half of the cooking time. Halve the turkey tenderloins crosswise.

To serve, place the cooked pasta on a serving platter. Arrange the turkey on top of the pasta. Spoon the sauce over the turkey and pasta. Garnish with the orange wedges.

Makes 4 servings.

VARIATION

If you'd rather grill the turkey instead of broiling it, place the tenderloins on the grill rack directly over medium coals. Grill 12 to 16 minutes or until the turkey is cooked through, turning the turkey and brushing with the orange juice after half of the cooking time.

◆ TIP

A turkey tenderloin is the whole muscle taken from the inside of the turkey breast. It is a long, tapered piece that is thinner at the narrow end.

Braised Turkey Tenderloins with Vegetables and Sour Cream–Mustard Sauce

Rosemary recalls, "When I was a kid, the only time we had turkey was when my mom roasted a whole bird. But since then, the turkey industry has developed a variety of different smaller cuts, so I make turkey dishes a lot more often. This recipe features the turkey breast tenderloin. Look for it in the poultry section of your supermarket's meat case."

1 pound turkey breast tenderloins (see Tip, page 105) or boneless skinless chicken breast halves
2 tablespoons olive oil or vegetable oil
2 medium-size yellow summer squash or zucchini, cut into ½-inch-thick slices
2 stalks celery, sliced
1 medium-size onion, halved lengthwise and thinly sliced
¾ cup dry white wine
¾ cup chicken broth
1½ teaspoons dried basil leaves
¾ teaspoon dried dill weed
¼ teaspoon salt
¼ teaspoon ground black pepper
⅓ cup sour cream
2 tablespoons Dijon mustard
2 to 3 teaspoons prepared horseradish
1 teaspoon all-purpose flour

Rinse the turkey or chicken and pat dry with paper towels. Place 1 piece of turkey between sheets of plastic wrap. Using the flat side of a meat mallet, pound lightly from the center to the edges until ½ inch thick. Remove the plastic wrap. Repeat with the remaining turkey pieces. Cut the turkey into 4 portions.

In a 12-inch nonstick skillet, heat the oil over medium heat. Add the turkey and cook 5 minutes or until the turkey is browned on both sides. Remove the turkey from skillet.

Add the yellow squash or zucchini, celery, and onion to the skillet. Stir in the wine, chicken broth, basil, dill weed, salt, and pepper and bring to a boil. Return the turkey to the skillet. Reduce heat, cover, and simmer 5 to 7 minutes or until the turkey is cooked through.

Transfer the turkey to a serving platter. Using a slotted spoon, arrange the vegetables alongside the turkey; cover with foil and keep warm.

For the sauce, bring the wine mixture in the skillet to a boil over high heat. Reduce heat to medium-high and cook 5 minutes or until the wine mixture is reduced to about ⅔ cup. In a small bowl, combine the sour cream, mustard, horseradish, and flour. Whisk the sour cream mixture into the wine mixture in the skillet. Heat through, but do not boil.

To serve, spoon the sauce over the turkey and vegetables.

Makes 4 servings.

Smoked Turkey with Walnuts, Sherried Apricots, and Angel Hair Pasta

We created the rich pasta sauce to go with one of the smoked turkey drumsticks we found at our local supermarket. The smoked flavor of the meat blends well with the subtle sweetness of the apricots and the crunchiness of the walnuts.

½ cup chopped dried apricots or peaches
½ cup dry sherry
3 tablespoons butter
1 cup coarsely chopped walnuts
1 large green bell pepper, cut into ¾-inch pieces
½ cup thinly sliced green onions
3 tablespoons all-purpose flour
¼ teaspoon salt

¼ teaspoon freshly ground black pepper
2 cups half-and-half
½ cup low-fat (1%) milk
1½ pounds smoked turkey drumstick, skin removed and cubed (about 2 cups)
1 (9-ounce) package refrigerated angel hair pasta
2 tablespoons minced fresh parsley

In a small saucepan, combine the apricots or peaches and sherry. Bring to a boil, reduce heat, and simmer 1 minute. Remove from heat; set aside.

In a medium-size saucepan, melt the butter over medium-high heat. Add the walnuts and cook, stirring constantly, 1 minute. Add the bell pepper and green onions and cook, stirring constantly, 3 to 4 minutes or until the walnuts are golden brown and the bell pepper is crisp-tender.

Stir the flour, salt, and black pepper into the walnut mixture. Add the half-and-half and milk. Cook over medium heat, stirring constantly, until the mixture thickens. Cook, stirring constantly, 1 minute. Stir in the smoked turkey and the apricot mixture. Cook, stirring occasionally, 1 to 2 minutes or until the turkey is heated through.

Meanwhile, cook the angel hair pasta according to the package directions; drain. Rinse under hot running water and drain again.

To serve, place the pasta on a serving platter. Spoon the turkey mixture over the pasta. Sprinkle with the parsley.

Makes 4 servings.

VARIATION
Another time, spoon the turkey sauce over baked puff pastry shells.

Cornish Game Hens with Sausage, Apple, and Date Dressing

The contrast between the tart apples, the savory sausage, and the sweet dates makes the stuffing sensational. If you like very tart apples, use McIntoshes or Granny Smiths. For apples that are just a little sweeter, try Cortlands, Empires, Jonathans, or Rome Beauties.

4 (1¼- to 1½-pound) Cornish game hens
Salt
2 tablespoons butter, melted
¾ teaspoon lemon pepper
4 ounces bulk pork sausage
1 medium-size onion, chopped
1 stalk celery, chopped

3 cups toasted soft bread crumbs
2 medium-size tart apples, peeled, cored, and chopped
½ cup finely chopped dates
½ teaspoon ground cinnamon
¼ teaspoon ground nutmeg
1 (5½-ounce) can apple juice or ⅔ cup chicken broth

Preheat the oven to 375°F (190°C). Rinse the Cornish hens and pat dry with paper towels. Sprinkle the body cavities with a little salt. To truss each hen, pull the neck skin over the opening and secure it to the back with a small skewer. Tie the drumsticks together with cotton string. Twist the wing tips behind the back.

Place the hens, breast side up, on a rack in a shallow roasting pan. Brush the hens with the melted butter. Sprinkle with ½ teaspoon salt and ½ teaspoon of the lemon pepper. Cover loosely with foil. Roast 1¼ hours or until the juices run clear when the hens are pierced with a fork and the drumsticks move easily in their sockets. Remove the foil after 30 minutes of roasting.

While the hens are roasting, prepare the dressing. Lightly grease a 1½-quart casserole dish; set aside. In a large skillet, cook the pork sausage, onion, and celery until the meat is browned, breaking up the meat as it cooks. Drain off fat.

In a large bowl, combine the sausage mixture, bread crumbs, apples, dates, cinnamon, the remaining ¼ teaspoon salt, the nutmeg, and the remaining ¼ teaspoon lemon pepper. Gradually add the apple juice or chicken broth, tossing gently to moisten. Spoon the dressing into the prepared casserole dish.

Cover and bake alongside the hens during the last 25 to 30 minutes of roasting time. Serve the stuffing with the Cornish hens.

Makes 4 servings.

Country French Duck with Calvados Sauce

Meaty, trumpet-shaped chanterelle mushrooms impart a nutty flavor to this cider-simmered duck, while crème fraîche laced with apples and Calvados adds the finishing touch.

Crème Fraîche (page 78)
1 (4½- to 5-pound) ready-to-cook duck, quartered and wings and skin removed
¼ cup (½ stick) butter
3 cups coarsely chopped fresh chanterelle, oyster, and/or shiitake mushrooms
2 cups apple cider or apple juice

1 stalk celery, sliced
2 medium-size tart apples, peeled, cored, and thinly sliced
¼ cup Calvados, applejack, or brandy
2 tablespoons minced fresh tarragon or 2 teaspoons dried tarragon leaves
⅛ teaspoon salt
⅛ teaspoon ground white pepper or black pepper

Prepare the Crème Fraîche. Rinse the duck pieces and pat dry with paper towels. In a 12-inch nonstick skillet, melt 2 tablespoons of the butter over medium heat. Add the duck pieces and cook 10 to 12 minutes or until the duck is browned on all sides. Remove the duck from skillet.

Add the mushrooms, apple cider or juice, and celery to the skillet and bring to a boil. Return the duck to skillet. Reduce heat, cover, and simmer 30 to 35 minutes or until the duck is tender. Transfer the duck and vegetables to a serving platter; cover with foil and keep warm.

For the sauce, melt the remaining 2 tablespoons butter in a medium-size saucepan over medium heat. Add the apples and cook, stirring frequently, 5 minutes or until the apples are tender. Stir in the crème fraîche; Calvados, applejack, or brandy; tarragon; salt; and white or black pepper. Heat through.

To serve, spoon the sauce over the duck and vegetables.
Makes 4 servings.

✦ TIP

To quarter and skin the duck, use sturdy poultry shears to cut along each side of the duck's backbone; remove and discard the backbone. Cut lengthwise through the breastbone. Then, cut each duck half crosswise to make two quarters. Cut off and discard the wings. Finally, carefully pull the skin and underlayer of fat away from the meat; use the shears to cut through the membrane so you can remove the skin and fat.

Smoked Pheasant with Onion and Caper Sauce

"Although we once dined at a restaurant claiming to have the best pheasant in the Black Hills, my husband, George, insists my recipe featuring smoked pheasant in a Parmesan cheese-and-caper sauce is better," boasts Sandra.

1 (1¾- to 2-pound) smoked pheasant
1 orange, sliced
1¾ cups Chicken Stock (page 42)
   or 1 (14½-ounce) can chicken broth
1¼ cups low-fat (1%) milk
1 large onion, halved lengthwise and
   thinly sliced
2 bay leaves

¼ teaspoon white pepper or black
   pepper
¼ cup (½ stick) unsalted butter
⅓ cup all-purpose flour
½ cup freshly grated Parmesan
   cheese or Romano cheese
2 tablespoons drained capers
Cooked linguine or fettuccine

Preheat the oven to 325°F (165°C). Place the pheasant in a 3-quart casserole dish. Arrange the orange slices on top of the pheasant. Cover and bake 55 to 60 minutes or until the pheasant is heated through.

Meanwhile, for the sauce, combine the Chicken Stock or broth, milk, onion, bay leaves, and pepper in a medium-size saucepan and bring nearly to a boil. Reduce heat, cover, and simmer 15 to 20 minutes or until the onion is very soft. Discard the bay leaves.

In a large saucepan, melt the butter over medium-high heat. Stir in the flour. Add the hot milk mixture and cook, stirring constantly, until the mixture thickens. Add the Parmesan or Romano cheese. Cook, stirring constantly, 1 minute. Stir in the capers.

Remove the pheasant from the oven. Let stand 5 minutes before carving the pheasant. Discard the orange slices.

To serve, place the cooked linguine or fettuccine on a serving platter. Arrange the pheasant pieces on top of the pasta. Spoon the sauce over the pheasant and pasta.

Makes 4 servings.

MOUTHWATERING MEATS

When you're searching for that truly impressive entree or just for something a little different, turn to this chapter. Here are some delectable beef, veal, pork, ham, sausage, lamb, and rabbit main dishes. Each one was designed to employ intriguing flavor combinations and to satisfy even the most discriminating palate.

Meat is so versatile that the methods of preparing it are innumerable. If the occasion calls for a flamboyant showstopper, there's Scallop- and Spinach-Stuffed Filet, Lyonnaise Style. The decadent duo of beef tenderloin and scallops is irresistible. When you want to try something a little unusual, opt for Cuban-Style Shredded Flank Steak with Plantain Crisps, a recipe that highlights a host of Caribbean seasonings as well as browned plantain slices. For a homey, yet classic dish, simmer veal shanks and fennel into Milanese-Style Osso Buco with Risotto and Tomato Gremolata. When you want to grill outdoors, remember Smoked Jamaican Jerk Pork Ribs. The jerk seasoning with habanero chiles is delicious and like none other. To feed the gang, turn a ham shank into Ham in Horseradish Crust with Roasted Shallots, Turnips, and Carrots. Or, for a Mexican-influenced meal, roll up Chorizo and Pinto Bean Burritos with Sour Cream Velouté Sauce. Discriminating lamb fans will love Butterflied Leg of Lamb with Dried Peach Stuffing and Peach Cognac Sauce, while rabbit enthusiasts will lean toward Wine-Marinated Rabbit with Fennel and Red-Pepper Sauce.

Thumb through this amazing assortment of meat recipes as you plan meals. With these creative entrees, you'll find putting together memorable menus is a breeze.

Scallop- and Spinach-Stuffed Filet, Lyonnaise-Style

This sophisticated scallop-stuffed beef tenderloin recipe is ideal for entertaining in grand style. Serve it with a full-flavored red wine.

8 ounces fresh or thawed frozen sea scallops or peeled, deveined, fresh or thawed frozen shrimp
2 (2½-pound) beef tenderloins, trimmed of fat
½ cup (1 stick) butter, at room temperature
¼ cup finely chopped shallots
2 tablespoons Dijon mustard
1 teaspoon minced garlic
1 (10-ounce) package frozen chopped spinach, thawed and well drained
¾ cup soft bread crumbs
2 eggs, lightly beaten

⅓ cup freshly grated Parmesan cheese
Lyonnaise Sauce (see below)
5 pounds tiny new potatoes
¼ cup minced fresh parsley

LYONNAISE SAUCE
2 tablespoons butter
4 medium-size onions, cut into very thin wedges
2 teaspoons minced garlic
1½ cups dry white wine
1 (10½-ounce) can condensed beef broth
2 tablespoons minced fresh parsley

Preheat the oven to 400°F (205°C). In a medium-size saucepan, bring a moderate amount of water to a boil over high heat. Add the scallops or shrimp and cook 1 to 3 minutes or just until the scallops or shrimp are opaque throughout. Drain and coarsely chop; set aside.

Rinse the beef tenderloins and pat dry with paper towels. Make a double butterfly cut in each tenderloin (see Tip, opposite page). Using the flat side of a meat mallet, pound each tenderloin lightly from the center to the edges to form a 9 x 8-inch rectangle. In a small bowl, combine the butter, shallots, Dijon mustard, and garlic. Spread over the meat to within 1 inch of the edges.

For the filling, combine the spinach, bread crumbs, eggs, and Parmesan cheese in a medium-size bowl; stir in the scallops or shrimp. Spread the filling over the butter mixture. Beginning on a long side, roll each tenderloin tightly, jelly-roll style. Place the meat rolls, seam side down, on a rack in a shallow roasting pan. Roast 50 to 55 minutes or until the internal temperature reaches 160°F (70°C) for medium or until done as desired. (An instant-read thermometer inserted into the center of each meat roll works well for checking the temperature of the meat.)

While the meat rolls are roasting, prepare the Lyonnaise Sauce; cover and keep warm.

Wash and lightly scrub the new potatoes (because the skin is so tender, don't peel the potatoes). Halve any large potatoes. In a Dutch oven, cover the potatoes with water, and bring to a boil. Reduce heat, cover, and simmer 12 to 14 minutes or until the potatoes are tender. Drain; cover and keep warm.

To serve, cut the meat rolls crosswise into 1-inch-thick slices. Overlap the slices on a serving platter. Place the potatoes in a large serving bowl. Sprinkle the potatoes with the ¼ cup parsley. Pass the sauce to spoon over the meat and potatoes.

Makes 14 servings.

Lyonnaise Sauce

In a large saucepan, melt the butter over medium heat. Add the onions and garlic and cook, stirring frequently, 10 minutes or until the onions are very tender. Add the wine and bring to a boil over high heat. Reduce heat to medium-high and cook 5 to 8 minutes or until the wine is reduced to about ¾ cup. Add the beef broth. Return to a boil. Reduce heat, and simmer 25 minutes or until the sauce is of desired consistency. Stir in the parsley. Transfer the sauce to a serving bowl.

Makes about 3 cups.

✦ TIP

For a double-butterfly cut, make a lengthwise cut down the center of the meat, cutting to within ½ inch of the other side. Make two more lengthwise cuts, one on each side of the first cut, cutting through the thickest portions of meat to within ½ inch of the other side.

Iowa Beef Tenderloin Steaks with Morel, Ricotta, and Red Bell Pepper Sauce

"In the spring, my dad and I would comb the thick woods on our farm looking for morel mushrooms," remembers Sandra. "He always knew the right spots to find them. Once we cleaned the mushrooms, my mom would fry them in butter. These days, I don't often have the luxury of fresh morels, so I created this recipe to take advantage of dried ones."

2 (½-ounce) packages dried morel mushrooms or 4 ounces fresh morel mushrooms, sliced
1 cup ricotta cheese
1 cup half-and-half
2 tablespoons loosely packed fresh parsley leaves
2 tablespoons minced fresh basil or 2 teaspoons dried basil leaves
1 clove garlic, peeled
¼ teaspoon salt
4 beef tenderloin steaks or 2 boneless beef top loin steaks (about 1½ pounds total), 1 inch thick and trimmed of fat

1 tablespoon whole black peppercorns
1 tablespoon olive oil or vegetable oil
1 medium-size red bell pepper, chopped
½ cup chopped sun-dried tomatoes (oil packed)
Fresh basil sprigs, for garnish
Cooked wild rice
Steamed asparagus spears

In a small bowl, cover the dried mushrooms, if using, with hot water. Let stand 20 minutes. Rinse under warm running water; squeeze out excess moisture. Slice the mushrooms into rings.

In a food processor or blender, combine the ricotta cheese, half-and-half, parsley leaves, basil, garlic, and salt. Cover and process until smooth. Set aside.

Rinse the beef steaks and pat dry with paper towels. In a small heavy plastic bag, place the peppercorns; seal bag. Using the flat side of a meat mallet, coarsely crack the peppercorns. Sprinkle the peppercorns on both sides of the meat. Using the heel of your hand, gently press the peppercorns into the surface of the meat.

In a 12-inch nonstick skillet, heat the oil over medium-high heat. Add the meat; reduce heat to medium. Cook 8 to 10 minutes for medium rare or until done as desired, turning the meat after half of the cooking time. Transfer the meat to a serving platter. If using the top loin steaks, cut each steak in half crosswise. Cover with foil and keep warm.

For the sauce, add the mushrooms, bell pepper, and sun-dried tomatoes to the drippings in the skillet. Cook, stirring frequently, 3 to 4 minutes or until the bell pepper is crisp-tender. Stir in the ricotta mixture and simmer, stirring occasionally, 3 minutes.

To serve, spoon the sauce over the meat. Garnish with the basil sprigs. Serve with the cooked wild rice and the steamed asparagus spears.

Makes 4 servings.

✦ TIP

If dried morel mushrooms aren't available at your store, substitute dried porcini mushrooms.

Cuban-Style Shredded Flank Steak with Plantain Crisps

The simmered Cuban classic, ropa vieja, *on which this recipe is based, was originally made with skirt steak, but we've used flank steak because it's easier to find at the store and cooks up to make tender savory shreds of meat.*

1 (1-pound) beef flank steak,
   trimmed of fat
3 cups water
2 medium-size carrots, cut up
1 large tomato, quartered
1 medium-size onion, quartered
2 cloves garlic, peeled
2 bay leaves
¼ teaspoon salt
¼ teaspoon ground black pepper
Plantain Crisps (see opposite)
2 tablespoons vegetable oil
1 medium-size green or red bell
   pepper, chopped
1 medium-size onion, chopped

1 teaspoon minced garlic
1 (15-ounce) can chunky salsa
   tomato sauce
1 teaspoon ground cumin
Cooked rice

PLANTAIN CRISPS
2 green plantains
1 teaspoon salt
Vegetable oil
½ teaspoon seasoned salt
½ teaspoon dried oregano leaves
¼ teaspoon garlic powder
¼ teaspoon onion powder

Rinse the beef steak and pat dry with paper towels. Cut the meat crosswise into thirds. In a Dutch oven, combine the meat, water, carrots, tomato, the quartered onion, the 2 cloves garlic, bay leaves, salt, and black pepper and bring to a boil. Reduce heat, cover, and simmer, occasionally skimming off any foam, 1½ to 1¾ hours or until the meat will shred easily.

While the meat is simmering, start preparing the Plantain Crisps, cooking and flattening the slices; set aside.

Using a slotted spoon, remove the meat from the Dutch oven. (If desired, strain and reserve the cooking liquid for another use; discard the vegetables and seasonings.) Using 2 forks, pull the meat apart, along the grain, into shreds; set aside.

In a large skillet, heat the vegetable oil over medium heat. Add the bell pepper, the chopped onion, and minced garlic and cook, stirring frequently, 5 minutes or until the vegetables are tender. Stir in the shredded meat, the tomato sauce, and cumin and bring to a boil. Reduce heat, cover, and simmer 10 minutes.

Meanwhile, finish preparing the plantains, cooking the flattened slices in the 1 to 1½ inches of hot oil and sprinkling them with the oregano mixture.

To serve, place the cooked rice on a serving platter. Spoon the meat mixture over the rice. Serve with the hot plantains.

Makes 4 servings.

PLANTAIN CRISPS

Using a sharp paring knife, cut off about 1 inch of the tapered ends of the plantains; cut the plantains in half crosswise. Make 4 lengthwise slits in each half, cutting just through the skin to the flesh. Using the tip of the knife, lift a corner of the skin and peel it away from the flesh. (Or, slide your thumbnail under the slit and pry off the skin.) Cut the peeled plantains crosswise into ¾-inch-thick slices.

In a large saucepan, bring a small amount of water and the salt to a boil over high heat. Add the plantains. Reduce heat, cover, and simmer 5 to 10 minutes or until the plantains are nearly tender. Drain well; pat dry with paper towels.

In a large skillet, heat 2 tablespoons vegetable oil over medium heat. Add the plantain slices and cook 4 minutes, turning the slices after half of the cooking time. (Do not brown.) Using a slotted spatula, remove the plantain slices. Drain on paper towels.

Place a large sheet of plastic wrap or waxed paper over the plantain slices. Using the bottom of a 10-ounce custard cup or a small heavy skillet, flatten each slice until ¼ to ⅛ inch thick.

In a small bowl, combine the seasoned salt, oregano, garlic powder, and onion powder; set aside. In a large heavy saucepan, heat 1 to 1½ inches of vegetable oil over medium-high heat to 375°F (190°C). Add the plantains, a few at a time, and cook 2 minutes or until the plantains are lightly browned and crisp, turning the pieces after half of the cooking time. Using a slotted spoon, remove the plantains from the hot oil. Drain well on paper towels. Sprinkle the hot plantains with the oregano mixture. Serve immediately.

Makes about 24.

◆ TIP

Plantains are a tropical fruit often used in Caribbean and South American cooking. Although they look like oversized bananas, they have a mild flavor and a very firm texture. You will find plantains in varying stages of ripeness. Some are green, others are yellow with spots, and still others are brown. For crisps with the sweetest flavor, choose brown plantains.

Milanese-Style Osso Buco with Risotto and Tomato Gremolata

To guarantee true Old World flavor, we simmered the veal shanks for this hearty entree long and slow so the meat ends up succulent and tender and we sprinkled on a topping (gremolata) of plum tomato, parsley, shallots, and lemon peel.

1 medium-size fennel bulb with tops
6 veal shanks, sawed into
    1½-inch-thick pieces by butcher
    (about 3 pounds total)
2 tablespoons olive oil
1 medium-size onion, chopped
1 medium-size carrot, chopped
1 teaspoon minced garlic
1¾ cups chopped Italian plum
    tomatoes or 1 (14½-ounce) can
    diced tomatoes, with juice
1¾ cups Beef Stock (page 42) or
    1 (14½-ounce) can beef broth
1 cup dry white wine
1 tablespoon minced fresh marjoram
    or 1 teaspoon dried marjoram
    leaves
1 tablespoon minced fresh thyme or
    1 teaspoon dried thyme leaves
2 bay leaves

1 teaspoon freshly grated lemon peel
½ teaspoon salt
½ teaspoon freshly ground black
    pepper
Tomato Gremolata (see below)
Milanese-Style Risotto (page 173)
    or cooked rice
¼ cup cold water
2 tablespoons all-purpose flour

TOMATO GREMOLATA
¼ cup finely chopped Italian plum
    tomato
¼ cup minced fresh parsley
2 tablespoons finely chopped shallots
2 teaspoons freshly grated
    lemon peel
1 teaspoon balsamic vinegar
½ teaspoon minced garlic

Remove any tough or bruised outer leaves from the fennel bulb. Trim off the root end; discard. Pull off the feathery tops from the stems. Finely chop the tops; reserve 2 tablespoons of the tops. Trim off the stems; discard. Thoroughly rinse the trimmed bulb and halve the bulb lengthwise; remove the core. Cut the bulb crosswise into ¼-inch-thick slices. Set aside.

Rinse the veal shanks and pat dry with paper towels. In a Dutch oven, heat the olive oil over medium heat. Add the veal shanks and cook 10 minutes or until browned on both sides. Remove the veal shanks from the Dutch oven.

Add the fennel slices, onion, carrot, and the garlic to the drippings in the Dutch oven. Cook, stirring frequently, 5 minutes or until the vegetables are tender. Stir in the reserved 2 tablespoons fennel tops, the tomatoes with their juice, the Beef Stock or broth, wine, marjoram, thyme, bay leaves, lemon peel, salt, and pepper and bring to a boil. Return the veal shanks to the Dutch oven. Reduce heat, cover, and simmer 1 to 1¼ hours or until the meat is tender.

While the veal shanks are simmering, prepare the Tomato Gremolata; cover and refrigerate. Prepare the Milanese-Style Risotto or cooked rice.

Remove the veal shanks from the Dutch oven; cover with foil and keep warm. For the sauce, combine the cold water and flour in a small bowl; stir into the tomato mixture in the Dutch oven. Cook, stirring constantly, until the mixture thickens. Cook, stirring constantly, 1 minute. Discard the bay leaves.

To serve, spoon the risotto or rice onto dinner plates. Arrange the veal shanks on top of the risotto. Spoon the sauce over the veal shanks and risotto. Sprinkle with the gremolata.

Makes 6 servings.

TOMATO GREMOLATA

In a small bowl, combine the tomato, parsley, shallots, lemon peel, balsamic vinegar, and garlic.

Makes about ⅔ cup.

✦ TIP

If you like, substitute 3 (1-pound) beef shanks for the 6 veal shanks.

Honey-Balsamic Beef Stir-Fry in Black Bean–Garlic Sauce

Black bean–garlic sauce blends deliciously with the flavors of the honey and balsamic vinegar in this robust stir-fry. Look for the sauce in the Asian food section of your supermarket or at an Asian grocery store.

1 pound boneless beef sirloin steak
   or top round steak, trimmed of fat
1 egg white, lightly beaten
4 tablespoons soy sauce
4 tablespoons balsamic vinegar
7 teaspoons cornstarch
1/4 teaspoon crushed red pepper
3/4 cup beef broth
3 tablespoons honey

3 tablespoons black bean–garlic sauce
2 tablespoons vegetable oil
4 cups sliced bok choy
1 large onion, cut into thin wedges
2 medium-size tomatoes, cut into
   thin wedges
Soaked bean threads (cellophane
   noodles) or cooked rice

Rinse the beef steak and pat dry with paper towels. Partially freeze the meat, then thinly slice across the grain into bite-size strips (see Tip, page 57).

For the marinade, combine the egg white, 1 tablespoon of the soy sauce, 1 tablespoon of the balsamic vinegar, 2 teaspoons of the cornstarch, and the crushed red pepper in a medium-size bowl. Stir in the meat. Cover and let stand at room temperature, stirring occasionally, while preparing the stir-fry. (Or, cover and refrigerate up to 2 hours.)

For the sauce, combine the beef broth, honey, black bean–garlic sauce, the remaining 3 tablespoons soy sauce, the remaining 3 tablespoons balsamic vinegar, and the remaining 5 teaspoons cornstarch in a small bowl; set aside.

In a wok or large nonstick skillet, heat 1 tablespoon of the oil over medium-high heat. Add the bok choy and onion and stir-fry 3 minutes or until the vegetables are crisp-tender. Remove the vegetables from the wok.

Add the remaining 1 tablespoon oil to the hot wok. (If needed, add more oil during cooking.) Add half of the meat and stir-fry 2 to 3 minutes or until the meat is cooked through, but still slightly pink on the inside. Remove the meat from the wok. Add the remaining meat and stir-fry 2 to 3 minutes. Return all of the meat to the wok. Push the meat against the side of the wok.

Stir the sauce; add to the center of the wok. Cook, stirring constantly, 1 to 2 minutes or until the sauce thickens. Stir the meat into the sauce until coated. Return the vegetables to the wok. Stir in the tomatoes and cook, stirring constantly, 1 minute longer or until all the vegetables are heated through.

Serve immediately over the soaked bean threads or cooked rice.

Makes 4 servings.

✦ TIP
To soak the bean threads, cover them with warm water. Let stand 15 minutes. Drain well.

Grilled Rib Eye Steaks with Firecracker Barbecue Butter

Jalapeño chile and ground red pepper put the fire in this colorful butter. Rosemary suggests it also tastes great on burgers or pork chops.

1 tablespoon butter	½ cup (1 stick) butter, at room
2 tablespoons thinly sliced green	temperature
onion	1 teaspoon brown sugar
1 teaspoon paprika	1 teaspoon Worcestershire sauce
1 teaspoon chili powder	¼ teaspoon ground red (cayenne)
½ teaspoon dry mustard	pepper
½ teaspoon minced garlic	3 (12-ounce) beef rib eye steaks,
1 fresh jalapeño chile	1¼ inches thick and trimmed of fat

For the barbecue butter, melt the 1 tablespoon butter in a small saucepan over medium heat. Add the green onion, paprika, chili powder, dry mustard, and garlic and cook, stirring frequently, 2 to 3 minutes or until the green onion is tender. Remove from heat; cool to room temperature.

Wearing plastic or rubber gloves to protect your skin from the oils in the chile, halve the jalapeño chile lengthwise; discard the stem, seeds, and membranes. Mince the chile. In a small bowl, combine the jalapeño chile, the green onion mixture, the ½ cup butter, brown sugar, Worcestershire sauce, and cayenne. Using a wooden spoon, beat until well mixed. Transfer to a sheet of waxed paper. Shape into a 4-inch-long roll. Wrap in the waxed paper and refrigerate at least 1 hour or until firm.

In an uncovered grill, arrange preheated coals in the firebox; test the coals for medium heat (see Tip, page 18). Rinse the beef steaks and pat dry with paper towels. Place the meat on the grill rack directly over the coals. Grill 12 to 15 minutes for medium rare or until done as desired, turning the meat after half of the cooking time. (Or, place the meat on the unheated rack of a broiler pan. Broil 4 to 5 inches from the heat 12 to 14 minutes for medium rare or until done as desired, turning after half of the cooking time.)

To serve, place the steaks on a serving platter. Cut each steak in half crosswise. Cut the barbecue butter into 6 slices. Place a slice of butter on top of each portion of meat.

Makes 6 servings.

VARIATION

To grill the steaks by indirect heat, in a covered grill, arrange preheated coals in the firebox around a drip pan; test the coals for medium heat above the pan (see Tip, page 18). Place the meat on the grill rack directly over the drip pan. Cover and grill 18 to 20 minutes for medium rare or until done as desired, turning the meat after half of the cooking time.

Roast Pork Tenderloin with Hot Black Bean and Papaya Salsa

Chunky tomato sauce gives the refreshing papaya-and-bean salsa just the right amount of body without a lot of simmering. Another time, team the salsa with grilled fish or chicken.

6 dried pasilla chiles
2 (12-ounce) pork tenderloins, trimmed of fat
¼ teaspoon salt
⅛ teaspoon ground black pepper
1 tablespoon olive oil
6 green onions, sliced
1 stalk celery, thinly sliced
1 teaspoon minced garlic
1 (15-ounce) can black beans, rinsed and drained

1 (15-ounce) can chunky salsa tomato sauce
1 ripe medium-size papaya, peeled, seeded, and chopped
2 tablespoons minced fresh cilantro or parsley
2 tablespoons fresh lime juice
Cooked rice

In a small bowl, cover the dried chiles with boiling water. Let stand 1 hour. Rinse under cold running water. Wearing plastic or rubber gloves to protect your skin from the oils in the chiles, halve the pasilla chiles lengthwise; discard the stems, seeds, and membranes. Chop the chiles; set aside.

Preheat the oven to 425°F (220°C). Rinse the pork tenderloins and pat dry with paper towels. Sprinkle the meat with the salt and black pepper. Place the meat on a rack in a shallow roasting pan. Roast 20 to 30 minutes or until the internal temperature reaches 155°F (70°C). (An instant-read thermometer inserted into the center of each tenderloin works well for checking the temperature of the meat.) Remove the meat from the oven. Cover with foil and let stand 15 minutes before slicing the meat.

Meanwhile, for the salsa, heat the olive oil in a large saucepan over medium heat. Add the green onions, celery, and garlic and cook, stirring frequently, 5 to 6 minutes or until the celery is tender.

Stir in the pasilla chiles, black beans, tomato sauce, papaya, cilantro or parsley, and lime juice. Bring to a boil, stirring frequently. Reduce heat, cover, and simmer, stirring frequently, 5 minutes or until the salsa is heated through. Transfer the salsa to a serving bowl.

To serve, pass the salsa to spoon over the meat and the cooked rice.

Makes 8 servings.

VARIATION

ROAST BEEF TENDERLOIN WITH HOT BLACK BEAN AND PAPAYA SALSA

Substitute 1 (1½-pound) beef tenderloin for the pork tenderloins. Roast 55 to 65 minutes or until the internal temperature reaches 155°F (70°C) for medium.

When fresh papayas aren't available, look for refrigerated papaya slices in a jar. Chop enough of the slices to make 1 cup.

Veal Chops with Dried Cherry and Green Peppercorn Sauce

The combination of cherries and green peppercorns makes this creamy wine sauce exceptional. Not only is it delicious over veal or lamb, but it's also first-rate with beef, pork, or chicken.

4 veal loin chops or 8 lamb loin chops, 1 inch thick and trimmed of fat
2 tablespoons olive oil
1 cup sliced leek
½ cup dry white wine
1 tablespoon crushed green peppercorns
1 teaspoon minced garlic

¼ teaspoon ground white pepper or black pepper
⅛ teaspoon salt
¼ cup cubed cream cheese, at room temperature
1 (3-ounce) package dried tart red cherries or cranberries
½ cup whipping cream
Cooked linguine

Rinse the veal or lamb chops and pat dry with paper towels. Brush both sides of the meat with 1 tablespoon of the olive oil.

To pan-broil the meat, heat a 12-inch nonstick heavy skillet over medium-high heat until very hot. Reduce heat to medium. Add the meat and cook 8 to 10 minutes for medium, turning the meat after half of the cooking time. (Do not add water or fat. Do not cover. If the meat browns too quickly, reduce the heat to medium-low.) Transfer the meat to a serving platter; cover with foil and keep warm.

For the sauce, heat the remaining 1 tablespoon olive oil in the same skillet over medium heat. Add the leek and cook, stirring frequently, 5 minutes or until the leek is tender. Add the wine, green peppercorns, garlic, pepper, and salt. Bring to a boil over high heat; reduce heat to medium. Stir the cream cheese into the wine mixture until smooth. Stir in the dried cherries or cranberries and whipping cream. Heat through, but do not boil.

To serve, pass the sauce to spoon over the meat and the cooked linguine.

Makes 4 servings.

◆ TIP
When you shop for veal, look for pieces that are fine-textured and creamy pink in color, with as little fat as possible.

Pork Loin Roast with Garlic and Peppery Herb Rub

"Remember this roast when you're having company for the weekend. Serve the roast one night for dinner, then slice the leftover cold meat to make sandwiches for lunch the next day," suggests Sharyl.

1 (3- to 3½-pound) boneless pork single-loin roast, trimmed of fat
½ teaspoon fennel seeds
3 cloves garlic, cut into slivers
1 tablespoon olive oil
2 tablespoons paprika
2 tablespoons minced fresh thyme or 2 teaspoons dried thyme leaves
1 tablespoon sea salt or 1½ teaspoons salt

2 teaspoons coarsely ground black pepper
1 teaspoon ground red (cayenne) pepper
½ teaspoon dry mustard
2 tablespoons minced fresh parsley, for garnish

Rinse the pork roast and pat dry with paper towels. Using a sharp paring knife, cut about 12 small slits randomly around the meat. Insert the tip of the knife into each slit, then push 5 or 6 fennel seeds and 1 or 2 garlic slivers into the slit as you remove the knife. Rub the surface of the meat with the olive oil.

In a small bowl, combine the paprika, thyme, salt, black pepper, cayenne, and dry mustard. Rub the paprika mixture over the surface of the meat. Place the meat in a shallow dish. Cover and marinate in the refrigerator 8 hours or overnight.

Preheat the oven to 325°F (165°C). Remove the meat from the refrigerator. Place the meat on a rack in a shallow roasting pan. Insert a meat thermometer into the center of the meat. Roast 1¼ to 1½ hours or until the internal temperature reaches 155°F (70°C). Remove the meat from the oven. Cover with foil and let stand 15 minutes before carving the meat into thin slices.

To serve, arrange the meat slices on a serving platter. Sprinkle with the parsley.
Makes 8 to 10 servings.

◆ TIP
Letting the roast stand 15 minutes before carving allows the meat to firm up. This way, the pieces will hold together better as you carve and will look more attractive.

Polynesian-Spiced Pot Roast and Vegetables

This peppy pot roast has a gingery flavor reminiscent of sauerbraten. The colorful carrots, sweet potatoes, and onions make it a satisfying family supper dish.

1 (3- to 3¼-pound) boneless pork double-loin roast, trimmed of fat and tied by butcher
2 tablespoons vegetable oil
1 tablespoon minced gingerroot
2 teaspoons minced garlic
1¾ cups Chicken Stock (page 42) or 1 (14½-ounce) can chicken broth
⅓ cup soy sauce
⅓ cup red wine vinegar or fresh lemon juice
¼ cup turbinado sugar, Hawaiian raw sugar, or packed light brown sugar

1 teaspoon dry mustard
½ teaspoon ground cinnamon
¼ teaspoon salt
8 medium-size sweet potatoes, peeled and quartered
4 cups baby-cut carrots (see Tip, page 80)
1 (16-ounce) package frozen small whole onions
½ cup cold water
¼ cup all-purpose flour
Cooked rice

Rinse the pork roast and pat dry with paper towels. In a large Dutch oven, heat the oil over medium heat. Add the gingerroot and garlic and cook, stirring constantly, 30 seconds. Add the meat and cook until browned on all sides. Drain off fat.

Add the Chicken Stock or broth, soy sauce, vinegar or lemon juice, sugar, dry mustard, cinnamon, and salt. Bring to a boil. Reduce heat, cover, and simmer 1¼ hours. Turn the meat over. Add the sweet potatoes, carrots, and onions to the Dutch oven and return to a boil. Reduce heat, cover, and simmer 25 to 30 minutes or until the meat and vegetables are tender. Transfer the meat and vegetables to a large serving platter; cover with foil and keep warm.

For the gravy, measure the pan juices. Skim the fat. If needed, add extra stock, broth, or water to make 2½ cups; return to the Dutch oven. In a small bowl, stir together the ½ cup cold water and the flour; stir mixture into the pan juices in the Dutch oven. Cook, stirring constantly, until the mixture thickens. Cook, stirring constantly, 1 minute. Transfer the gravy to a serving bowl.

To serve, pass the gravy to spoon over the meat and vegetables. Serve with the cooked rice. **Makes 8 servings.**

◆ TIP
Turbinado sugar is raw sugar that's been steam-processed so the golden crystals are coarse and have a mild molasses flavor.

Sweet-and-Tangy Raspberry-Sauced Medallions of Pork

We designed this raspberry-and-orange sauce especially to go with pork. But once we tasted it, we decided it would be dynamite with duck, too.

1 pound pork tenderloin, trimmed of fat	1 tablespoon light brown sugar
2 teaspoons lemon pepper	2 teaspoons cornstarch
3 tablespoons butter	1/8 teaspoon ground cinnamon
2/3 cup fresh orange juice	1/8 teaspoon ground nutmeg
2 tablespoons raspberry vinegar or balsamic vinegar	1/4 cup thinly sliced green onions
	2/3 cup seedless raspberry jam
	Cooked brown rice

Rinse the pork tenderloin and pat dry with paper towels. Cut the meat crosswise into 8 pieces. Place 1 piece of meat between sheets of plastic wrap. Using the flat side of a meat mallet, pound lightly from the center to the edges until about 1/4 inch thick. Remove the plastic wrap. Repeat with the remaining meat pieces. Sprinkle both sides of the meat with the lemon pepper.

In a large skillet, melt 2 tablespoons of the butter over medium-high heat. Add the meat and cook 3 to 4 minutes or until the meat is cooked through, but still slightly pink on the inside, turning after half of the cooking time. Transfer the meat to a serving platter; cover with foil and keep warm.

For the sauce, combine the orange juice, vinegar, brown sugar, cornstarch, cinnamon, and nutmeg in a small bowl. In the same skillet, melt the remaining 1 tablespoon butter over medium heat. Add the green onions and cook, stirring frequently, 1 minute. Add the orange juice mixture. Cook, stirring constantly, until the mixture thickens. Stir in the raspberry jam. Cook, stirring constantly, 2 minutes. Transfer the sauce to a serving bowl.

To serve, pass the sauce to spoon over the meat and the cooked brown rice.

Makes 4 servings.

VARIATION

Use 4 boneless pork chops, cut 3/4 inch thick and trimmed of fat, in place of the pork tenderloin. Pound the chops as directed and cook 2 chops at a time.

Pork Chops with Caramelized Onion and Shallots

Cooking the onions and shallots in a mixture of butter and sugar turns them a golden caramel color and gives them a subtle sweetness.

3 tablespoons butter
1 tablespoon sugar
1 large onion, coarsely chopped
8 large shallots, thinly sliced
2 tablespoons balsamic vinegar

1 tablespoon minced fresh savory
   or 1 teaspoon dried savory leaves
4 boneless pork chops, ¾ inch thick
   and trimmed of fat
1 tablespoon olive oil

In a medium-size saucepan, melt the butter over medium heat. Sprinkle the sugar over the melted butter. Add the onion and shallots and cook, stirring frequently, 15 minutes. Increase heat to medium-high. Cook, stirring constantly, 5 minutes or until the vegetables are golden brown. Remove from heat. Stir in the balsamic vinegar and savory. Transfer the onion mixture to a serving bowl.

Meanwhile, rinse the pork chops and pat dry with paper towels. Brush both sides of the meat with the olive oil.

To pan-broil the meat, heat a 12-inch nonstick heavy skillet over medium-high heat until very hot. Reduce heat to medium. Add the meat and cook 5 to 7 minutes or until the meat is cooked through, but still slightly pink on the inside, turning the meat after half of the cooking time. (Do not add water or fat. Do not cover. If the meat browns too quickly, reduce the heat to medium-low.)

To serve, pass the onion mixture to spoon over the meat.

Makes 4 servings.

Pork Chops with Cognac Cream Sauce

"The combination of Muscat wine and Cognac in the creamy herb sauce is exquisite!" exclaims Rosemary.

4 boneless pork chops, ¾ inch thick
   and trimmed of fat
1 tablespoon olive oil
2 teaspoons butter
¾ cup thinly sliced celery
¾ cup sweet Muscat wine
2 tablespoons Cognac or other
   brandy

¾ cup half-and-half
4 teaspoons all-purpose flour
¼ teaspoon salt
¼ teaspoon ground white pepper
2 tablespoons minced fresh parsley
1 tablespoon minced fresh thyme or
   1 teaspoon dried thyme leaves
Cooked noodles

Rinse the pork chops and pat dry with paper towels. Brush both sides of the meat with the olive oil.

To pan-broil the meat, heat a 12-inch nonstick heavy skillet over medium-high heat until very hot. Reduce heat to medium. Add the meat and cook 5 to 7 minutes or until the meat is cooked through, but still slightly pink on the inside, turning the meat after half of the cooking time. (Do not add water or fat. Do not cover. If the meat browns too quickly, reduce the heat to medium-low.) Transfer the meat to a serving platter; cover with foil and keep warm.

For the sauce, melt the butter in a medium-size saucepan over medium heat. Add the celery and cook, stirring frequently, 5 to 6 minutes or until the celery is tender. Add the wine and Cognac or other brandy. Bring to a boil over high heat. Reduce heat to medium-high and cook 4 minutes or until the wine mixture is reduced to about ⅔ cup.

In a small bowl, stir together the half-and-half, flour, salt, and white pepper. Stir into the wine mixture in saucepan. Cook, stirring constantly, until the mixture thickens. Cook, stirring constantly, 1 minute. Stir in the parsley and thyme. Transfer the sauce to a serving bowl.

To serve, pass the sauce to spoon over the meat and the cooked noodles.

Makes 4 servings.

Peppery Pork Chops with Brown Mushrooms

The pine-scented flavor of rosemary and the wallop of cracked pepper make a zesty rub for succulent pork chops.

1 teaspoon cracked black pepper
1 teaspoon dried rosemary leaves, crushed
½ teaspoon dry mustard
¼ teaspoon onion salt
4 bone-in pork chops, ¾ inch thick and trimmed of fat

2 tablespoons butter
2 cups halved fresh brown mushrooms
1 large leek, thinly sliced
1 (5½-ounce) can spicy vegetable juice

In a small bowl, combine the pepper, rosemary, dry mustard, and onion salt. Rinse the pork chops and pat dry with paper towels. Sprinkle the pepper mixture on both sides of the meat. Using the heel of your hand, gently press the mixture into the surface of the meat.

In a large skillet, melt 1 tablespoon of the butter over medium heat. Add the meat and cook until browned on both sides. Remove the meat from skillet.

In the same skillet, melt the remaining 1 tablespoon butter over medium heat. Add the mushrooms and leek and cook, stirring frequently, 3 minutes or until the leek is nearly tender. Stir in the vegetable juice and bring to a boil. Return the meat to the skillet. Reduce heat, cover, and simmer 5 minutes or until the meat is cooked through, but still slightly pink on the inside.

To serve, spoon the mushroom mixture over the meat.

Makes 4 servings.

✦ TIP

Because dried rosemary leaves are too hard and sharp to crush with your fingers, be sure to use a mortar and pestle.

Smoked Jamaican Jerk Pork Ribs

The mixture that's used to "jerk" or marinate these meaty ribs contains ten different seasonings—everything from tongue-tingling habanero chiles to simple sugar.

2 dried habanero chiles
½ cup minced red onion
2 tablespoons minced fresh thyme
   or 2 teaspoons dried thyme leaves
2 teaspoons sugar
2 teaspoons minced gingerroot
2 teaspoons minced garlic
1 teaspoon ground allspice

½ teaspoon salt
½ teaspoon ground cinnamon
½ teaspoon ground nutmeg
2½ to 3 pounds country-style
   pork ribs
4 cups hickory wood chunks or
   chips

In a small bowl, cover the dried chiles with boiling water. Let stand 30 minutes. Rinse under cold running water. Wearing plastic or rubber gloves to protect your skin from the oils in the chiles, halve the habanero chiles lengthwise; discard the stems, seeds, and membranes. Mince the chiles.

For the jerk seasoning, combine the habanero chiles, red onion, thyme, sugar, gingerroot, garlic, allspice, salt, cinnamon, and nutmeg in a small bowl.

Rinse the pork ribs and pat dry with paper towels. Spread the jerk seasoning over the meaty side of the ribs. Place the ribs in a large shallow dish, cover, and marinate in the refrigerator 8 hours or overnight.

In a large bowl, cover the wood chunks or chips with water. Let stand at least 1 hour; drain well.

In a covered grill, arrange preheated coals in the firebox around a drip pan; test the coals for medium heat above the pan (see Tip, page 18). Sprinkle the wood chunks on the hot coals. Place the ribs, meaty side up, on the grill rack directly over the drip pan. Cover and grill 1½ to 2 hours or until the ribs are cooked through.

Makes 4 servings.

◆ TIP

To avoid contaminating the cooked ribs with bacteria from the raw meat, always use a clean platter to carry the cooked ribs from the grill to the dinner table.

Sweet and Hot Barbecue-Sauced Ribs with Tortillas

Ultra-hot, dark brown pasilla chiles add a fiery flavor to this honey barbecue sauce. Slather it on ribs, burgers, or chops to make them finger-lickin' good.

3 dried pasilla chiles
6 pounds pork loin back ribs, cut
    into 2-rib portions
1 tablespoon vegetable oil
1 large onion, finely chopped
2 teaspoons minced garlic
1¾ cups chopped tomatoes or
    1 (14½-ounce) can diced
    tomatoes, with juice

1 (12-ounce) can beer
1 (6-ounce) can tomato paste
½ cup honey
2 teaspoons celery seeds
1 teaspoon ground cumin
1 teaspoon dry mustard
12 flour tortillas, warmed

In a small bowl, cover the dried chiles with boiling water. Let stand 1 hour. Rinse under cold running water. Wearing plastic or rubber gloves to protect your skin from the oils in the chiles, halve the pasilla chiles lengthwise; discard the stems, seeds, and membranes. Chop the chiles; set aside.

Meanwhile, preheat the oven to 350°F (175°C). Rinse the pork ribs and pat dry with paper towels. Place the ribs, meaty side up, in a large shallow roasting pan. Bake 1¼ to 1½ hours or until the ribs are cooked through. Drain off fat.

While the ribs are baking, prepare the barbecue sauce: In a large saucepan, heat the oil over medium heat. Add the onion and garlic and cook, stirring frequently, 5 minutes or until the onion is tender. Stir in the pasilla chiles, tomatoes with their juice, beer, tomato paste, honey, celery seeds, cumin, and dry mustard and bring to a boil. Reduce heat and simmer, stirring frequently, 25 minutes or until the sauce is of desired consistency.

Transfer half of the barbecue sauce to a serving bowl; set aside. Brush the ribs with some of the remaining sauce. Bake 15 minutes, brushing once or twice with the sauce.

To serve, pass the reserved barbecue sauce to serve with the ribs and the warmed tortillas.
Makes 6 servings.

✦ TIP
To warm the tortillas, wrap them in foil and place them in a 350°F (175°C) oven for 10 minutes or until heated through.

Chorizo and Pinto Bean Burritos with Sour Cream Velouté Sauce

Deep reddish-black guajillo chiles have a lot of fire power. Because they're so hot, they're sometimes called travieso, *which is Spanish for "mischievous." You'll find them at Mexican food stores.*

3 dried guajillo chiles
Sour Cream Velouté Sauce
   (see opposite)
8 (10-inch) flour tortillas
8 ounces bulk chorizo or hot Italian
   sausage
2 medium-size onions, cut into very
   thin wedges
1 medium-size red or green bell
   pepper, cut into ¾-inch pieces
1 teaspoon minced garlic
½ cup dry red wine or water
1 cup ricotta cheese
1 (15-ounce) can pinto beans,
   rinsed and drained

1 medium-size tomato, chopped
Shredded lettuce
Avocado wedges, for garnish

SOUR CREAM VELOUTÉ SAUCE
2 tablespoons butter
3 tablespoons all-purpose flour
¼ teaspoon salt
⅛ teaspoon ground black pepper
1¼ cups chicken broth
1 (8-ounce) container sour cream
2 tablespoons minced fresh cilantro
   or parsley

In a small bowl, cover the dried chiles with boiling water. Let stand 1 hour. Rinse under cold running water. Wearing plastic or rubber gloves to protect your skin from the oils in the chiles, halve the guajillo chiles lengthwise; discard the stems, seeds, and membranes. Chop the chiles; set aside.

Meanwhile, prepare the Sour Cream Velouté Sauce; cover and keep warm. Preheat the oven to 350°F (175°C). Stack the tortillas and wrap tightly in foil. Heat in the oven 10 minutes or until softened. (When ready to fill the tortillas, remove only half at a time, keeping the remaining tortillas warm in the oven.)

While the tortillas are heating, prepare the filling. In a large skillet, cook the sausage, onions, bell pepper, and garlic over medium heat until the meat is browned, breaking up the meat as it cooks. Drain well. Stir in the red wine or water and cook 5 minutes or until most of the wine has evaporated. Remove the skillet from the heat. Stir in the ricotta cheese, guajillo chiles, and ½ cup of the sauce.

Spoon about ½ cup of the filling onto each tortilla just below the center of the tortilla. Top each with some of the pinto beans and tomato. Fold up the bottom edge over the filling just until the mixture is covered. Fold in the opposite sides, then roll up the tortilla from the bottom.

Arrange the burritos, seam side down, on a baking sheet. Bake 15 minutes or until the burritos are heated through.

To serve, arrange the shredded lettuce on a serving platter. Arrange the burritos on top of the lettuce. Garnish with the avocado wedges. Serve with the remaining sauce.

Makes 4 servings.

SOUR CREAM VELOUTÉ SAUCE

In a medium-size saucepan, melt the butter over medium heat. Stir in 1 tablespoon of the flour, the salt, and black pepper. Add the chicken broth and cook, stirring constantly, until the mixture thickens.

In a small bowl, combine the sour cream and the remaining 2 tablespoons flour. Stir into the broth mixture. Cook, stirring constantly, 1 minute or until hot. Do not boil. Stir in the cilantro or parsley.

Makes about 2¼ cups.

✦ TIP

Chorizo is a spicy fresh pork sausage that's flavored with garlic, chili powder, and other seasonings. It's sold both in bulk and link forms at Mexican food stores and some supermarkets.

Ham in Horseradish Crust with Roasted Shallots, Turnips, and Carrots

"If you're a horseradish lover like I am, you can never have too many recipes that use horseradish," says Sandra. "I'm always inventing different ways to use it. I'm especially fond of this recipe because everyone, even the horseradish novice, enjoys it."

20 medium-size shallots, peeled
10 medium-size turnips, peeled and
    quartered
10 medium-size carrots, cut into
    3-inch pieces
$\frac{1}{3}$ cup olive oil
2 tablespoons minced fresh dill or
    2 teaspoons dried dill weed

2 tablespoons fresh lemon juice
$1\frac{1}{2}$ cups soft bread crumbs (about
    2 slices)
3 tablespoons prepared horseradish
$\frac{1}{8}$ teaspoon ground black pepper
1 (4- to $4\frac{1}{2}$-pound) cooked ham,
    shank portion
$\frac{1}{4}$ cup Dijon mustard

In a Dutch oven, cover the shallots, turnips, and carrots with water and bring to a boil. Reduce heat, cover, and simmer 10 minutes: drain. Transfer the vegetables to a 13 x 9-inch baking dish. In a small bowl, combine the olive oil, half of the dill, and the lemon juice. Pour over the vegetables, tossing to coat; set aside.

Preheat the oven to 325°F (165°C). Spread the bread crumbs in a shallow baking pan. Bake, stirring occasionally, 10 to 12 minutes or until lightly toasted. In a medium-size bowl, combine the toasted bread crumbs, the horseradish, the remaining dill, and the pepper; set aside.

Score the top of the ham into diamonds. Insert a meat thermometer into the center of the thickest portion of the ham. Do not allow the thermometer to touch bone. Using a pastry brush, spread the Dijon mustard over the top and uncut sides of the ham. Using your fingers, press the bread crumb mixture evenly over the mustard.

Place the ham on a rack in a shallow baking pan. Place the ham in the oven. Place the vegetables in the oven alongside the ham. Bake $1\frac{1}{2}$ to $1\frac{3}{4}$ hours or until the internal temperature of the ham reaches 135°F (55°C). Stir the vegetables after half of the baking time.

Remove the ham and vegetables from the oven. Cover the ham with foil and let stand 15 minutes before carving. Transfer the vegetables to a serving bowl; cover with foil and keep warm. Serve the vegetables with the ham.

Makes 10 servings.

✦ TIP

Scoring the ham allows the mustard to penetrate the meat. Use a small sharp knife to score diagonal lines into the surface of the ham, cutting them about $\frac{1}{4}$ inch deep and 1 inch apart. Make another series of cuts at right angles to the first ones to form a diamond pattern.

Ham and Shiitake Mushroom–Stuffed Puff Pastry

We used shiitake mushrooms in this elegant giant turnover to boost the flavor, but you can use the milder white mushrooms, if you prefer.

1 tablespoon butter
3 cups coarsely chopped fresh
    shiitake mushrooms
8 medium-size green onions, sliced
1 (7-ounce) jar roasted peppers,
    drained and coarsely chopped
¼ cup minced fresh parsley
1 tablespoon minced fresh basil or
    1 teaspoon dried basil leaves
1 tablespoon minced fresh oregano
    or 1 teaspoon dried oregano leaves

¼ teaspoon ground red (cayenne)
    pepper
1 (17¼-ounce) package frozen puff
    pastry, thawed 30 minutes
1 egg mixed with 1 teaspoon water,
    for glaze
2 cups (8 ounces) shredded
    provolone cheese or mozzarella
    cheese
1½ cups (8 ounces) cooked ham cut
    into thin strips

Preheat the oven to 400°F (205°C). For the filling, melt the butter in a large skillet over medium heat. Add the mushrooms and green onions and cook, stirring frequently, 5 minutes or until the mushrooms are tender; drain well. Stir in the roasted peppers, parsley, basil, oregano, and cayenne; set aside.

Line a 15 x 10-inch jelly roll pan with foil. Lightly grease the foil; set aside. On a lightly floured surface, roll 1 sheet of the puff pastry into a 14 x 10-inch rectangle. Place the pastry on the prepared pan; set aside. Roll the remaining sheet of puff pastry into a 12 x 9½-inch rectangle. Cut slits in the pastry or prick with a fork to let steam escape.

Lightly brush the pastry on the pan with some of the egg glaze. Spread the filling over the pastry to within 1 inch of the edges. Sprinkle with the cheese. Arrange the ham strips over the cheese.

Moisten the edges of the pastry on the pan with some of the egg glaze; place the remaining pastry over the filling. Overlap the edges of the pastry rectangles by holding onto the foil on 1 side of the pan and lifting the foil until the edge of the bottom pastry overlaps the edge of the top pastry. Repeat on the remaining 3 sides. Using a fork, press the edges together to seal. Lightly brush the top pastry with the remaining egg glaze. Bake 30 minutes or until the pastry is golden brown.

Makes 6 servings.

✦ TIP
The mushroom mixture, ham strips, and cheese from this recipe make great toppers for pizza.

Wine-Marinated Rabbit with Fennel and Red-Pepper Sauce

This recipe is our version of the German classic, hasenpfeffer. *Originally wild rabbits were marinated to make them more tender, but we've marinated the already-tender domestic rabbit to add lots of sassy flavor.*

1 (2½- to 3-pound) whole domestic rabbit, ready to cook
2 cups dry white wine
½ cup tarragon vinegar or cider vinegar
1 small onion, thinly sliced and separated into rings
2 large fresh parsley sprigs
2 fresh thyme sprigs
2 bay leaves
6 cloves garlic, crushed

1 teaspoon hot pepper sauce
1 medium-size fennel bulb with tops
3 tablespoons olive oil
1 cup sliced leek
1 medium-size red or green bell pepper, cut into ¾-inch pieces
2 tablespoons all-purpose flour
2 tablespoons sugar
½ teaspoon salt
½ teaspoon crushed red pepper
Cooked wild rice

Cut the rabbit into 4 pieces. Rinse the rabbit pieces and pat dry with paper towels. Place the rabbit pieces in a large heavy plastic bag.

For the marinade, combine the wine, vinegar, onion, parsley sprigs, thyme sprigs, bay leaves, garlic, and hot pepper sauce in a medium-size bowl. Pour over the rabbit; seal bag. Marinate in the refrigerator 8 hours or overnight, turning occasionally.

Remove any tough or bruised outer leaves from the fennel bulb. Trim off the root end; discard. Pull off the feathery tops from the stems. Finely chop the tops; reserve 2 tablespoons of the tops. Trim off the stems; discard. Thoroughly rinse the trimmed bulb and halve the bulb lengthwise; remove the core. Cut the bulb crosswise into ¼-inch-thick slices. Set aside.

Remove the rabbit from the bag, reserving the marinade. Pat the rabbit pieces dry with paper towels. Strain the marinade through a sieve; discard the onion and seasonings.

In a 12-inch nonstick skillet, heat 2 tablespoons of the olive oil over medium heat. Add the rabbit pieces and cook 5 minutes or until browned on both sides. Add the marinade and the fennel slices and bring to a boil. Reduce heat, cover, and simmer 35 to 45 minutes or until the rabbit is tender. Using a slotted spoon, transfer the rabbit and fennel to a serving platter; cover with foil and keep warm.

Strain the pan juices through a sieve; measure the pan juices. Skim off fat. If needed, add enough water to make 1½ cups; set aside.

For the sauce, heat the remaining 1 tablespoon olive oil in a medium-size saucepan over medium heat. Add the leek and bell pepper and cook, stirring frequently, 5 minutes or until the vegetables are tender. Stir in the flour, sugar, salt, and crushed red pepper. Add the reserved

1½ cups pan juices and the reserved 2 tablespoons fennel tops. Cook, stirring constantly, until the mixture thickens. Cook, stirring constantly, 1 minute.

To serve, spoon the sauce over the rabbit and fennel. Serve with the cooked wild rice.
Makes 4 servings.

VARIATION

Substitute 2½ to 3 pounds of chicken breasts, thighs, and/or drumsticks for the rabbit.

Hoppin' Habanero Lamb with Roasted Rhubarb–Orange Sauce

"I came up with this piquant fruity dish one day in May when I was planning a special Mother's Day dinner. I guess you could say it's a celebration of spring because it features two of my spring favorites—lamb and rhubarb. The sharp bite of the rhubarb is simply fantastic combined with the hot and sweet marinade," proclaims Sandra.

1½ cups extra-dry vermouth
1 cup fresh orange juice
2 tablespoons fresh lime juice
2 tablespoons red wine vinegar
2 tablespoons hot habanero pepper
   sauce
2 teaspoons minced garlic
1 (4- to 4½-pound) leg of lamb,
   boned, trimmed of fat, rolled,
   and tied by butcher

2 pounds fresh rhubarb, cut into
   1-inch pieces (6 cups)
½ cup apricot jam or peach jam
2 tablespoons butter, cut into small
   pieces

For the marinade, combine the vermouth, orange juice, lime juice, vinegar, habanero pepper sauce, and garlic in a small saucepan and bring to a boil. Reduce heat, and simmer 10 minutes. Cool slightly. Reserve ½ cup of the marinade for the rhubarb sauce; cover and refrigerate.

Rinse the leg of lamb and pat dry with paper towels. Place the lamb in a large heavy plastic bag; set the bag in a bowl. Pour the remaining marinade over the lamb; seal bag. Marinate in the refrigerator 8 hours or overnight, turning occasionally.

Preheat the oven to 325° (165°C). Remove the lamb from the marinade, discarding the marinade. Place the lamb on a rack in a shallow roasting pan. Insert a meat thermometer into the center of the lamb. Roast 1¼ to 1¾ hours or until the internal temperature reaches 140°F (60°C) for medium rare.

Meanwhile, for the rhubarb sauce, combine the rhubarb and jam in a 9-inch-square baking pan. Add the reserved ½ cup marinade and dot with the butter. Place the rhubarb mixture in the oven alongside the lamb during the last 20 minutes of roasting.

Remove the lamb and rhubarb sauce from the oven. Cover the lamb with foil and let stand 15 to 20 minutes before carving. Transfer the sauce to a serving bowl; cover with foil and keep warm. Serve the sauce with the lamb.

Makes 12 servings.

Lamb Chops with Parsley–Bread Crumb Crust and Baked Chèvre

This super-easy entree looks sophisticated and tastes terrific.

1½ cups soft sourdough bread crumbs or home-style white bread crumbs (about 2 slices)
¼ cup minced fresh parsley
1 tablespoon finely chopped shallot
1½ teaspoons paprika
1 teaspoon coarsely ground black pepper
¼ cup (½ stick) butter, melted

1 teaspoon dry mustard
1 teaspoon minced garlic
1 teaspoon fresh lemon juice
¼ teaspoon salt
¼ teaspoon hot pepper sauce
8 lamb top loin chops, ¾ inch thick and trimmed of fat
4 ounces herbed chèvre cheese (goat cheese)

Preheat the oven to 400°F (205°C). Spread the bread crumbs in a shallow baking pan. Bake 2 to 3 minutes or until lightly toasted, stirring once.

In a shallow dish, stir together the toasted bread crumbs, the parsley, shallot, paprika, and pepper. Set aside ¼ cup of the bread crumb mixture for the topping. In another shallow dish, combine the melted butter, dry mustard, garlic, lemon juice, salt, and hot pepper sauce.

Rinse the lamb chops and pat dry with paper towels. Dip the lamb into the butter mixture, then into the remaining bread crumb mixture to coat. Place the lamb on the unheated rack of a broiler pan or on a rack in a shallow roasting pan.

Slice or shape the cheese into 4 (½-inch-thick) rounds; halve the rounds crosswise. Place the half-circles of cheese on top of the lamb. Spoon the reserved bread crumb mixture over the cheese. Bake 25 minutes or until the lamb is cooked through but still slightly pink on the inside and the bread crumbs are golden brown.

Makes 4 servings.

VARIATION

Substitute 1 (4½-ounce) package Brie cheese for the goat cheese. Quarter the round of brie, then cut the wedges in half horizontally to form 8 thin wedges.

Butterflied Leg of Lamb with Dried Peach Stuffing and Peach-Cognac Sauce

Plan to prepare this spectacular roast with its unforgettable walnut and peach stuffing for a very special gathering.

1 (5½-pound) leg of lamb, boned, trimmed of fat, and butterflied by butcher
¼ teaspoon salt
¼ teaspoon ground black pepper
3 tablespoons butter
1 medium-size onion, finely chopped
1 stalk celery, thinly sliced
1 egg, lightly beaten
2 tablespoons freshly grated orange peel
6 slices firm-textured cinnamon-raisin bread, cut into cubes and dried (4½ cups)
½ cup finely chopped dried peaches or apricots
½ cup walnut pieces

1 tablespoon olive oil
Peach-Cognac Sauce (see below)

PEACH-COGNAC SAUCE
⅓ cup packed light brown sugar
2 tablespoons cornstarch
½ teaspoon ground cinnamon
¼ teaspoon salt
¼ teaspoon ground ginger
3 (5½-ounce) cans peach nectar or apricot nectar
⅓ cup Cognac or other brandy
1 tablespoon freshly grated orange peel
⅔ cup chopped dried peaches or apricots
2 tablespoons butter

Rinse the lamb and pat dry with paper towels. Using the fine-toothed side of a meat mallet, pound the lamb from the center to the edges until about ¾ inch thick. Sprinkle both sides of the lamb with the salt and pepper.

Preheat the oven to 450°F (230°C). For the stuffing, melt the butter in a small saucepan over medium heat. Add the onion and celery and cook, stirring frequently, 5 to 6 minutes or until the vegetables are tender. Remove from heat. Stir in the egg and orange peel. In a large bowl, combine the bread cubes, dried peaches or apricots, and the walnuts. Add the onion mixture, tossing gently to moisten.

Spread the stuffing over the lamb to within 1 inch of the edges. (If you spread the stuffing too close to the edges, it will ooze out as you roll up the lamb.) Beginning on a short side, roll tightly, jelly-roll style. Using cotton string, tie the lamb roll securely.

Place the lamb on a rack in a shallow roasting pan. Brush the lamb with the olive oil. Insert a meat thermometer into the center of the lamb. Roast 20 minutes. Reduce the oven temperature to 350°F (175°C). Roast ¾ to 1¼ hours longer or until the internal temperature reaches 140°F (60°C) for medium-rare.

While the lamb is roasting, prepare the Peach-Cognac Sauce; cover and keep warm. Remove the lamb from the oven. Cover lamb with foil and let stand 15 to 20 minutes before carving. Serve the sauce with the lamb.

Makes 12 servings.

Peach-Cognac Sauce

In a medium-size saucepan, combine the brown sugar, cornstarch, cinnamon, salt, and ginger. Stir in the peach or apricot nectar, cognac or other brandy, and the orange peel. Cook, stirring constantly, until the mixture thickens. Stir in the dried peaches or apricots and butter. Cook, stirring constantly, 2 minutes.

Makes about 2½ cups sauce.

Lamb Chops with Smoky Basil-Tomato Cream Sauce

Flavorful summertime tomatoes and basil are ideal for making this wickedly wonderful cream sauce. Try it over grilled fish, steaks, or pork chops, too.

4 thick slices bacon, chopped
1 large onion, chopped
2 pounds garden-ripe Italian plum tomatoes, peeled and coarsely chopped
½ cup dry red wine
2 tablespoons minced fresh basil or 2 teaspoons dried basil leaves
2 teaspoons minced garlic
½ teaspoon sugar

¼ teaspoon salt
¼ teaspoon ground black pepper
½ cup whipping cream or half-and-half
2 tablespoons minced fresh parsley
4 lamb sirloin chops, ½ inch thick and trimmed of fat
1 tablespoon olive oil
Cooked spaghetti or linguine

For the sauce, cook the bacon in a large saucepan over medium heat until crisp. Remove the bacon, reserving 2 tablespoons of the drippings. Drain the bacon on paper towels; set aside. Add the onion to the reserved drippings and cook, stirring frequently, 5 minutes or until the onion is tender.

Stir in the tomatoes, red wine, basil, garlic, sugar, salt, and pepper and bring to a boil. Reduce heat and simmer gently, stirring occasionally, 20 minutes.

Slowly add the whipping cream or half-and-half to the tomato mixture, stirring constantly. Cook, stirring constantly, 3 minutes. Remove from heat. Stir in the reserved bacon and the parsley. Transfer the sauce to a serving bowl.

Meanwhile, rinse the lamb chops and pat dry with paper towels. Brush both sides of the lamb with the olive oil.

To pan-broil the lamb, heat a 12-inch nonstick heavy skillet over medium-high heat until very hot. Reduce heat to medium. Add the lamb and cook 4 to 6 minutes for medium, turning the lamb after half of the cooking time. (Do not add water or fat. Do not cover. If the lamb browns too quickly. Reduce heat to medium-low.)

To serve, pass the sauce to spoon over the lamb and the cooked spaghetti or linguine.

Makes 4 servings.

⬦ TIP

To peel fresh tomatoes, place the whole tomatoes in a large saucepan of boiling water 30 seconds or until the skins split. Using a slotted spoon, immediately transfer the tomatoes to a bowl of ice water. When the tomatoes are cool enough to handle, peel off the skins with your fingers or a small knife.

SUCCULENT FISH AND SEAFOOD

Seafood lovers, we invite you to sink your teeth into some of our finest fish, shrimp, lobster, crab, and scallop dishes. We look upon good seafood as a precious commodity, so we've done our best to cook it up proud in ways we think you'll love. We've added vibrant seasonings and ingredients that enhance the flavors of the fish and seafood and used preparation techniques that carefully preserve their toothsome textures.

Whole Baked Tilefish with Garden Fresh Ratatouille is a case in point. We've gently baked the mild-flavored whole fish on a bed of eggplant, plum tomatoes, zucchini, and yellow summer squash. The colorful vegetables are first-rate with the succulent fish. Braised Shark Steaks with Chipotle Chile Sauce, another one of our favorites, is an easy entree that looks and tastes spectacular. If you're looking for a new way to serve shrimp, try Brazilian Soufflé-Topped Shrimp Pies. You'll find it hard to decide which you like better, the coconut-milk sauce or the fluffy parsnip soufflé topper. Together they're superb. And, with Sizzled Soft-Shell Blue Crabs with Pistachio-Browned Butter Sauce, you don't have to wait for a vacation by the ocean to enjoy these incredible crustacean delicacies. You can fry them up right in your own kitchen.

So accept our invitation and serve some seafood soon. Any of these top-notch fish and seafood dishes will make you glad you did.

Red Snapper with Couscous, Feta, and Sun-Dried Tomato Stuffing

This flavorful stuffing goes well with all types of fish. Not only is it tasty inside a whole red snapper or pike, it's also marvelous served as a side dish with poached orange roughy or grilled salmon.

1 tablespoon oil from sun-dried tomatoes
1 cup shredded carrot
½ cup thinly sliced green onions
1 teaspoon minced garlic
1¾ cups Chicken Stock (page 42) or 1 (14½-ounce) can chicken broth
1 tablespoon butter
¼ teaspoon ground red (cayenne) pepper

1 cup couscous
1 cup (4 ounces) crumbled feta cheese
¼ cup finely chopped sun-dried tomatoes (oil packed)
¼ cup minced fresh parsley
1 (3¼- to 3½-pound) fresh or thawed frozen dressed red snapper, pike, lake trout, rockfish, or whitefish
1 tablespoon olive oil

Preheat the oven to 400°F (205°C). For the stuffing, heat the oil from sun-dried tomatoes in a large saucepan over medium heat. Add the carrot, green onions, and garlic and cook, stirring frequently, 5 minutes or until the carrot is tender.

Add the Chicken Stock or broth, butter, and cayenne and bring to a boil. Stir in the couscous, cover, and remove from heat. Let stand 5 minutes. Stir in the feta cheese, sun-dried tomatoes, and parsley; set aside.

Lightly grease a large shallow baking pan. Rinse the fish and pat dry with paper towels. Place the fish in the prepared baking pan. To stuff the fish, fill the fish cavity with some of the stuffing, lightly patting the stuffing to flatten evenly. (Spoon the remaining stuffing into a lightly greased casserole dish; cover the casserole.) Tie or skewer the fish closed.

Brush the outside of the fish with the olive oil. Bake 40 to 45 minutes or until the fish is opaque, but still moist, throughout. Place the covered casserole of stuffing in the oven alongside the fish during the last 15 minutes of baking. Serve the fish with the stuffing.

Makes 4 servings.

+ TIP

Don't let fish terminology confuse you. To make this recipe, purchase a *dressed,* not a *drawn,* fish. A dressed fish has had its organs, scales, fins, tail, and head removed. A drawn fish has only its organs removed.

Whole Baked Tilefish with Garden Fresh Ratatouille

*L*iz *highly recommends this easy oven meal. "I've always been a fan of dishes where everything cooks together. In this dish, the ratatouille-style vegetables absorb a wonderful flavor from the fish as they bake."*

2 tablespoons olive oil

1 large red, yellow, or green bell pepper, cut into 1-inch pieces

1 large onion, coarsely chopped

1 tablespoon minced garlic

1 small eggplant (about 1 pound), quartered lengthwise and cut into ½-inch-thick slices

8 medium-size garden-ripe Italian plum tomatoes or 3 medium-size garden-ripe tomatoes, seeded and coarsely chopped

2 medium-size zucchini, cut crosswise into ½-inch-thick slices

2 medium-size yellow summer squash, cut crosswise into ½-inch-thick slices

2 tablespoons minced fresh basil or 2 teaspoons dried basil leaves

2 tablespoons minced fresh oregano or 2 teaspoons dried oregano leaves

1 teaspoon sea salt or ½ teaspoon salt

½ teaspoon freshly ground black pepper

1 (3¾- to 4-pound) fresh or thawed frozen dressed tilefish, rockfish, sea bass, sea trout, cod, or orange roughy

1 tablespoon butter, melted

Preheat the oven to 400°F (205°C). In a Dutch oven, heat the olive oil over medium heat. Add the bell pepper, onion, and garlic and cook, stirring frequently, 5 minutes or until the vegetables are tender.

Stir in the eggplant, tomatoes, zucchini, yellow squash, basil, oregano, salt, and black pepper and bring to a boil. Reduce heat, cover, and simmer 15 minutes. Lightly grease a roasting pan. Transfer the vegetable mixture to the roasting pan, spreading the mixture in an even layer.

Rinse the fish and pat dry with paper towels. Place the fish on top of the vegetable mixture. Brush the outside of the fish with the melted butter. Bake 35 to 40 minutes or until the fish is opaque, but still moist, throughout. Serve the fish with the vegetables.

Makes 6 servings.

✦ TIP

When selecting a whole fish, look for one with shiny, fresh-looking skin (any skin coloring should be bright) and firm flesh that springs back when you touch it.

Crispy Trout with Saffron Corn Sauce

You'll be amazed at how the peppery coating and delicate saffron-and-wine cream sauce dress up this prize catch.

Saffron Corn Sauce (see opposite)
1/3 cup buttermilk
1 egg white, lightly beaten
1/3 cup seasoned dry bread crumbs
1/3 cup yellow cornmeal or
   white cornmeal
2 tablespoons minced fresh parsley
1 teaspoon dry mustard
1/4 teaspoon salt
1/4 teaspoon ground red (cayenne)
   pepper
4 (8- to 10-ounce) fresh or thawed
   frozen pan-dressed trout, catfish,
   or other small fish
2 tablespoons butter, melted
Mashed parsnips or potatoes

SAFFRON CORN SAUCE
1 tablespoon hot water
1/2 teaspoon thread saffron, crushed
1 ear of corn or 1/2 cup frozen
   whole-kernel corn
2 tablespoons butter
1/4 cup finely chopped shallots
1/4 cup thinly sliced celery
2 teaspoons minced garlic
3/4 cup dry white wine
3/4 cup half-and-half
4 teaspoons all-purpose flour
1/4 teaspoon salt
1/4 teaspoon white pepper

Prepare the Saffron Corn Sauce. Remove from heat; cover and keep warm while preparing the fish.

Preheat the oven to 500°F (260°C). In a pie pan or shallow dish, combine the buttermilk and egg white. In another pie pan or shallow dish, combine the bread crumbs, cornmeal, parsley, dry mustard, salt, and cayenne.

Place a wire rack in a large shallow baking pan; lightly grease the rack. Rinse the fish and pat dry with paper towels. Using tongs, dip each fish into the buttermilk mixture, turning to coat both sides. Hold the fish over the pan for a few seconds to allow the excess mixture to drip back into the pan. Then, roll the fish in the crumb mixture, coating both sides evenly.

Place the fish on the prepared rack in the baking pan. Using a small spoon, drizzle the 2 tablespoons melted butter evenly over the fish. Bake 12 to 14 minutes or until the coating is golden brown and the fish is opaque, but still moist, throughout.

Transfer the fish to a serving platter. Spoon the sauce around the fish. Serve with the mashed parsnips or potatoes.

Makes 4 servings.

SAFFRON CORN SAUCE

In a small bowl, combine the hot water and saffron; let stand 15 minutes. If using the fresh ear of corn, place the ear of corn in a shallow pan. Holding the ear at an angle, use a sharp knife to cut down across the tips of the kernels. Using the dull side of the knife, scrape the ear to release the milky juices into the pan. Measure ½ cup of the corn with its juices.

In a medium-size saucepan, melt the butter over medium heat. Add the shallots, celery, and garlic and cook, stirring frequently, 5 to 6 minutes or until the vegetables are tender. Stir in the fresh or frozen corn. Cook, stirring occasionally, 10 minutes or until the corn is crisp-tender.

Add the wine and bring to a boil over high heat. Reduce heat to medium-high and cook 5 minutes or until the wine mixture is reduced to about ⅔ cup. In a small bowl, stir together the saffron mixture, the half-and-half, flour, salt, and white pepper. Stir the saffron mixture into the wine mixture. Cook over medium heat, stirring constantly, until the mixture thickens. Cook, stirring constantly, 1 minute.

Makes about 2 cups.

VARIATION

CRISPY FISH FILLETS WITH SAFFRON CORN SAUCE

Substitute 4 (5- to 6-ounce) fresh or thawed frozen fish fillets, ¼ to ½ inch thick, for the pan-dressed trout. Coat the fish and bake 7 to 8 minutes.

◆ TIP

Great-tasting trout can range from white to a deep-salmon color, depending largely on what the fish eat. So, when shopping for trout, use freshness, rather than color as a guide to quality.

Cajun Redfish with Sauce Piquante

"While vacationing in New Orleans, my husband and I ate bowl after bowl of redfish cooked in a tomatoey, roux-based sauce. The memory of this delightfully peppery concoction inspired me to create this recipe," proclaims Sandra.

2 or 3 fresh serrano chiles or
    jalapeño chiles
¼ cup all-purpose flour
¼ cup vegetable oil
1 large green bell pepper, finely
    chopped
2 stalks celery, sliced
1 large onion, chopped
1 tablespoon minced garlic
½ teaspoon salt
½ teaspoon hot pepper sauce
1¾ cups chopped Italian plum
    tomatoes or 1 (14½-ounce) can
    diced tomatoes, with juice

1¾ cups Chicken Stock (page 42)
    or 1 (14½-ounce) can chicken broth
1 tablespoon minced fresh thyme or
    1 teaspoon dried thyme leaves
2 bay leaves
1 (2- to 2½-pound) fresh or thawed
    frozen dressed redfish, yellowtail,
    snapper, croaker, cusk, or drum
    (with head and tail)
Cooked rice
¼ cup minced fresh parsley
Lemon slices, for garnish

Preheat the oven to 400°F (205°C). Wearing plastic or rubber gloves to protect your skin from the oils in the chiles, halve the serrano or jalapeño chiles lengthwise; discard the stems, seeds, and membranes. Mince the chiles; set aside.

For the sauce, stir together the flour and oil in a large heavy saucepan until smooth. Cook over medium heat, stirring constantly with a wooden spoon, 10 minutes or until a dark, reddish brown roux is formed.

Add the chiles, bell pepper, celery, onion, garlic, salt, and hot pepper sauce amd cook, stirring frequently, 5 to 6 minutes or until the vegetables are tender. Gradually stir in the tomatoes with their juice, Chicken Stock or broth, thyme, and bay leaves and bring to a boil. Reduce heat and simmer 30 to 35 minutes or until the mixture slightly thickens. Remove from heat; discard the bay leaves.

Lightly grease a large shallow baking pan. Rinse the fish and pat dry with paper towels. Place the fish in the prepared baking pan. Pour the sauce over the fish. Bake 30 to 35 minutes or until the fish is opaque, but still moist, throughout.

To serve, arrange the cooked rice on a serving platter. Carefully place the fish on top of the rice; spoon the sauce over the fish and rice. Sprinkle with the parsley. Garnish with the lemon slices.

Makes 4 servings.

✦ TIP

Slowly cooking the roux so it takes on a nutty flavor and a coppery color is the secret to this recipe. When the roux is just right, it should be the color of a tarnished penny.

Braised Shark Steaks with Chipotle Chile Sauce

The first time we tasted this recipe, we couldn't praise it enough. It's so easy, yet looks and tastes so great, that it's become one of our favorites.

2 tablespoons butter
1 medium-size onion, chopped
¼ cup chopped carrot
¼ cup sliced celery
¼ cup sliced green onions
2 teaspoons minced garlic
1¾ cups chopped tomatoes or
    1 (14½-ounce) can diced
    tomatoes, with juice
1 cup dry white wine

1½ teaspoons sugar
½ teaspoon bottled crushed
    chipotle chile
¼ teaspoon salt
2 tablespoons minced fresh cilantro
    or parsley
6 (5- to 6-ounce) fresh or thawed
    frozen shark, salmon, halibut, or
    swordfish steaks, cut ½ inch thick

For the sauce, melt the butter in a 12-inch nonstick skillet over medium heat. Add the onion, carrot, celery, green onions, and garlic and cook, stirring frequently, 5 to 6 minutes or until the vegetables are tender.

Stir in the tomatoes with their juice, white wine, sugar, chipotle chile, and salt and bring to a boil. Reduce heat, and simmer 15 minutes. Stir in the cilantro or parsley.

Rinse the fish and pat dry with paper towels. Place the fish on top of the tomato mixture and return to a boil. Reduce heat, cover, and simmer 5 to 6 minutes or until the fish is opaque, but still moist, throughout.

Using a wide, slotted spatula, carefully transfer the fish to a serving platter. Spoon the sauce over the fish.

Makes 6 servings.

Broiled Halibut with Basil
and Sun-Dried Tomato Mayonnaise

"Even though she lived in the heart of Chicago, my grandmother had fresh basil growing in her yard," recalls Rosemary. "As a child, I remember she and I always made a special point of stopping to smell the basil. To this day, basil is my favorite herb, especially when it's used in an enchanting dish like this one."

Basil and Sun-Dried Tomato
   Mayonnaise (see opposite)
4 (7- to 8-ounce) fresh or thawed
   frozen halibut, salmon, shark, or
   swordfish steaks, 1 inch thick
2 tablespoons butter, melted
1 tablespoon finely chopped green
   onion
1 tablespoon fresh lime juice
½ teaspoon minced garlic
¼ teaspoon salt
⅛ teaspoon ground black pepper

BASIL AND SUN-DRIED TOMATO
MAYONNAISE
¼ cup loosely packed fresh basil
   leaves
1 teaspoon oil from sun-dried
   tomatoes
¾ cup mayonnaise
¼ cup finely chopped sun-dried
   tomatoes (oil packed)
2 tablespoons finely chopped green
   onion
2 tablespoons fresh lime juice
⅛ teaspoon salt
⅛ teaspoon ground black pepper

Prepare the Basil and Sun-Dried Tomato Mayonnaise and refrigerate.

Preheat the broiler. Lightly grease the unheated rack of a broiler pan. Rinse the fish and pat dry with paper towels. Place the fish on the prepared rack of the broiler pan.

For the basting sauce, combine the melted butter, green onion, lime juice, garlic, salt, and pepper in a small bowl. Brush the fish with about half of the basting sauce.

Broil fish 5 inches from the heat 10 to 12 minutes or until opaque, but still moist, throughout, turning the fish with a wide spatula and brushing with the remaining basting sauce after half of the cooking time. Serve the fish with the mayonnaise.

Makes 4 servings.

BASIL AND SUN-DRIED TOMATO MAYONNAISE

In a small bowl, stir together the basil leaves and the oil from sun-dried tomatoes until the leaves are coated. Turn the basil leaves out onto a cutting board. Using a very sharp knife, mince the basil leaves.

In a medium-size bowl, combine the minced basil, the mayonnaise, sun-dried tomatoes, green onion, lime juice, salt, and pepper. Cover and refrigerate at least 4 hours or up to 1 week.

Makes about 1¼ cups.

◆ TIP

The basil you see most often is sweet basil. It has bright green leaves and a slightly peppery flavor. Other basils include purple basil, with deep-red-accented leaves, as well as lemon basil, with a lemony aroma, and cinnamon basil, with a spicy scent. Any of the basils will work well in this mayonnaise.

Tuna Steaks with East Indian Spice Puree

The daring flavors of ginger, red chiles, and cilantro are well suited to the robust flavor of tuna. Because the steaks are baked quickly at a very high temperature, they turn out tender and succulent.

4 small dried red chiles
1 medium-size onion, cut into
   wedges
3 tablespoons loosely packed fresh
   cilantro leaves
2 tablespoons white wine vinegar
2 teaspoons sugar
2 teaspoons minced gingerroot
1 teaspoon ground turmeric

2 cloves garlic, halved
1/2 teaspoon salt
1/2 teaspoon ground cumin
1/2 teaspoon ground mace
4 (7- to 8-ounce) fresh or thawed
   frozen tuna, salmon, halibut,
   shark, or swordfish steaks,
   1 inch thick

In a small bowl, cover the dried chiles with boiling water. Let stand 30 minutes. Rinse under cold running water. Wearing plastic or rubber gloves to protect your skin from the oils in the chiles, halve the red chiles lengthwise; discard the stems, seeds, and membranes. Mince the chiles.

For the spice puree, combine the red chiles, onion, cilantro leaves, vinegar, sugar, gingerroot, turmeric, garlic, salt, cumin, and mace in a food processor or blender. Cover and process until nearly smooth.

Rinse the fish and pat dry with paper towels. Place the fish in a shallow dish. Spoon some spice puree onto 1 side of each fish steak. Cover and marinate in the refrigerator 1 to 2 hours.

Preheat the oven to 500°F (260°C). Place a wire rack in a large shallow baking pan; lightly grease the rack. Place the fish steaks, puree side up, on the prepared rack in the baking pan. Bake 22 to 25 minutes or until the fish is opaque, but still moist, throughout.

Makes 4 servings.

VARIATION
Use 1/2 teaspoon crushed red pepper in place of the 4 dried red chiles.

Thai-Spiced Grilled Swordfish Brochettes

Sharyl points out that the firm, meaty texture of swordfish is ideal for these garlic and ginger–seasoned kabobs. She also says the trick to keeping the fish from sticking during grilling is to spray the unheated grill rack with nonstick cooking spray (or brush it with vegetable oil) before you place it over the coals.

1 pound fresh or thawed frozen
    swordfish, tuna, halibut, shark, or
    sea bass steaks, 1 inch thick
¼ cup thinly sliced green onions
3 tablespoons fish sauce (nam pla)
    or soy sauce
3 tablespoons fresh lime juice
2 tablespoons vegetable oil
2 teaspoons minced gingerroot

2 teaspoons minced garlic
16 fresh pineapple chunks
1 medium-size orange, cut into
    8 chunks
8 green onions, sliced diagonally
    into 1½-inch pieces
Lime slices and red bell pepper
    strips, for garnish

Rinse the fish and pat dry with paper towels. Remove any skin and bones from fish. Cut the fish into 1-inch pieces. Place the fish in a heavy plastic bag.

For the marinade, combine the thinly sliced green onions, fish sauce or soy sauce, lime juice, oil, gingerroot, and garlic in a small bowl. Pour over the fish; seal bag. Marinate in the refrigerator 3 to 4 hours, turning occasionally.

Cover 8 (10-inch) bamboo skewers with water. Let stand 30 minutes; drain. Remove the fish from the bag, reserving the marinade. For the fish skewers, thread the fish, pineapple chunks, orange chunks, and green onion pieces on the bamboo skewers, leaving ¼ inch space between the pieces. (Leaving a little space between the pieces allows the fish to cook evenly.) Brush the skewers with some of the marinade.

In an uncovered grill, arrange preheated coals in the firebox; test the coals for medium-hot heat (see Tip, page 18). Place the fish skewers on the lightly greased grill rack directly over the coals. Grill 8 to 10 minutes or until the fish is opaque, but still moist, throughout, turning the skewers and brushing with some of the marinade after half of the cooking time. (Or, place the fish skewers on the lightly greased unheated rack of a broiler pan. Broil 4 to 5 inches from the heat 6 to 8 minutes or until the fish is opaque, but still moist, throughout, turning and brushing with some of the marinade after half of the cooking time.) Discard the remaining marinade.

To serve, arrange the fish skewers on a serving platter. Garnish with the lime slices and bell pepper strips.

Makes 4 servings.

✦ TIP

To choose the perfect pineapple, look for one that's well-rounded and heavy for its size and has a fresh-looking green top. Its aroma should be sweet, not perfumey or fermented, and it should yield slightly to gentle pressure.

Mediterranean Pike with Herbed White Bean Puree

These pike rolls get a triple-flavor whammy. First, they're sprinkled with oregano and orange peel. Then, they're simmered with tomatoes, onion, carrots, and fennel. And finally, they're served with a creamy bean, basil, and garlic puree.

2 medium-size fennel bulbs
2 tablespoons olive oil
1 large onion, halved lengthwise
   and thinly sliced
1¾ cups chopped tomatoes or
   1 (14½-ounce) can diced
   tomatoes, with juice
2 medium-size carrots, thinly sliced
1 cup fresh orange juice
¼ cup coarsely chopped pitted
   kalamata olives or sliced pitted
   ripe olives

½ teaspoon crushed red pepper
4 (5- to 6-ounce) fresh or thawed
   frozen skinless pike, flounder,
   sole, orange roughy, or other fish
   fillets, ¼ to ½ inch thick
1 tablespoon minced fresh oregano
   or 1 teaspoon dried oregano leaves
1 teaspoon freshly grated orange peel
⅛ teaspoon salt
Herbed White Bean Puree
   (page 187)
2 tablespoons crumbled feta cheese

Remove any tough or bruised outer leaves from the fennel bulbs. Trim off the root ends and the stems; discard. Thoroughly rinse the trimmed bulbs and quarter each bulb lengthwise; remove the core. Cut the fennel crosswise into thin slices.

In a large skillet, heat the olive oil over medium heat. Add the fennel and onion and cook, stirring frequently, 5 minutes or until the vegetables are tender. Add the tomatoes with their juice, carrots, orange juice, olives, and crushed red pepper and bring to a boil. Reduce heat and simmer 20 minutes.

Meanwhile, rinse the fish and pat dry with paper towels. Sprinkle the fish with the oregano, orange peel, and salt. Beginning from the narrow end, roll up each fillet and secure with wooden picks. Place the fish rolls, seam side down, in the tomato mixture. Cover and simmer 8 to 9 minutes or until the fish is opaque, but still moist, throughout.

While the fish rolls are simmering, prepare the Herbed White Bean Puree. Remove from heat; cover and keep warm.

To serve, using a slotted spatula, transfer the fish rolls to a serving platter. Carefully remove the wooden picks from the fish rolls. Spoon the tomato mixture over the fish rolls. Sprinkle with the feta cheese. Serve with the bean puree.

Makes 4 servings.

Goat Cheese and Pesto–Stuffed Orange Roughy

Liz relies on this recipe as a favorite company dish: "It's elegant, flavor-packed, and just right for four people."

1 egg, lightly beaten
6 ounces chèvre cheese (goat cheese), at room temperature
²⁄₃ cup bottled pesto
6 tablespoons minced fresh parsley
¹⁄₃ cup toasted pine nuts (see Tip, page 47)
¹⁄₄ cup seasoned dry bread crumbs
1 teaspoon dry mustard

¹⁄₄ teaspoon ground black pepper
4 (6-ounce) fresh or thawed frozen skinless orange roughy, sole, flounder, pike, or other fish fillets, ¹⁄₄ to ¹⁄₂ inch thick
8 ounces dried fettuccine
2 tablespoons fresh lime juice
Lime wedges and carrot curls, for garnish

For the filling, combine the egg, cheese, ¹⁄₃ cup of the pesto, 4 tablespoons of the parsley, the pine nuts, bread crumbs, dry mustard, and pepper in a medium-size bowl; mix well.

Preheat the oven to 375°F (190°C). Lightly grease a 13 x 9-inch baking dish; set aside. Rinse the fish and pat dry with paper towels. Spread about ¹⁄₂ cup of the filling evenly along the length of each fish fillet. Beginning from the narrow end, roll up each fillet and secure with wooden picks. Place the fish rolls, seam side down, in the prepared baking dish. Bake 20 to 25 minutes or until the fish is opaque, but still moist, throughout.

Meanwhile, cook the fettuccine according to the package directions; drain.

To serve, combine the cooked fettuccine, the remaining ¹⁄₃ cup pesto, and the lime juice. Toss gently to coat. Divide the pasta mixture evenly among 4 dinner plates. Using a slotted spatula, place the baked fish rolls on top of the pasta. Carefully remove the wooden picks from the fish rolls. Sprinkle the fish rolls with the remaining 2 tablespoons parsley. Garnish with the lime wedges and carrot curls.

Makes 4 servings.

✦ TIP
To make sure your fish rolls look company perfect, choose fish fillets that are uniform in size and thickness.

Fillet of Grouper with Sherry Vinaigrette and Stir-Fried Baby Corn

Delicate grouper, nutty sesame seeds, and fresh-tasting baby corn all team up to make this entree a true work of culinary art.

Stir-Fried Baby Corn (see opposite)
2 tablespoons dry sherry
1 tablespoon balsamic vinegar
1 tablespoon soy sauce
1½ teaspoons sesame oil
4 (5- to 6-ounce) fresh or thawed
   frozen skinless grouper, cod,
   orange roughy, monkfish, tilefish,
   sea bass, or other fish fillets, ¼ to
   ½ inch thick
¼ teaspoon ground white pepper
⅛ teaspoon salt
1 tablespoon toasted sesame seeds

STIR-FRIED BABY CORN
1 (14-ounce) can whole baby sweet
   corn, drained
½ cup chicken broth
1 tablespoon dry sherry
2 teaspoons cornstarch
⅛ teaspoon white pepper
1 tablespoon vegetable oil
1 large red or orange bell pepper,
   cut into thin 2-inch-long sticks
1 large onion, cut into thin wedges
1 teaspoon minced gingerroot

Preheat the oven to 500°F (260°C). Assemble and prepare the ingredients for the Stir-Fried Baby Corn; set aside.

In a pie pan or shallow dish, combine the sherry, balsamic vinegar, soy sauce, and sesame oil; set aside.

Place a wire rack in a large shallow baking pan; lightly grease the rack. Rinse the fish and pat dry with paper towels. Using tongs, dip each fish fillet into the sherry mixture, turning to coat both sides. Place the fish on the prepared rack in the baking pan.

Drizzle the remaining sherry mixture over the fish. Sprinkle with the white pepper and salt. Bake 7 to 8 minutes or until the fish is opaque, but still moist, throughout.

While the fish is baking, cook the stir-fried corn. Transfer the fish to a serving platter. Sprinkle the fish with the sesame seeds. Serve the fish with the stir-fried corn.

Makes 4 servings.

STIR-FRIED BABY CORN

Cut the baby corn into 1-inch pieces. For the sauce, in a small bowl, stir together the chicken broth, sherry, cornstarch, and white pepper; set aside.

In a wok or large nonstick skillet, heat the vegetable oil over medium-high heat. Add the corn, bell pepper, onion, and gingerroot and stir-fry 3 to 4 minutes or until the vegetables are crisp-tender. Push the vegetables against the side of the wok.

Stir the sauce; add to the center of the wok. Cook, stirring constantly, until the sauce thickens. Stir the vegetables into the sauce until coated. Cook, stirring constantly, 1 minute longer. Serve immediately.

Makes about 3½ cups.

+ TIP

Because grouper is part of the sea bass family, it may be sold as bass at your store. Look for fillets with bright red coloring on the skin side of each fillet. If the coloring has darkened to brown, the fish is not fresh.

Broiled Tuna with Wine and Rosemary

Heating the marinade helps marry the flavors of the fresh rosemary, gingerroot, wine, and lemon juice. Serve these satisfying fish fillets with nutty wild rice on the side.

½ cup dry white wine
2 tablespoons fresh lemon juice
1 tablespoon olive oil
2 teaspoons minced fresh rosemary
   or ½ teaspoon dried rosemary
   leaves
2 teaspoons minced gingerroot
1 teaspoon freshly grated lemon peel

½ teaspoon salt
4 (5- to 6-ounce) fresh or thawed
   frozen tuna, salmon, swordfish,
   trout, or shad fillets, ¼ to ½ inch
   thick
Lemon slices and fresh rosemary
   sprigs, for garnish

For the marinade, combine the wine, lemon juice, olive oil, rosemary, gingerroot, lemon peel, and salt in a small saucepan and bring to a boil. Reduce heat, and simmer 5 minutes. Cool slightly.

Rinse the fish and pat dry with paper towels. Place the fish in a heavy plastic bag. Pour the marinade over the fish; seal bag. Marinate in the refrigerator 4 to 6 hours, turning occasionally.

Preheat the broiler. Lightly grease the unheated rack of a broiler pan. Remove the fish from the bag, reserving the marinade. Place the fish on the prepared rack of the broiler pan. Tuck under the thin edges of the fish. Brush the fish with some of the marinade.

Broil 5 inches from the heat 5 to 7 minutes or until the fish is opaque, but still moist, throughout, brushing with some of the marinade after half of the cooking time. Discard the remaining marinade.

Using a wide spatula, transfer the fish to a serving platter. Garnish with the lemon slices and rosemary sprigs.

Makes 4 servings.

◆ TIP
The fresher the fish when you cook it, the better. Try to use fresh fish within 2 days.

Shrimp with Chiles and Angel Hair Pasta

"A friend and I shared a delightfully spicy-hot shrimp appetizer with serrano chiles and fresh cilantro at a restaurant," remembers Sandra. *"We both agreed that we'd never tasted shrimp so good! Here's my own version of that sumptuous recipe. I turned it into an impressive main dish by increasing the portion size and serving it over angel hair pasta."*

1½ pounds fresh or thawed frozen
   large shrimp, shelled and
   deveined, with tails left on
4 fresh serrano chiles
¼ cup (½ stick) butter
1 tablespoon oil from sun-dried
   tomatoes
½ cup chopped shallots
2 teaspoons minced garlic
½ cup finely chopped sun-dried
   tomatoes (oil packed)

¼ cup minced fresh cilantro or
   parsley
2 tablespoons fresh lime juice
1 tablespoon minced fresh oregano
   or 1 teaspoon dried oregano leaves
½ teaspoon hot pepper sauce
1 (9-ounce) package refrigerated
   angel hair pasta
Lime wedges, for garnish

Rinse the shrimp and pat dry with paper towels. Wearing plastic or rubber gloves to protect your skin from the oils in the chiles, halve the serrano chiles lengthwise; discard the stems, seeds, and membranes. Mince the chiles.

In a large skillet, heat the butter and oil over medium heat. Add the shallots and garlic and cook, stirring frequently, 1 minute.

Stir in the shrimp, serrano chiles, sun-dried tomatoes, cilantro or parsley, lime juice, oregano, and hot pepper sauce. Cover and cook over medium-low heat, stirring occasionally, 4 to 5 minutes or just until the shrimp are opaque throughout.

Meanwhile, cook the angel hair pasta according to the package directions; drain well.

To serve, pour the shrimp mixture over the cooked pasta. Toss gently to coat. Transfer the pasta mixture to a serving platter. Garnish with the lime wedges.

Makes 4 servings.

◆ TIP

How large is a large shrimp? As a general rule, you'll get between 21 and 30 to the pound.

Brazilian Soufflé-Topped Shrimp Pies

We took ingredients and seasonings that are typical of the cooking of northern Brazil and combined them with our own parsnip puff. The delicious result is these elegant individual casseroles.

12 ounces fresh or thawed frozen
   shelled and deveined medium
   shrimp
6 tablespoons butter
1 large onion, chopped
1 stalk celery, sliced
1¼ cups chopped tomatoes
¼ cup minced fresh parsley
1 tablespoon minced fresh thyme or
   1 teaspoon dried thyme leaves

½ teaspoon salt
½ teaspoon crushed red pepper
1 (13½-ounce) can coconut milk or
   1¾ cups low-fat (1%) milk
3 tablespoons all-purpose flour
1½ pounds parsnips, peeled and
   sliced (about 4 cups)
¼ teaspoon ground black pepper
2 eggs, separated

Rinse the shrimp. Halve the shrimp lengthwise and pat dry with paper towels; set aside.

In a medium-size saucepan, melt 2 tablespoons of the butter over medium heat. Add the onion and celery and cook, stirring frequently, 5 to 6 minutes or until the vegetables are tender. Stir in the tomatoes, parsley, thyme, ¼ teaspoon of the salt, and the crushed red pepper and bring to a boil. Reduce heat and simmer 10 minutes.

In a medium-size bowl, combine 1¼ cups of the coconut or low-fat milk and the flour. Stir into the simmering tomato mixture and cook over medium heat, stirring constantly, until the mixture thickens. Cook, stirring constantly, 1 minute. Stir the shrimp into the tomato mixture and bring to a boil. Reduce heat, cover, and simmer, stirring occasionally, 3 minutes or just until the shrimp are opaque throughout. Remove from heat; set aside.

Meanwhile, preheat the oven to 400°F (205°C). In another medium-size saucepan, bring a moderate amount of water to a boil over high heat. Add the parsnips. Reduce heat, cover, and simmer 9 to 11 minutes or until the parsnips are very tender. Drain well. Transfer the parsnips to a large bowl. Beat with an electric mixer at low speed until nearly smooth. Add the remaining 4 tablespoons butter, the remaining coconut or low-fat milk, the remaining ¼ teaspoon salt, and the black pepper. Beat until light and fluffy.

In a small bowl, beat the egg yolks with the electric mixer at medium speed 6 minutes or until the egg yolks are very thick and light colored. Gently fold about ½ cup of the parsnip mixture into the beaten egg yolks. Then, gently fold all of the beaten egg yolks into the remaining parsnip mixture.

Wash the small bowl and mixer beaters well in hot soapy water. In the clean bowl, beat the egg whites with the electric mixer at medium to high speed until the egg whites are stiff but not dry. Add the beaten egg whites to the parsnip mixture, then gently fold together.

To assemble the pies, divide the shrimp mixture among 4 (16-ounce) au gratin dishes or individual casserole dishes. Spread or dollop the parsnip mixture on top of the shrimp mixture. Place the au gratin dishes on a large baking sheet. Bake 20 to 25 minutes or until the parsnip mixture is golden brown. Let stand 5 minutes before serving.

Makes 4 servings.

Green Peppercorn Shrimp in Mushroom-Vermouth Sauce

Vermouth, green peppercorns, and Dijon mustard are a winning taste trio in this easy shrimp dish, which is especially good over cooked brown rice.

12 ounces fresh or thawed frozen shelled and deveined medium shrimp
2 tablespoons butter
12 green onions, sliced diagonally into 1-inch pieces
1¾ cups Beef Stock (page 42) or 1 (14½-ounce) can beef broth
⅔ cup extra-dry vermouth or dry white wine

1 tablespoon crushed green peppercorns
1 tablespoon Dijon mustard
2 tablespoons cornstarch
2 cups sliced fresh shiitake mushrooms or brown mushrooms
Cooked rice or noodles

Rinse the shrimp. Halve the shrimp lengthwise and pat dry with paper towels; set aside.

In a large skillet, melt the butter over medium heat. Add the green onions and cook, stirring frequently, 1 minute. Stir in 1¼ cups of the Beef Stock or broth, the vermouth or wine, green peppercorns, and Dijon mustard and bring to a boil. Reduce heat and simmer 5 minutes.

Stir the cornstarch into the remaining ½ cup Beef Stock or broth until dissolved. Stir into the mixture in skillet. Cook, stirring constantly, until the mixture thickens. Cook, stirring constantly, 2 minutes.

Stir the shrimp and mushrooms into the vermouth mixture and bring to a boil. Reduce heat, cover, and simmer, stirring occasionally, 3 minutes or just until the shrimp are opaque throughout. Serve the shrimp mixture over the cooked rice or noodles.

Makes 4 servings.

✦ TIP

To devein a shrimp, cut a slit along the back of the shrimp with a sharp knife. Then, use the tip of the knife to remove the vein. Rinse the shrimp under cold running water.

Sizzled Soft-Shell Blue Crabs with Pistachio-Browned Butter Sauce

"*My first encounter with soft-shell crabs was at a restaurant in New Orleans. I was captivated by their sweet flavor and unique texture. Unfortunately, I live a long way from Louisiana, so I decided to come up with a way to make them at home,*" confesses Sandra. "*This recipe tops the tender crabs with pistachio nuts and browned butter. It's absolutely scrumptious!*"

½ cup buttermilk
½ teaspoon hot pepper sauce
1¼ cups finely crushed saltine
   crackers
3 tablespoons all-purpose flour
1 tablespoon minced fresh oregano
   or 1½ teaspoons dried oregano
   leaves
1½ teaspoons dry mustard
1 teaspoon paprika

¼ teaspoon ground black pepper
8 cleaned soft-shell blue crabs
4 tablespoons olive oil
1 lemon, quartered
¼ cup (½ stick) unsalted butter
½ cup coarsely chopped pistachio
   nuts, pecans, or slivered almonds
2 tablespoons minced fresh parsley,
   for garnish

Preheat the oven to 300°F (150°C) to holding cooked crabs. In a pie pan or shallow dish, combine the buttermilk and hot pepper sauce. In another pie pan or shallow dish, combine the crackers, flour, oregano, dry mustard, paprika, and black pepper.

Thoroughly rinse the crabs under cold running water to remove the mustard-colored substance. (Handle the crabs carefully.) Pat dry with paper towels. Using tongs, dip each crab into the buttermilk mixture, turning to coat both sides. Hold the crab over the pan for a few seconds to allow the excess mixture to drip back into the pan. Then, roll the crab in the cracker mixture, coating both sides evenly.

In a 12-inch nonstick skillet, heat 2 tablespoons of the olive oil over medium heat. Add half of the crabs, back side down, and cook 6 to 8 minutes or until the crabs are golden brown, carefully turning the crabs with a wide spatula after half of the cooking time. Drain on paper towels. Transfer the cooked crabs to an oven-safe platter and keep warm in the oven. Repeat with the remaining crabs in the remaining 2 tablespoons olive oil. Squeeze the lemon over the cooked crabs.

For the sauce, melt the butter in a small skillet over medium heat until it starts to turn brown. Stir in the nuts. Pour the sauce over the crabs. Garnish with the parsley.

Makes 4 servings.

✦ TIP

We've found the easiest way to clean soft-shell crabs is to have someone at our fish market do it. But, if you'd like to clean the crabs yourself, grasp each one between the back legs. With the other hand, remove the face by cutting about ½ inch behind the protruding eyes with kitchen shears. Lift one side of the pointed soft top shell. Push up and remove the spongy gill tissue with your fingers. Return the soft top shell to its original position and repeat on the other side. Turning the crab over on its back, pull up and discard the triangular apron. Rinse crabs well under cold running water; pat dry with paper towels.

Lobster and Asparagus in Black Bean–Garlic Sauce

Sharyl says, "This fragrant dish is a variation of classic lobster Cantonese. We've added asparagus and leeks for a unique flavor twist and pine nuts for a pleasing crunch."

8 ounces lean boneless pork,
   trimmed of fat
½ cup chicken broth
½ cup dry sherry
3 tablespoons black bean–garlic
   sauce
2 tablespoons soy sauce
1 tablespoon cornstarch
2 tablespoons vegetable oil
1 pound fresh asparagus, cut into
   1-inch pieces, or 1 (10-ounce)
   package frozen cut asparagus,
   thawed

3 medium-size leeks, thinly sliced
8 ounces cooked lobster meat,
   cut into bite-size pieces
   (about 1½ cups)
⅓ cup toasted pine nuts (see Tip,
   page 47)
Cooked rice

Rinse the pork and pat dry with paper towels. Partially freeze the pork, then thinly slice across the grain into bite-size strips (see Tip, page 57).

For the sauce, combine the chicken broth, sherry, black bean–garlic sauce, soy sauce, and cornstarch in a small bowl; set aside.

In a wok or large nonstick skillet, heat the oil over medium-high heat. (If needed, add more oil during cooking.) Add the fresh asparagus, if using, and stir-fry 3 minutes. Add the leeks and thawed frozen asparagus, if using, and stir-fry 2 minutes or until the asparagus is crisp-tender. Remove the vegetables from the wok.

Add the pork and stir-fry 2 to 3 minutes or until the meat is cooked through, but still slightly pink on the inside. Push the pork against the side of the wok.

Stir the sauce mixture; add to the center of the wok. Cook, stirring constantly, 1 minute or until the sauce thickens. Stir the pork into the sauce until coated. Return the vegetables to the wok. Stir in the lobster meat and pine nuts. Cook, stirring constantly, 1 minute or until heated through.

Serve immediately over the cooked rice.

Makes 4 servings.

✦ TIP
   For 8 ounces of cooked lobster meat, start with two 8-ounce lobster tails.

Curried Scallops with Arugula

*M*ild *scallops, eye-catching vegetables, spicy arugula, and high-powered curry seasoning make up this impressive stir-fry.*

1 pound fresh or thawed frozen
   sea scallops
½ cup water
3 tablespoons fish sauce (nam pla)
   or soy sauce
2 tablespoons chili-garlic sauce
1 tablespoon cornstarch
1 tablespoon curry powder
½ teaspoon sugar
1 tablespoon vegetable oil
2 medium-size carrots, cut into thin
   2-inch-long sticks

2 stalks celery, cut into thin 2-inch
   sticks
1 (8-ounce) can bamboo shoots,
   drained
4 cups bite-size pieces arugula or
   spinach
Cooked rice
Lime wedges and fresh cilantro
   sprigs, for garnish

Rinse the scallops and pat dry with paper towels. For the sauce, stir together the water, fish sauce or soy sauce, chili-garlic sauce, cornstarch, curry powder, and sugar in a small bowl; set aside.

In a wok or large nonstick skillet, heat the oil over medium-high heat. (If needed, add more oil during cooking.) Add the carrots and celery and stir-fry 5 minutes. Add the bamboo shoots and stir-fry 1 minute or until the vegetables are crisp-tender. Remove the vegetables from the wok.

Add half of the scallops and stir-fry 3 minutes or until the scallops are opaque throughout. Remove the scallops from the wok. Add the remaining scallops and stir-fry 3 minutes. Return all of the scallops to the wok. Push the scallops against the side of the wok.

Stir the sauce; add to the center of the wok. Cook, stirring constantly, 1 minute or until the sauce thickens. Stir the scallops into the sauce until coated. Return the vegetables to the wok. Cook, stirring constantly, 1 minute or until the vegetables are heated through. Add the arugula or spinach. Cook, stirring constantly, just until the arugula starts to wilt.

Serve immediately over the cooked rice. Garnish with the lime wedges and cilantro sprigs.
Makes 4 servings.

✦ TIP
Sea scallops should be creamy or slightly pink in color, with a slight sheen. Avoid very white, dull-looking ones.

Savory Pasta, Pizza, and Meatless Dishes

We'll let you in on a secret. This chapter was one of our favorites because it allowed us to throw caution to the wind and create some snappy sensations with some of our favorite foods. We tossed pasta, rolled out pizza, and juggled eggs, cheese, beans, and grains into meatless dishes. The result was this good-looking, great-tasting batch of recipes.

Gorgonzola 'n' Fettuccine with Broiled Portobello Mushrooms is just one of our chock-full-of-flavor pasta dishes. It showcases meaty portobello mushrooms on top of creamy pasta loaded with sour cream, leeks, and Gorgonzola cheese. It's a blue-cheese lover's delight. As for grains, you can choose traditional dishes such as Milanese-Style Risotto, with its mellow saffron-and-shallot seasoning, or go for creative ethnic choices, such as Chinese Noodle Cake with Stir-Fried Vegetables.

If you're bored with ordinary pizza, try one of our bold innovations, such as Shiitake Mushroom, Pork, and Shrimp Teriyaki Pizza or Basil-Scented Tomato and Caramelized Onion Pizza. Or, sample one of our bean or cheese dishes. Jarlsberg Cheese and Watercress Soufflé is the ultimate meatless main dish and Sicilian Fava Beans in Plum Tomato–Fennel Sauce is a very satisfying alternative to baked beans.

Rely on any of these lively dishes to add flair to your menus. From the first forkful to the last bite, all of them stack up to flavor-packed meals.

Gorgonzola 'n' Fettuccine with Broiled Portobello Mushrooms

"I have a weakness for all kinds of blue cheese," confesses Rosemary. "I especially like this recipe because the aromatic, wonderfully pungent tang of the Gorgonzola cheese contrasts dramatically with the rich, meaty flavor of the portobello mushrooms. I couldn't get enough of this exquisite side dish!"

6 ounces dried whole-wheat, spinach, or plain fettuccine
8 ounces fresh portobello mushrooms
1 tablespoon olive oil
Salt and white pepper
2 tablespoons butter

1 medium-size leek, thinly sliced
1 tablespoon all-purpose flour
½ cup low-fat (1%) milk
½ cup sour cream
½ cup (2 ounces) crumbled Gorgonzola cheese or other blue cheese

Cook the pasta according to the package directions; drain. Return the cooked pasta to the saucepan; cover and keep warm.

Meanwhile, preheat the broiler. Cut off the mushroom stems; discard. Using a damp paper towel, wipe the mushroom caps clean. Cut the mushroom caps into ½-inch-thick slices.

Place the mushroom slices on the unheated rack of a broiler pan. Brush with the olive oil and sprinkle with a little salt and white pepper. Broil 4 to 5 inches from the heat 9 to 10 minutes or until the mushrooms are lightly charred and tender, turning the mushrooms after half of the cooking time. Cover with foil and keep warm.

For the sauce, melt the butter in a medium-size saucepan over medium heat. Add the leek and cook, stirring frequently, 5 minutes or until the leek is tender. Stir in the flour, ¼ teaspoon salt, and ¼ teaspoon white pepper. Add the milk and cook, stirring constantly, until the mixture thickens. Cook, stirring constantly, 1 minute.

Gradually stir about ½ cup of the hot mixture into the sour cream, then return it to the remaining hot mixture. Reduce heat to low. Stir in the cheese until the cheese is nearly melted, but do not boil.

To serve, pour the sauce over the cooked pasta. Toss gently to coat. Transfer the pasta mixture to a serving platter. Place the broiled mushrooms on top of the pasta mixture.

Makes 6 side-dish servings.

Ricotta-Smothered Pasta with Marsala Tomato Sauce

Marsala wine adds a mellow richness to the chunky tomato sauce, while bacon adds a hint of smoky flavor. Serve this spirited side dish with roasted or grilled beef or lamb.

2 thick slices bacon, chopped
1 large onion, chopped
1 (15-ounce) can chunky Italian
   tomato sauce
½ cup dry Marsala or dry red wine
1 tablespoon minced fresh marjoram
   or 1 teaspoon dried marjoram leaves
1 teaspoon sugar
1 teaspoon minced garlic

¼ teaspoon ground black pepper
8 ounces dried rigatoni or ziti pasta
1 cup ricotta cheese
3 tablespoons low-fat (1%) milk
2 tablespoons minced fresh parsley
2 tablespoons minced fresh oregano
   or 2 teaspoons dried oregano leaves
¼ teaspoon salt

For the sauce, cook the bacon in a large saucepan over medium heat until crisp. Remove the bacon, reserving the drippings. Drain the bacon on paper towels; set aside. Add the onion to the reserved drippings and cook, stirring frequently, 5 minutes or until the onion is tender.

Stir in the tomato sauce, Marsala or red wine, marjoram, sugar, garlic, and pepper and bring to a boil. Reduce heat and simmer, stirring occasionally, 10 minutes.

Meanwhile, cook the pasta according to the package directions; drain. Return the cooked pasta to the saucepan. Stir in the ricotta cheese, milk, parsley, oregano, and salt and cook, stirring occasionally, until the mixture is heated through.

To serve, transfer the pasta mixture to a warm serving bowl. Pour the sauce over the pasta mixture. Sprinkle with the cooked bacon.

Makes 4 or 5 side-dish servings.

✦ TIP

To help keep pasta just the right eating temperature, serve it in a warm dish. Heat your serving dish by filling it with hot water and letting it stand for a few minutes. Then, drain the dish, dry it, and add the hot pasta.

Chinese Noodle Cake with Stir-Fried Vegetables

Sharyl advises that soaking the Chinese egg noodles helps to soften the strands so they separate more easily and cook in single ribbons rather than in clumps.

4 ounces dried Chinese egg noodles
   or fine egg noodles
12 cups water
1 tablespoon salt
4 tablespoons peanut oil or
   vegetable oil
½ cup chicken broth
3 tablespoons soy sauce

3 tablespoons rice wine or dry sherry
1 tablespoon cornstarch
1 cup fresh snow peas
2 medium-size carrots, cut into thin
   2-inch-long sticks
4 cups sliced bok choy
1 tablespoon minced gingerroot
1 tablespoon minced garlic

Preheat the oven to 300°F (150°C). For the noodle cake, place the Chinese egg noodles, if using, in a large bowl and cover the noodles with hot water. Let stand 10 minutes. Stir to untangle the noodles. Drain well.

In a Dutch oven, bring the 12 cups water and the salt to a boil. Add the Chinese or fine egg noodles. Return to a boil, reduce heat, and simmer 6 minutes for the Chinese noodles or 4 minutes for the fine egg noodles or until the noodles are tender; drain. Rinse under cold running water; drain well.

In a heavy, 10-inch, oven-safe, nonstick skillet, heat 2 tablespoons of the oil over medium heat. Carefully place the noodles in the skillet. Using the back of a wooden spoon, gently pat the noodles to make the top as smooth as possible. Cook 7 to 8 minutes or until the bottom of the noodle cake is golden brown. Run a large spatula around the edge of the skillet to loosen the noodles. Invert a baking sheet or large plate over the skillet. Holding the baking sheet and skillet together, invert the skillet onto the baking sheet to remove the noodle cake; remove the skillet.

To brown the other side, heat another 1 tablespoon of the oil in the same skillet. Slide the noodle cake from the baking sheet into the skillet, pushing gently with the wooden spoon. Cook 7 to 8 minutes or until the bottom is golden brown. Remove from heat. Place the skillet in the oven to keep the noodle cake warm while stir-frying the vegetables.

For the sauce, combine the chicken broth, soy sauce, rice wine or dry sherry, and cornstarch in a small bowl; set aside.

To remove the strings from the snow peas, use your fingers or a paring knife to pull off the tip of each pod without breaking the string, then gently pull the string down the length of the pod; discard the string. Cut the pea pods in half crosswise.

In a wok or large nonstick skillet, heat the remaining 1 tablespoon oil over medium-high heat. (If needed, add more oil during cooking.) Add the carrots and stir-fry 4 minutes. Add the snow peas, bok choy, gingerroot, and garlic and stir-fry 2 minutes or until the vegetables are crisp-tender. Push the vegetables against the side of the wok.

Stir the sauce; add to the center of the wok. Cook, stirring constantly, until the sauce thickens. Stir the vegetables into the sauce until coated. Cook, stirring constantly, 1 minute.

To serve, slide the noodle cake from the skillet onto a serving platter. Spoon some of the stir-fried vegetables over the noodle cake. Pass the remaining stir-fried vegetables. Serve immediately.

Makes 4 side-dish servings.

✦ TIP

Bok choy is a type of Chinese cabbage with white celerylike stalks and vivid green leaves. It has a mild flavor much like that of cabbage. You may find it labeled Chinese mustard cabbage, Chinese chard cabbage, or Chinese white cabbage.

Cheese Tortellini with Artichoke Hearts and Cannellini Beans

Rosemary and Liz both love this lively dish, but each adds her own special touch. Rosemary serves it with the sharp, almost pungent, Romano cheese, while Liz sprinkles on the more subtle Parmesan cheese. You'll have to decide for yourself which is your favorite.

2 tablespoons olive oil
1 large green bell pepper, cut into
   1-inch pieces
6 green onions, sliced diagonally
   into 1-inch pieces
2 pounds plum tomatoes, chopped
   (about 3½ cups), or 2 (14½-ounce)
   cans diced tomatoes, with juice
1 (6-ounce) can tomato paste
2 tablespoons minced fresh basil or
   2 teaspoons dried basil leaves
1 teaspoon sugar
¼ teaspoon ground red (cayenne)
   pepper

⅛ teaspoon salt
1 (15-ounce) can cannellini (white
   kidney) beans or great Northern
   beans, rinsed and drained
1 (6-ounce) jar marinated artichoke
   hearts, drained
1 (8-ounce) package dried cheese
   tortellini or 1 (9-ounce) package
   refrigerated cheese tortellini
Freshly grated Romano cheese or
   Parmesan cheese

For the sauce, heat the olive oil in a large saucepan over medium heat. Add the bell pepper and green onions and cook, stirring frequently, 5 minutes or until the vegetables are tender.

Stir in the tomatoes with their juice, tomato paste, basil, sugar, cayenne, and salt and bring to a boil. Reduce heat and simmer, stirring occasionally, 20 minutes or until the mixture is of desired consistency. Stir in the beans and artichoke hearts. Cook, stirring occasionally, until the mixture is heated through.

Meanwhile, cook the pasta according to the package directions; drain. Return the cooked pasta to the saucepan. Pour the sauce over the cooked pasta. Toss gently to coat. Transfer the pasta mixture to a warm serving bowl. Serve with the Romano or Parmesan cheese.

Makes 8 side-dish servings or 4 main-dish servings.

⬥ TIP

Because plum tomatoes are meatier than other tomatoes, we used them in this fresh-tasting sauce to give it plenty of body.

Milanese-Style Risotto

Creamy rice accented with saffron is a classic with cooks who live around Milan. We dressed up our version of risotto with shallots and a little nutmeg. This cheese-laden side dish is delicious with all types of meats and poultry, but in Italy, it's traditionally served with osso buco *(our recipe is on page 118).*

1 tablespoon hot water
½ teaspoon thread saffron, crushed
1¾ cups Chicken Stock (page 42)
    or 1 (14½-ounce) can chicken broth
3 tablespoons butter
1 cup Arborio rice or short-grain
    white rice

2 tablespoons chopped shallots
½ cup dry white wine
¼ teaspoon ground white pepper or
    black pepper
⅛ teaspoon ground nutmeg
¼ cup freshly grated Parmesan
    cheese

In a small bowl, combine the hot water and saffron; let stand 15 minutes. In a small saucepan, bring the Chicken Stock or broth to a boil over high heat. Reduce heat to low, cover, and keep warm.

In a large saucepan, melt 2 tablespoons of the butter over medium heat. Add the rice and cook, stirring frequently, 3 minutes. Add the shallots and cook, stirring frequently, 2 minutes or until the rice is lightly browned. Add the wine and cook, stirring constantly, until most of the wine is absorbed.

Add half of the hot stock and cook, stirring constantly to prevent sticking and browning, until most of the stock is absorbed. Add the remaining stock, saffron mixture, pepper, and nutmeg and bring to a boil. Reduce heat, cover, and simmer, without stirring, 12 to 15 minutes or until the rice is firm-tender. (The rice should be tender, yet it should offer a slight resistance when you bite into it.)

Stir in the Parmesan cheese and the remaining 1 tablespoon butter. If needed, stir in a little extra stock or water to make the rice mixture creamy and moist.

Makes 4 to 6 side-dish servings.

• TIP
Short-grain, Arborio rice from Italy is suggested for making risotto because the grains have a high starch content that allows them to absorb a lot of liquid without becoming mushy. This quality gives risotto its famous creamy texture.

Garlicky Brown Rice with Spinach and Fontina

Smooth-melting fontina cheese gives this risottolike dish a nutty accent to complement the full-flavored spinach, robust garlic, tangy dried tomatoes, and wonderfully salty ripe olives.

2 tablespoons butter
1 cup chopped fresh spinach
1 medium-size carrot, shredded
1 small onion, finely chopped
1 tablespoon minced garlic
¾ cup long-grain brown rice
1¾ cups Chicken Stock (page 42) or 1 (14½-ounce) can chicken broth
½ cup extra-dry vermouth or dry white wine

1 tablespoon minced fresh basil or 1 teaspoon dried basil leaves
¼ teaspoon ground red (cayenne) pepper
½ cup (2 ounces) shredded fontina cheese or Swiss cheese
¼ cup coarsely chopped sun-dried tomatoes (oil packed)
2 tablespoons sliced pitted ripe olives

In a large saucepan, melt the butter over medium heat. Add the spinach, carrot, onion, and garlic and cook, stirring frequently, 3 to 4 minutes or until the vegetables are tender. Stir in the brown rice.

Add the Chicken Stock or broth, vermouth or white wine, basil, and cayenne and bring to a boil. Reduce heat, cover, and simmer, without stirring, 45 minutes or until the rice is tender (not all of the liquid will be absorbed).

Stir in the cheese, sun-dried tomatoes, and olives. Cook, uncovered, 1 to 2 minutes or until the mixture is heated through.

Makes 4 or 5 side-dish servings.

✦ TIP

To tell if the rice is tender, press a piece with your fingers. It should be tender in the center with no hard spots.

Ginger-Lemon Wild Rice with Shiitake Mushrooms

Liz, a Minnesota-native and wild-rice fan, says this is one of her favorite ways to serve the grain: "The nutty flavor of the wild rice is fabulous with the earthy shiitake mushrooms, subtle lemon, spicy gingerroot, and fresh-tasting thyme."

1 cup wild rice
2 tablespoons butter
1¾ cups Chicken Stock (page 42) or 1 (14½-ounce) can chicken broth
1 medium-size onion, chopped
1 stalk celery, thinly sliced
2 teaspoons minced gingerroot
3 cups sliced fresh shiitake mushrooms or chanterelle mushrooms

⅓ cup dry sherry
2 tablespoons minced fresh thyme or 2 teaspoons dried thyme leaves
2 teaspoons freshly grated lemon peel
¼ teaspoon salt
¼ teaspoon freshly ground black pepper

Rinse the wild rice under cold running water, lifting the rice with your fingers to clean thoroughly. Drain.

In a medium-size saucepan, melt 1 tablespoon of the butter over medium heat. Add the wild rice and cook, stirring frequently, 5 minutes or until the rice is toasted.

Add the Chicken Stock or broth and bring to a boil. Reduce heat, cover, and simmer, without stirring, 40 to 50 minutes or until the rice is tender. If needed, drain off the liquid.

Meanwhile, melt the remaining 1 tablespoon butter in a large saucepan over medium heat. Add the onion, celery, and gingerroot and cook, stirring frequently, 5 to 6 minutes or until the vegetables are tender. Stir in the mushrooms, sherry, thyme, lemon peel, salt, and pepper. Cook, stirring frequently, 2 minutes.

Stir the cooked wild rice into the mushroom mixture. Cook, stirring frequently, 2 to 3 minutes or until the mixture is heated through.

Makes 4 side-dish servings.

✦ TIP

Test the doneness of wild rice as you do pasta. When it's done, it should be tender, but slightly chewy.

Bulgur, Almond, and Red Pepper Pilaf

"I love the myriad of spice and nut combinations found in Middle Eastern pilafs, so I created this toasted-bulgur pilaf for a dinner party to go with grilled lamb kabobs. Since then, I've served it with grilled chicken and poached fish, too," explains Sandra.

3 tablespoons butter
¾ cup bulgur (cracked wheat)
⅓ cup slivered almonds or pine nuts
1 large yellow or green bell pepper, chopped
1 large onion, chopped
1¾ cups Chicken Stock (page 42) or 1 (14½-ounce) can chicken broth

¼ teaspoon kosher salt or ⅛ teaspoon salt
¼ teaspoon ground cardamom
¼ teaspoon ground cinnamon
1 pound plum tomatoes, chopped (about 1¾ cups), or 1 (14½-ounce) can diced tomatoes, with juice

In a large saucepan, melt 2 tablespoons of the butter over medium heat. Add the bulgur and nuts and cook, stirring frequently, 5 minutes or until the bulgur and nuts are toasted. Remove the bulgur mixture from the saucepan.

In the same saucepan, melt the remaining 1 tablespoon butter over medium heat. Add the bell pepper and onion and cook, stirring frequently, 5 minutes or until the vegetables are tender.

Return the bulgur mixture to the saucepan. Add the Chicken Stock or broth, salt, cardamom, and cinnamon and bring to a boil. Reduce heat, cover, and simmer 18 minutes or until the bulgur is tender and most of the liquid is absorbed.

Stir in the tomatoes with their juice and return to a boil. Reduce heat, cover, and simmer 2 to 3 minutes or until the mixture is heated through. Let stand, covered, 5 minutes before serving.

Makes 6 side-dish servings.

+ TIP

Bulgur consists of whole-wheat kernels that have been cooked, dried, and cracked. It's tan in color and has a slightly nutty flavor. Look for it in the rice and other grains section of your supermarket. Once you get it home, you can store it in an airtight container for as long as 6 months.

Shiitake Mushroom, Pork, and Shrimp Teriyaki Pizza

"My son Erik loves my egg rolls and is always begging me to make them," says Sandra. "So, one day, I used the pork-and-shrimp filling from my egg roll recipe and an Italian bread shell to make pizza. The combination was an instant hit. Now, instead of wrapping and frying egg rolls, I make pizza."

3 cups sliced fresh shiitake
   mushrooms or brown mushrooms
2 cups thinly sliced bok choy
1 medium-size carrot, shredded
2 green onions, thinly sliced
¼ cup dry sherry
2 tablespoons water
1 tablespoon light brown sugar
1 tablespoon soy sauce
1 teaspoon minced garlic

1 teaspoon minced gingerroot
½ teaspoon dry mustard
8 ounces fresh or thawed frozen
   shelled and deveined medium
   shrimp
8 ounces ground pork
1 (16-ounce) Boboli or other Italian
   bread shell
2 cups (8 ounces) shredded
   mozzarella cheese

Place the mushrooms, bok choy, carrot, and green onions in a heavy plastic bag. For the marinade, combine the sherry, water, brown sugar, soy sauce, garlic, gingerroot, and dry mustard in a small bowl. Pour over the vegetables; seal bag. Marinate in the refrigerator 2 to 4 hours, turning occasionally. Drain the vegetables, discarding the marinade.

Preheat the oven to 400°F (205°C). Rinse the shrimp. Halve the shrimp lengthwise and pat dry with paper towels; set aside.

In a large skillet, cook the ground pork over medium heat until the meat is cooked through, breaking up the meat as it cooks. Using a slotted spoon, remove the meat, reserving the drippings. Drain the meat on paper towels; set aside.

Increase heat to medium high. Add the vegetables to the reserved drippings and cook, stirring frequently, 4 minutes or until the vegetables are crisp-tender. Bring to a boil over high heat and cook, stirring frequently, 2 to 3 minutes or until most of the liquid has evaporated. Add the shrimp and cook, stirring frequently, 1 to 2 minutes or just until the shrimp are opaque throughout. Remove from heat. Stir in the meat.

Place the Boboli or other bread shell on a large baking sheet. Sprinkle half of the mozzarella cheese over the bread shell. Top with the shrimp mixture. Sprinkle with the remaining mozzarella cheese. Bake 15 minutes or until the cheese is golden brown and the pizza is heated through.

Makes 4 main-dish servings.

Roasted Red Pepper, Ricotta, and Artichoke Pizza

Two cheeses, red bell pepper, yellow summer squash, and pale-green artichoke hearts make this pizza as great-tasting as it is eye-catching. Serve it as a side dish with poultry or fish or as a hearty appetizer.

2 medium-size red bell peppers
Garlic and Herb Whole-Wheat
    Pizza Dough (page 180)
2 tablespoons cornmeal
1 (15-ounce) container ricotta cheese
1 cup (4 ounces) crumbled feta
    cheese
1/4 cup minced fresh parsley
1/4 cup low-fat (1%) milk
1/4 teaspoon ground red (cayenne)
    pepper

1 small yellow summer squash,
    thinly sliced
2 tablespoons olive oil
1 tablespoon minced fresh marjoram
    or 1 teaspoon dried marjoram
    leaves
1 (6-ounce) jar marinated artichoke
    hearts, drained and coarsely
    chopped
1 tablespoon drained capers

Preheat the oven to 425°F (220°C). To roast the bell peppers, line a baking sheet with foil; set aside. Quarter the peppers lengthwise; discard the stems, seeds, and membranes. Cut small slits in the ends of the pepper pieces to make them lie flat. Place the pepper pieces, smooth side up, on the prepared baking sheet. Bake 20 to 25 minutes or until the skins are blistered and dark brown. Immediately place the peppers in a paper or heavy plastic bag; seal the bag. Let stand 20 to 30 minutes or until the peppers are cool enough to handle. Using a sharp knife, carefully peel the peppers. Cut into 1/4-inch-wide strips.

Meanwhile, prepare the Garlic and Herb Whole-Wheat Pizza Dough. Lightly grease 2 (11- to 12-inch) pizza pans; sprinkle the pans with the cornmeal. Divide the dough in half. On a lightly floured surface, roll each half of dough into a circle 1 inch larger than pizza pan. Transfer dough to the prepared pans. Build up the edges slightly. Using a fork, prick the dough generously. Bake 10 to 12 minutes or until the pizza crusts are lightly browned. Remove from oven.

In a medium-size bowl, stir together the ricotta cheese, feta cheese, parsley, milk, and cayenne. In a small bowl, combine the yellow squash, olive oil, and marjoram; toss gently to coat.

Spread the ricotta mixture over the hot pizza crusts. Arrange the roasted pepper strips, the herb-coated squash slices, and the artichoke hearts on top of the ricotta mixture. Sprinkle with the capers. Bake 10 to 12 minutes or until the pizzas are heated through.

Makes 8 side-dish servings.

VARIATION

We liked this pizza best made with roasted fresh red bell peppers. But if you're in a rush, use 1 (7-ounce) jar roasted sweet red peppers. Drain the peppers and cut them into 1/4-inch-wide strips.

Basil-Scented Tomato and Caramelized Onion Pizza

"Whenever my grandmother made homemade bread, she always made pizza, too. She never used a recipe, she just took some of the bread dough and layered on whatever was handy in the refrigerator," remembers Rosemary. *"This recipe grew out of my memories of those pizzas of days gone by."*

3 tablespoons butter
4 medium-size onions, halved
   lengthwise and thinly sliced
1 tablespoon sugar
Cheese and Pepperoni Pizza Dough
   (page 180)
3 cups (12 ounces) shredded Gruyère
   cheese or Muenster cheese

2 medium-size garden-ripe red
   tomatoes, thinly sliced and halved
1 medium-size garden-ripe yellow
   tomato, thinly sliced and halved
⅓ cup minced fresh basil
¾ cup finely shredded Parmesan
   cheese

In a large skillet, melt the butter over medium heat. Add the onions, reduce heat to medium-low and cook, stirring frequently, 20 minutes or until the onions are very soft and golden. Sprinkle the sugar over the onions and cook, stirring frequently, 10 to 15 minutes or until the onions start to brown.

Meanwhile, preheat the oven to 425°F (220°C). Prepare the Cheese and Pepperoni Pizza Dough. Lightly grease 2 large baking sheets; set aside. Divide the dough into 8 pieces. On a lightly floured surface, roll each piece of dough into a 7-inch circle. Transfer dough to the prepared baking sheets. Build up the edges slightly. Decorate the edges of the crusts by snipping the dough with kitchen scissors at 1-inch intervals. Using a fork, prick the dough generously. Bake 8 to 10 minutes or until the pizza crusts are lightly browned. Remove from oven.

Sprinkle the Gruyère or Muenster cheese over the hot crusts. Arrange the red and yellow tomato slices in a circular pattern on top of the cheese. Sprinkle with the basil. Top with the caramelized onions. Sprinkle with the Parmesan cheese. Bake 8 to 10 minutes or until the pizzas are heated through.

Makes 8 side-dish servings.

VARIATION

If you like, substitute 8 (6-inch) individual Boboli or other Italian bread shells for the Cheese and Pepperoni Pizza Dough, and omit the prebaking.

Garlic and Herb Whole-Wheat Pizza Dough

This food-processor method lets you assemble the pizza dough in next to no time.

2 cups all-purpose flour
1 cup whole-wheat flour
1 (¼-ounce) package active dry yeast
2 cloves garlic, halved
2 teaspoons dried Italian seasoning

¼ teaspoon kosher salt or
  ⅛ teaspoon salt
2 tablespoons olive oil
¾ to 1 cup warm water
  (105 to 115°F, 40 to 45°C)

In a food processor, combine the all-purpose flour, whole-wheat flour, yeast, garlic, Italian seasoning, and salt. Cover and process 10 seconds or until the ingredients are combined. Add the olive oil.

With the machine running, pour only enough of the warm water through the feed tube to form a ball of dough (you may not need all of the water). To knead the dough, process 1 minute.

Turn the dough out onto a lightly floured surface; shape into a ball. Cover with a slightly damp towel. Let rise in a warm place, free from drafts, 10 minutes. Continue as directed in pizza recipe. Makes 2 (11- to 12-inch) pizza crusts or 8 (7-inch) individual pizza crusts.

VARIATION

CHEESE AND PEPPERONI PIZZA DOUGH
Substitute 3 cups all-purpose flour for the 2 cups all-purpose flour and the 1 cup whole-wheat flour; omit the salt. Add 2 tablespoons finely shredded Parmesan cheese and ½ ounce sliced pepperoni, halved.

◆ TIP
If you like, freeze one of the pizza crusts for later. Just knead the dough in the food processor, then divide it in half. Use half to make 1 crust and shape the other half into a ball. Wrap the ball in plastic wrap and place it in a freezer bag. Seal and label the bag. Then, freeze for up to 8 months. To use, thaw the dough overnight in the refrigerator.

Jarlsberg Cheese and Watercress Soufflé

With three cups of nutty Jarlsberg cheese, this soufflé is one of the cheesiest ever. To serve the soufflé, use two forks to gently break the top into servings. Then, scoop out the soufflé with a large spoon.

1 bunch watercress or fresh parsley	3 cups (12 ounces) shredded
1/3 cup unsalted butter	Jarlsberg cheese or Swiss cheese
1/3 cup all-purpose flour	6 eggs, separated
1½ cups low-fat (1%) milk	¼ teaspoon cream of tartar

Rinse the watercress or parsley under cold running water. Pull the thin leafy watercress branches or the parsley leaves from the large stems and pat dry with paper towels; discard the large stems. In a food processor, process the watercress or parsley with on/off pulses until coarsely chopped. Measure ½ cup; set aside.

Preheat the oven to 350°F (175°C). Attach a foil collar to a 2-quart soufflé dish. (The collar supports the soufflé as it puffs above the top of the dish during baking.) Generously butter the foil collar and the dish.

In a large saucepan, melt the butter over medium heat. Stir in the flour. Add the milk and cook, stirring constantly, until the mixture thickens. Cook, stirring constantly, 1 minute. Remove from heat. Stir in the cheese until cheese is nearly melted.

In a large bowl, beat the egg yolks with an electric mixer at medium speed 6 minutes or until the egg yolks are very thick and light colored. Slowly stir the cheese mixture into the beaten egg yolks. Let stand at room temperature 5 minutes to cool slightly. Stir in the reserved ½ cup watercress or parsley.

Wash the mixer beaters well in hot soapy water; dry thoroughly. In another large bowl, beat the egg whites with the electric mixer at medium to high speed until frothy. Add the cream of tartar and continue beating until the egg whites are stiff but not dry.

Slowly pour the cheese mixture over the beaten egg whites. Using a wooden spoon, gently fold together until the mixture is an even light yellow color. Gently spoon the mixture into the prepared soufflé dish. Bake 50 to 60 minutes or until a wooden skewer inserted off-center comes out clean.

To serve, carefully remove the foil collar from the soufflé. Serve immediately.
Makes 6 main-dish servings.

+ TIP
To make a foil collar, cut a piece of foil 6 inches longer than you'll need to wrap around the soufflé dish. Fold the foil lengthwise into thirds. Wrap the strip around the top edge of the dish, making sure the foil extends about 2 inches above the dish. Secure the foil strip with masking tape or cotton string.

Havarti Cheese and Sweet-Onion Tart

Sharyl points out, "This savory tart is extra scrumptious when you make it with one of the super sweet onions, such as Georgia Vidalia, Texas Supersweet, Washington Walla Walla, or Hawaiian Maui Sweet." She also suggests using a 10-inch quiche dish, if you don't have an 11-inch tart pan with a removable bottom.

Rich Tart Pastry (see opposite)
1 tablespoon butter
1 cup chopped sweet yellow onion
3 eggs, lightly beaten
¾ cup half-and-half
¾ cup low-fat (1%) milk
¼ cup coarsely chopped sun-dried
    tomatoes (oil packed)
¼ teaspoon salt
1½ cups (6 ounces) shredded
    Havarti cheese, Swiss cheese, or
    Monterey Jack cheese
1 tablespoon all-purpose flour

RICH TART PASTRY
1 cup all-purpose flour
¼ teaspoon salt
¼ cup (½ stick) cold unsalted butter,
    cut into 1-tablespoon-size pieces
1 tablespoon vegetable shortening
1 egg yolk
2 tablespoons ice cold water

Preheat the oven to 450°F (230°C). Prepare the Rich Tart Pastry. Line the bottom and side of the pastry-lined tart pan or quiche dish with a double thickness of heavy foil. Bake 10 minutes. Remove the foil. Bake 7 to 9 minutes or until the pastry is golden brown. Remove from oven; set aside. Reduce the oven temperature to 325°F (165°C).

For the filling, melt the 1 tablespoon butter in a small saucepan over medium heat. Add the onion and cook, stirring frequently, 5 minutes or until the onion is tender.

In a large bowl, stir together the cooked onion, eggs, half-and-half, milk, sun-dried tomatoes, and salt. In a small bowl, toss together the cheese and flour. Sprinkle the cheese mixture over the bottom of the hot pastry shell. Pour the egg mixture over the cheese.

Place the tart pan on a 12-inch pizza pan. (The pizza pan will catch any spills that may occur.) Bake 25 to 30 minutes for the tart pan or 30 to 35 minutes for the quiche dish or until a wooden pick inserted in the center comes out clean. Let stand on a wire rack 10 minutes.

To serve, remove the side of the tart pan. Cut the tart into wedges.

Makes 6 main-dish servings.

RICH TART PASTRY

In a medium-size bowl, combine the flour and salt. Using a pastry cutter or 2 knives, cut in the butter and shortening until the mixture resembles coarse crumbs. Make a well in the center. In a small bowl, combine the egg yolk and water; add to the flour mixture. Using a fork, stir until the dry ingredients are moistened. Shape the dough into a ball. Wrap in plastic wrap and chill in the freezer 20 minutes or in the refrigerator 1½ hours before rolling.

On a lightly floured surface, roll out the dough into a 13-inch circle. Line an 11-inch tart pan with a removable bottom or a 10-inch quiche dish with the pastry (see Tip, page 236). Fold the extra pastry to the inside and press it against the side of the pan. (Be sure the edge of the pastry is high enough to reach the top edge of the pan.) Using a fork, prick the side of the pastry to prevent puffing. (If the pastry is quite soft, chill in the freezer 30 minutes.)

Southwestern Christmas Limas with Goat Cheese

The traditional name for the Christmas lima is Anasazi. These white kidney-shaped beans have deep-red spots that disappear when the beans are cooked. They add a mild chestnutlike flavor to this zesty sausage and beer–accented dish.

1½ cups dried Christmas lima
   (Anasazi) beans or pinto beans
3½ cups Beef Stock (page 42) or
   2 (14½-ounce) cans beef broth
2 (12-ounce) bottles dark Mexican
   beer
8 ounces bulk pork sausage
1 large red bell pepper, chopped
1 large onion, chopped

1 tablespoon minced garlic
2 fresh jalapeño chiles
1 tablespoon dry mustard
1 tablespoon minced fresh oregano
   or 1 teaspoon dried oregano leaves
1½ teaspoons ground cumin
4 ounces chèvre cheese (goat cheese)
   or feta cheese, crumbled

Sort and rinse the beans. In a large saucepan, cover the beans generously with cold water. Cover and let stand overnight. (Or, bring to a boil. Reduce heat, and simmer 2 minutes. Remove from heat; cover and let stand 1 hour.) Drain and rinse the beans.

In the large saucepan, combine the soaked beans, the Beef Stock or broth, and beer and bring to a boil. Reduce heat, cover, and simmer 1 to 1¼ hours or until the beans are tender. Drain the beans, reserving 1¼ cups of the liquid. Return the beans and the reserved liquid to the saucepan.

Meanwhile, in a large skillet, cook the pork sausage over medium heat until the meat is cooked through, breaking up the meat as it cooks. Using a slotted spoon, remove the meat, reserving the drippings. Drain the meat on paper towels; set aside.

Add the bell pepper, onion, and garlic to the reserved drippings and cook, stirring frequently, 5 minutes or until the vegetables are tender; set aside.

Wearing plastic or rubber gloves to protect your skin from the oils in the chiles, halve the jalapeño chiles lengthwise; discard the stems, seeds, and membranes. Mince the chiles.

Stir the meat, the bell pepper mixture, the minced jalapeño chiles, the dry mustard, oregano, and cumin into the bean mixture and bring to a boil. Reduce heat, cover, and simmer, stirring occasionally, 15 minutes.

To serve, transfer the bean mixture to a serving bowl. Sprinkle with the crumbled cheese.
Makes 8 side-dish servings or 4 main-dish servings.

✦ TIP
   The Christmas limas are cooked through when you can press them easily between your fingers.

Tongues-of-Fire Beans with Rice

This kissing cousin to the Caribbean dish, black beans and rice, gets its name from the beans used to make it. Tongues-of-fire beans are a type of cranberry bean and are beige with flecks of red. Despite their fiery name, the beans have a mild nutlike flavor.

1½ cups dried tongues-of-fire beans, cranberry beans, or red beans
3½ cups Chicken Stock (page 42) or 2 (14½-ounce) cans chicken broth
2½ cups water
3 bay leaves
1 large onion, chopped
1 medium-size green bell pepper, chopped
1 stalk celery, sliced
2 tablespoons fresh lime juice

2 teaspoons minced garlic
1½ teaspoons fennel seeds, crushed
1 teaspoon ground red (cayenne) pepper
¼ teaspoon salt
1 cup long-grain white rice
¼ cup minced fresh cilantro or parsley
Sour cream
Sliced green onions
Lime wedges

Sort and rinse the beans. In a large saucepan, cover the beans generously with cold water. Cover and let stand overnight. (Or, bring to a boil, reduce heat, and simmer 2 minutes. Remove from heat; cover and let stand 1 hour.) Drain and rinse the beans.

In the large saucepan, combine the soaked beans, the Chicken Stock or broth, the 2½ cups water, and the bay leaves and bring to a boil. Reduce heat, cover, and simmer 45 to 60 minutes or until the beans are tender. Drain the beans, reserving 1½ cups of the liquid. Return the beans and the reserved liquid to the saucepan.

Stir in the onion, green bell pepper, celery, lime juice, garlic, fennel seeds, cayenne, and salt and bring to a boil. Reduce heat, cover, and simmer, stirring occasionally, 30 minutes or until the vegetables are tender and the mixture thickens slightly. Discard the bay leaves.

Meanwhile, cook the rice according to the package directions, omitting the butter and salt.

To serve, spoon the bean mixture over the cooked rice. Sprinkle with the cilantro or parsley. Serve with the sour cream, green onions, and lime wedges.

Makes 8 side-dish servings or 4 main-dish servings.

VARIATION
For a heartier dish, add ½ cup cubed cooked ham.

Sicilian Fava Beans in Plum Tomato–Fennel Sauce

Originally cultivated by the ancient Egyptians, fava beans have been used for centuries in many Mediterranean cuisines. These large, oval beans are also called broad or horse beans. Their unique flavor blends nicely with the tomatoey fennel sauce in this enticing take-off on baked beans.

1½ cups dried fava (broad) beans
6 cups water
1 medium-size fennel bulb with tops
2 tablespoons olive oil
1 large onion, chopped
2 teaspoons minced garlic
2 pounds plum tomatoes, chopped
   (about 3½ cups), or 2 (14½-ounce)
   cans diced tomatoes, with juice

½ cup dry red wine
1 (6-ounce) can tomato paste
1 teaspoon sugar
¼ teaspoon ground black pepper
⅛ teaspoon salt

Sort and rinse the beans. In a large saucepan, cover the beans generously with cold water and bring to a boil. Reduce heat, and simmer 20 to 30 minutes or until the outer skins are soft. Remove from heat; let stand 1 hour. Drain. Using your fingers, slip off the outer skins by pressing each bean between your thumb and forefinger; discard the skins. Rinse the beans.

In the large saucepan, combine the skinned beans and the 6 cups water and bring to a boil. Reduce heat, cover, and simmer 40 minutes or until the beans are tender. Drain.

Meanwhile, remove any tough or bruised outer leaves from the fennel bulb. Trim off the root end; discard. Pull off the feathery tops from the stems. Finely chop the tops; reserve 2 tablespoons of the tops. Trim off the stems; discard. Thoroughly rinse the trimmed bulb and quarter the bulb lengthwise; remove the core. Cut the bulb crosswise into ¼-inch-thick slices.

In another large saucepan, heat the olive oil over medium heat. Add the onion and garlic and cook, stirring frequently, 5 minutes or until the onion is tender.

Stir in the fennel slices, the tomatoes with their juice, red wine, tomato paste, sugar, pepper, and salt and bring to a boil. Reduce heat and simmer, stirring occasionally, 20 minutes. Stir in the cooked beans. Cook, stirring occasionally, until the mixture is heated through.

To serve, transfer the bean mixture to a serving bowl. Sprinkle with the reserved 2 tablespoons fennel tops.

Makes 8 to 10 side-dish servings.

✦ TIP

Because the outer skins of fava beans are very tough, simmer them until the skins are soft. Then, let the beans cool and slip off the skins.

Herbed White Bean Puree

This Italian-style puree is reminiscent of refried beans. Serve it with grilled or broiled beef, pork, chicken, or fish. Or, use it as a dip for chips or vegetables.

2 (15-ounce) cans cannellini (white kidney) beans or great Northern beans, rinsed and drained
3 tablespoons chicken broth
3 cloves garlic, halved
1 tablespoon minced fresh basil or 1 teaspoon dried basil leaves
1 tablespoon olive oil
$\frac{1}{4}$ teaspoon ground black pepper
1 tablespoon minced fresh cilantro or thinly sliced green onion

In a food processor or blender, combine the beans, chicken broth, garlic, basil, olive oil, and pepper. Cover and process until smooth.

Transfer the bean mixture to a medium-size saucepan. Cook over medium heat, stirring frequently, until the mixture is heated through.

To serve, transfer the bean puree to a serving bowl. Sprinkle with the cilantro or green onion. **Makes 3 to 4 side-dish servings.**

● TIP

Cannellini beans are Italian white kidney beans. If you can't find them at your supermarket, look for them at an Italian specialty store. Or, substitute great Northern beans.

BOLD BREADS

*H*ow did we make breads truly astonishing? We threw out all the rules for seasoning breads and began improvising. The result is this sassy sampling of tantalizing homemade breads. We think they're some of the most varied and innovative bread taste sensations ever.

When the occasion calls for a savory old-fashioned bread, try Country Fennel-Rye Bread. We spiked the dough with fennel and molasses for a hearty, down-home flavor. For sophisticated sandwiches use Cracked Pepper–Cornmeal Brioche Loaf. Indulge yourself with Chèvre Cheese and Dried-Tomato Angel Biscuits—tangy, yeast biscuits that are dressed up with a splash of sun-dried tomatoes. Enjoy two of life's simple pleasures—Buttery Pineapple and Coconut Scones served warm from the oven and a cup of hot tea. Snack on Butter Almond Coffee Cake or Gingered Fig and Oatmeal Muffins for a luxurious midmorning break. Or, stack a plate high with Cracked-Wheat Yeast Waffles and dollop on creamy Apricot-Walnut Butter for a delightful breakfast or light supper.

Whichever recipes you choose, you'll discover these distinctive breads, warm and fragrant from the oven, will introduce you to new flavors and textures and will give you a whole new perspective on bread baking.

Walnut and Grape Focaccia

When friends come over for dinner, this honey-flavored version of the classic Italian peasant flat bread is an excellent accompaniment to a special meal. The combination of grapes, rosemary, toasted walnuts, and full-flavored cheese sprinkled on top is irresistible. Add grilled or roasted poultry and a romaine-radicchio salad and you've got a fabulous menu. This focaccia also makes a great cocktail party finger food.

1 cup warm water (105 to 115°F; 40 to 45°C)
1 tablespoon honey
1 (¼-ounce) package active dry yeast
3 to 3¼ cups all-purpose flour
3 tablespoons walnut oil or olive oil
1 teaspoon salt
1 tablespoon butter
2 cups seedless red grapes, halved
1 tablespoon minced fresh rosemary or 1 teaspoon dried rosemary leaves

½ teaspoon coarsely ground black pepper
½ cup toasted chopped walnuts
½ cup (2 ounces) shredded Gruyère cheese or Swiss cheese
½ cup (2 ounces) crumbled Gorgonzola cheese or other blue cheese
½ cup (2 ounces) crumbled semisoft chèvre cheese (goat cheese)

In a small bowl, combine the water, honey, and yeast; stir to dissolve the yeast. Let stand at room temperature 15 minutes.

In a large bowl, combine the yeast mixture, 1 cup of the flour, the oil, and salt. Beat with an electric mixer at low speed 30 seconds, scraping the bowl constantly. Beat at high speed 3 minutes. Using a wooden spoon, stir in as much of the remaining flour as possible.

Turn out onto a lightly floured surface. Knead 5 to 6 minutes or until the dough is smooth and elastic, adding only enough remaining flour to prevent sticking. Clean and butter the bowl. Place the dough in bowl, turning dough to coat all surfaces. Cover with a slightly damp towel. Let rise in a warm place, free from drafts, 1 hour or until doubled in bulk.

Punch down the dough. Turn out onto lightly floured surface. Divide the dough into thirds. Cover; let stand 10 minutes. Lightly grease 3 baking sheets or pizza pans. Roll out each portion of dough into a 10-inch round. Place on the prepared baking sheets; cover the dough.

In a medium-size skillet, melt the butter over medium heat. Add the grapes, rosemary, and pepper and cook 8 to 10 minutes or until the grapes are soft, stirring occasionally. Drain well.

Using your fingertips, press slight indentations into the dough rounds. Top evenly with the cooked grape mixture and the walnuts. Cover with buttered waxed paper. Let rise in a warm place, free from drafts, 30 to 40 minutes or until nearly doubled in bulk.

Preheat the oven to 375°F (190°C). Bake 12 to 15 minutes or until golden brown. Sprinkle 1 round with Gruyère or Swiss cheese, the second with blue cheese, and the third with chèvre cheese. Bake 4 to 6 minutes longer or until the cheese is golden brown. Remove from the baking sheets. Serve warm or at room temperature.

Makes 3 focaccia, about 12 servings.

✦ TIP

To simplify serving these flavorful wedges, make the bread ahead and top it with the cooked grape mixture and walnuts. Then, refrigerate it for a few hours and bake the rounds at the last minute.

Butter-Pecan Cinnamon Rolls with Three Chocolates

Sandra's husband, George, has made it his life-long mission to taste and critique cinnamon rolls. If he's at a family gathering, bakery, restaurant, truck stop, bake sale, or farmers' market and there is a batch of freshly baked cinnamon rolls, he will find them. Besides being a cinnamon-roll aficionado, he's also a chocoholic, so Sandra created this decadent butter-pecan cinnamon roll, using cocoa powder, semisweet chocolate, and milk chocolate. The results are so sensational, he thinks that she has a shot at culinary immortality.

6¾ to 7¼ cups all-purpose flour
1½ cups warm low-fat (1%) milk
    (105 to 115°F; 40 to 45°C)
½ cup plus 1 tablespoon sugar
2 (¼-ounce) packages active
    dry yeast
3 eggs
⅓ cup unsweetened cocoa powder
1 tablespoon freshly grated
    orange peel
1 teaspoon salt
½ cup (1 stick) butter, at room
    temperature and cut into small
    pieces
Sugar-Cinnamon Filling (see opposite)
½ cup miniature semisweet
    chocolate pieces

½ cup chopped pecans
Chocolate Icing (see below)

SUGAR-CINNAMON FILLING
½ cup sugar
¼ cup (½ stick) butter, melted
1 tablespoon ground cinnamon
2 teaspoons all-purpose flour

CHOCOLATE ICING
¾ cup milk chocolate pieces
3 tablespoons butter
1½ cups sifted powdered sugar
3 tablespoons hot water

In a large bowl, combine 3 cups of the flour, the milk, 1 tablespoon of the sugar, and the yeast. Beat with an electric mixer at medium speed 2 minutes or until smooth. (The mixture will be thick and sticky.) Cover with plastic wrap. Let stand at room temperature 30 minutes or until bubbly.

Add the eggs, cocoa powder, orange peel, salt, another 1 cup of the flour, and the remaining ½ cup sugar to the flour mixture. Beat with an electric mixer at medium speed 2 minutes or until smooth. Add the butter, a few pieces at a time, and beat until well combined. Using a wooden spoon, stir in as much of the remaining flour as needed to make a soft dough.

Turn out onto a lightly floured surface. Knead 5 to 6 minutes or until the dough is smooth and elastic, adding only enough of the remaining flour to prevent sticking. Clean and butter the bowl. Place the dough in bowl, turning dough to coat all surfaces. Cover with a slightly damp towel. Let rise in a warm place, free from drafts, 1 hour or until doubled in bulk.

While the dough is rising, prepare the Sugar-Cinnamon Filling; set aside. Lightly grease a 13 x 9-inch baking pan; set aside.

Punch down the dough. Turn out onto lightly floured surface. Cover the dough; let stand 10 minutes. Roll out the dough into a 16 x 12-inch rectangle. Spread the filling over the dough. Sprinkle with the miniature chocolate pieces and pecans. Beginning on a long side, roll tightly in jelly-roll fashion. Pinch the seam to seal. Cut the roll into 12 slices. Arrange, cut side down, in the prepared pan. Cover with a dry towel. Let rise in a warm place, free from drafts, 30 minutes or until nearly doubled in bulk.

Preheat the oven to 375°F (190°C). Bake 20 to 25 minutes or until browned. While the rolls are baking, prepare the Chocolate Icing. Invert the rolls onto a wire rack. Cool slightly. Spread the rolls with the icing.

Makes 12 rolls.

Sugar-Cinnamon Filling

In a small bowl, stir together the sugar, melted butter, cinnamon, and flour.

Chocolate Icing

In a small saucepan, melt the milk chocolate pieces and butter over low heat, stirring frequently. Remove from heat. Stir in the powdered sugar and hot water. If needed, stir in additional hot water to make a smooth and creamy icing of spreading consistency.

＊ TIP

To easily "cut" the dough into slices, place a piece of heavy thread under the roll where you want to make the cut. Pull the ends up and around the sides and crisscross the thread at the top. Then, pull quickly to make the cut (as if you were tying a knot). Or, use a serrated knife to slice the dough, dipping the knife into flour when it starts sticking to the dough.

Country Fennel-Rye Bread

"My memories of my childhood in St. Paul, Minnesota, are a happy blur of winter sports, summer days at our lake cabin, and the wonderful food from my mom's kitchen," explains Liz. "The recipe that I remember most is her hearty rye bread. The first year I was married I made my mom's rye bread with a few of my own personal touches as a Mother's Day gift for my mother-in-law. Her response was so enthusiastic, she wanted the recipe. Now it's a family Mother's Day tradition."

3½ to 4 cups all-purpose flour
¼ cup unsweetened cocoa powder
3 (¼-ounce) packages active
   dry yeast
1 tablespoon instant espresso coffee
   powder or instant coffee crystals
2 teaspoons sugar
2 teaspoons caraway seeds
1 teaspoon salt
1 teaspoon fennel seeds, crushed

1½ cups warm water (115 to 120°F;
   45 to 50°C)
⅓ cup molasses
3 tablespoons vegetable oil
2 tablespoons balsamic vinegar
2 cups rye flour
Yellow cornmeal
1 egg white mixed with 1 tablespoon
   water, for glaze

In a large bowl, combine 2½ cups of the all-purpose flour, the cocoa powder, yeast, coffee powder or crystals, sugar, caraway seeds, salt, and fennel seeds. Add the 1½ cups warm water, the molasses, oil, and balsamic vinegar. Beat with an electric mixer at low speed 30 seconds, scraping the bowl constantly. Beat at high speed 3 minutes. Using a wooden spoon, stir in the rye flour and as much of the remaining all-purpose flour as needed to make a moderately stiff dough.

Turn out onto a lightly floured surface. Knead 5 to 6 minutes or until the dough is smooth and elastic, adding only enough of the remaining all-purpose flour to prevent sticking. Clean and butter the bowl. Place the dough in bowl, turning dough to coat all surfaces. Cover with a slightly damp towel. Let rise in a warm place, free from drafts, 1 hour or until doubled in bulk.

Punch down the dough. Turn out onto lightly floured surface. Divide the dough in half. Cover; let stand 10 minutes.

Lightly grease a large baking sheet; sprinkle with cornmeal. Shape each half of dough into a ball. Place on the prepared baking sheet. Flatten each ball to 6 inches in diameter. Cover with a dry towel. Let rise in a warm place, free from drafts, 45 to 60 minutes or until nearly doubled in bulk.

Preheat the oven to 375°F (190°C). Brush the loaves with egg-white glaze. Bake 40 minutes or until the bread sounds hollow when tapped on the bottom. If needed, cover loosely with foil the last 15 minutes to keep bread from becoming too brown. Remove from the baking sheet. Cool on wire racks.

Makes 2 loaves.

✦ TIP

Your oven can be a good draft-free place for letting dough rise. Place the bowl of dough in the unheated oven, then set a large pan of hot water under the bowl on the oven's lowest rack.

Light Rye Rolls with Caramelized Onions

These earthy rye rolls—infused with the sweet flavors of fresh basil and caramelized onions—are one of our favorites and may easily become yours. They're especially good with homemade beef-and-vegetable soup or a chicken-and-spinach main-dish salad. To get the spiral of caramelized onion, you use the same shaping technique as for cinnamon rolls.

3 to 3½ cups all-purpose flour
1 (¼-ounce) package active dry yeast
1 cup low-fat (1%) milk
¼ cup packed light brown sugar
¼ cup (½ stick) unsalted butter
½ teaspoon salt
2 eggs
1 cup rye flour
2 tablespoons olive oil or
   vegetable oil

2 large onions, chopped (2 cups)
1 tablespoon minced fresh basil or
   1 teaspoon dried basil leaves
½ cup finely shredded Parmesan
   cheese or ⅓ cup grated Parmesan
   cheese
1 egg white mixed with 1 tablespoon
   water, for glaze

In a large bowl, combine 2 cups of the all-purpose flour and the yeast. In a medium-size saucepan, heat the milk, brown sugar, butter, and salt, stirring constantly, until warm (120 to 130°F; 50 to 55°C) and the butter is almost melted. Add to the flour mixture; add the eggs. Beat with an electric mixer at low speed 30 seconds, scraping the bowl constantly. Beat at high speed 3 minutes. Using a wooden spoon, stir in the rye flour and as much of the remaining all-purpose flour as needed to make a soft dough.

Turn out onto a lightly floured surface. Knead 5 to 6 minutes or until the dough is smooth and elastic, adding only enough of the remaining all-purpose flour to prevent sticking. Clean and butter the bowl. Place the dough in bowl, turning dough to coat all surfaces. Cover with a slightly damp towel. Let rise in a warm place, free from drafts, 1 hour or until doubled in bulk.

While the dough is rising, heat the oil in a large skillet over medium heat. Add the onions, reduce heat to medium-low and cook, stirring frequently, 20 minutes or until the onions are very soft and golden. Stir in the basil; set aside. Lightly grease a 13 x 9-inch baking pan; set aside.

Punch down the dough. Turn out onto lightly floured surface. Cover the dough; let stand 10 minutes. Roll out the dough into a 16 x 12-inch rectangle. Spread the onion mixture over the dough. Sprinkle with the Parmesan cheese. Beginning on a long side, roll tightly in jelly-roll fashion. Pinch the seam to seal. Cut the roll into 12 slices. Arrange, cut side down, in the prepared pan. Cover with a dry towel. Let rise in a warm place, free from drafts, 30 to 40 minutes or until nearly doubled in bulk.

Preheat the oven to 375°F (190°C). Brush the rolls with egg-white glaze. Bake 20 to 23 minutes or until golden brown. If needed, cover loosely with foil the last 15 minutes to keep from becoming too brown. Cool slightly; remove from the pan. Serve warm.

Makes 12 rolls.

✦ TIP

Brushing the rolls with a mixture of egg white and a little water gives them a glossy, crispy crust.

Cracked Pepper–Cornmeal Brioche Loaf

A sandwich just isn't complete without slices of Cracked–Pepper Cornmeal Brioche Loaf. You can use regular cornmeal for this egg- and butter-rich brioche, if you like, but we prefer the slightly coarser texture of stone-ground meal. Baked in a loaf pan for easy slicing, the brioche's texture is a cross between cake and bread, with an even crumb.

2 (¼-ounce) packages active
  dry yeast
¼ cup warm water (105 to 115°F;
  40 to 45°C)
¾ cup (1½ sticks) unsalted butter,
  at room temperature
2 tablespoons sugar
2 teaspoons cracked black pepper

¾ teaspoon salt
2¼ cups all-purpose flour
¾ cup yellow cornmeal
½ cup chopped sun-dried tomatoes
  (oil packed)
3 eggs, room temperature
Melted butter

In a small bowl, dissolve the yeast in the warm water; set aside 5 minutes. In a large bowl, beat the ¾ cup butter with an electric mixer at medium speed 30 seconds. Add the sugar, pepper, and salt; beat well.

Stir in 1 cup of the flour, the cornmeal, tomatoes, and eggs. Add the softened yeast. Beat until well combined, scraping the bowl constantly. Using a wooden spoon, stir in the remaining 1¼ cups flour until the dough is smooth. Butter a large bowl. Turn the dough into the bowl. Brush the top with a little melted butter. Cover with plastic wrap and refrigerate 12 to 48 hours.

Punch down the dough. Turn out onto a lightly floured surface. Cover the dough; let stand 20 minutes. Lightly grease a 9 x 5-inch loaf pan; set aside.

Gently shape the dough into a loaf, tucking the edges under. Place in prepared pan. Cover and let rise in a cool place, free from drafts, 45 to 60 minutes or until nearly doubled in bulk.

Preheat the oven to 375°F (190°C). Bake 40 minutes or until the crust is golden brown and firm on top. If needed, cover loosely with foil the last 15 minutes to keep bread from becoming too brown. Remove from the pan. Cool on a wire rack.

Makes 1 loaf.

☙ TIP

This rich dough needs to rise in a cool place rather than the traditional warm place so the butter doesn't separate from the dough.

Herbed Ricotta Batter Rolls with Pine Nuts

Nothing whets the appetite like the aroma of baking bread. And this rich, robust roll, embellished with ricotta cheese and fresh herbs, is especially fragrant. For a novel flavor accent, we used wheat germ and toasted pine nuts. These savory rolls are delicious served with marinara-sauced pasta.

2 cups all-purpose flour
1 tablespoon minced fresh oregano
   or ¾ teaspoon dried oregano
   leaves
1 tablespoon minced fresh marjoram
   or ¾ teaspoon dried marjoram
   leaves
1 (¼-ounce) package active dry yeast
½ teaspoon salt

1 cup ricotta cheese
½ cup water
¼ cup packed light brown sugar
1 tablespoon butter
1 egg
½ cup toasted wheat germ
⅓ cup toasted pine nuts (see Tip,
   page 47)

Generously grease 12 (2½-inch) muffin cups; set aside. In a large bowl, combine 1 cup of the flour, the oregano, marjoram, yeast, and salt. In a small saucepan, heat the ricotta cheese, water, brown sugar, and butter, stirring constantly, until warm (120 to 130°F; 50 to 55°C) and the butter is almost melted. Add to the flour mixture; add the egg. Beat with an electric mixer at low speed 30 seconds, scraping the bowl constantly. Beat at high speed 3 minutes. Beat or stir in the wheat germ, pine nuts, and the remaining 1 cup flour. (The batter will be stiff.)

Spoon the batter into the prepared muffin cups. Cover with a dry towel. Let rise in a warm place, free from drafts, 30 to 40 minutes or until nearly doubled in bulk.

Preheat the oven to 400°F (205°C). Bake 16 to 18 minutes or until golden brown. Remove from the muffin cups. Serve warm.

Makes 12 rolls.

+ TIP
Be careful when working with yeast; if it gets too hot or too cold, the dough won't rise. Use a thermometer to make sure you heat the liquid mixture to just the right temperature. And, let the dough rise in a warm, not hot, place.

Cracked-Wheat Yeast Waffles with Apricot-Walnut Butter

These are the crème de la crème of waffles. The wholesome flavors of whole wheat and brown sugar make this recipe the best around. Crisp on the outside and tender on the inside, these fine-textured waffles have a flavorful tang because they're made by the sponge method. This technique slightly ferments the batter, giving the waffles a sourdoughlike flavor—a most remarkable dimension. And, slathering on homemade apricot-walnut butter only makes the waffles taste even better.

Apricot-Walnut Butter (see opposite)
  or pure maple syrup
1½ cups warm low-fat (1%) milk
  (105 to 115°F; 40 to 45°C)
1 cup all-purpose flour
1 cup whole-wheat flour
½ cup warm water (105 to 115°F;
  40 to 45°C)
2 tablespoons light brown sugar
1 (¼-ounce) package active dry yeast
1 cup boiling water
¼ cup cracked wheat (bulgur)
2 eggs

½ teaspoon ground cinnamon
¼ teaspoon salt
½ cup (1 stick) unsalted butter, at
  room temperature and cut into
  small pieces

APRICOT-WALNUT BUTTER
1 cup walnuts
½ cup (1 stick) butter, at room
  temperature and cut into small
  pieces
½ cup apricot preserves, peach
  preserves, or orange marmalade

Prepare the Apricot-Walnut Butter (if using); refrigerate. In a large bowl, combine the milk, all-purpose flour, whole-wheat flour, the warm water, brown sugar, and yeast. Beat with an electric mixer at medium speed 2 minutes or until smooth. Cover with plastic wrap. Let stand at room temperature 30 minutes or until bubbly.

Meanwhile, in a small bowl, pour the 1 cup boiling water over the cracked wheat. Let stand at room temperature 30 minutes.

Add the cracked wheat, eggs, cinnamon, and salt to the flour mixture. Beat with an electric mixer at medium speed 2 minutes or until combined. Add the butter, a few pieces at a time, and beat until well combined. (The batter will be very thin.)

Follow the manufacturer's directions for preheating and greasing your waffle iron. Pour about ¾ cup of the batter onto the grids of the waffle iron. Close the lid quickly; do not open during baking. Bake according to the manufacturer's directions. When golden and crisp, use a fork to lift the waffle off the grid. Repeat with the remaining batter. (The batter will keep in the refrigerator for up to 3 days.) Serve warm with the apricot butter or maple syrup.

Makes 4 servings.

APRICOT-WALNUT BUTTER

In a food processor or blender, place the walnuts, butter, and the apricot preserves, peach preserves, or orange marmalade. Cover and process until well combined, stopping to scrape down the sides as necessary. Transfer to a small bowl. Cover and refrigerate at least 1 hour before serving.

Makes about 1½ cups.

◆ TIP

To store baked waffles, cool them on a wire rack. Wrap each waffle in plastic wrap, then place the wrapped waffles in freezer bags and freeze until firm and the waffles keep up to 1 month. To serve, reheat the frozen waffles in a toaster.

Butter-Almond Coffee Cake

*R*eminiscent of German and Austrian *kuchens, this eye-catching bread is great with coffee or tea for a midmorning or afternoon pick-me-up. When making it for company, sprinkle a few rose petals over the wedges of coffee cake. The petals make a lovely, fragrant garnish.*

Almond Filling (see opposite)
2¾ cups all-purpose flour
¾ cup sugar
¾ cup (1½ sticks) unsalted butter
½ cup sliced almonds
¾ teaspoon ground nutmeg
½ teaspoon baking powder
½ teaspoon baking soda
¼ teaspoon salt
1 egg, lightly beaten
¾ cup buttermilk

ALMOND FILLING
½ cup (1 stick) unsalted butter, at
    room temperature
½ cup sugar
2 tablespoons amaretto or fresh
    orange juice
1½ cups finely chopped almonds

Preheat the oven to 350°F (175°C). Grease and flour an 11-inch tart pan with a removable bottom or a 10-inch quiche dish; set aside. Prepare the Almond Filling; set aside.

In a large bowl, stir together the flour and sugar. Using a pastry cutter or 2 knives, cut in the butter until the mixture resembles coarse crumbs. For the crumb topping, measure ½ cup of the flour mixture; place in a small bowl. Stir in the sliced almonds; set aside.

Stir the nutmeg, baking powder, baking soda, and salt into the remaining flour mixture. In a small bowl, combine the egg and buttermilk. Add to the flour mixture, stirring only until the dry ingredients are moistened.

Using a narrow metal spatula, spread two-thirds of the batter over the bottom and about 1 inch up the side of the prepared pan. Spread the filling over the batter. Spoon the remaining batter in small mounds on top. Sprinkle with the crumb topping.

Bake 30 minutes or until a wooden pick inserted in the center comes out clean. Let stand in the pan on a wire rack 15 minutes. Remove the side of the tart pan (leave the coffee cake in the quiche dish). Cut into wedges. Serve warm or at room temperature.

Makes 8 servings.

ALMOND FILLING

In a medium-size bowl, beat the ½ cup butter with an electric mixer at medium speed 30 seconds. Add the sugar and the amaretto or orange juice. Beat well. Stir in the finely chopped almonds.

VARIATION

If you don't have any buttermilk, substitute soured milk. To make ¾ cup soured milk, place 2 teaspoons lemon juice in a glass measuring cup. Add enough low-fat (1%) milk to measure ¾ cup. Stir and let stand at room temperature 5 minutes.

Banana-Nut Gingerbread Loaf

A little tinkering can turn humble, homemade banana bread into an incredible taste sensation that's perfect with scrambled eggs and fresh fruit for a weekend brunch. We took our favorite gingerbread recipe, which is wonderfully embellished with fresh gingerroot and crystallized ginger, and mixed in some banana and cinnamon. Then, by adding a spicy, lemony glaze, we came up with a tempting loaf that borders on absolute perfection.

1¾ cups all-purpose flour
½ cup packed light brown sugar
1 tablespoon minced gingerroot or
   1 teaspoon ground ginger
2 teaspoons baking powder
¾ teaspoon ground cinnamon
½ teaspoon baking soda
¼ teaspoon salt
1 cup mashed ripe banana
   (2 to 3 medium-size bananas)
½ cup (1 stick) butter, at room
   temperature and cut into small
   pieces

¼ cup molasses
2 tablespoons low-fat (1%) milk
2 eggs
½ cup toasted chopped walnuts or
   pecans
3 tablespoons finely chopped
   crystallized ginger
Gingered Lemon Glaze (see below)

GINGERED LEMON GLAZE
⅓ cup sifted powdered sugar
⅛ teaspoon ground ginger
1 to 2 teaspoons fresh lemon juice

Preheat the oven to 350°F (175°C). Grease a 9 x 5-inch loaf pan; set aside.

In a large bowl, combine the flour, brown sugar, gingerroot or ground ginger, baking powder, cinnamon, baking soda, and salt. Add the mashed banana, butter, molasses, and milk. Beat with an electric mixer at low speed until combined. Beat at high speed 2 minutes. Add the eggs. Beat until blended. Stir in the walnuts or pecans and crystallized ginger. Pour the batter into the prepared loaf pan. Bake 55 to 60 minutes or until a wooden pick inserted off-center comes out clean.

Let stand in the pan on a wire rack 10 minutes. Remove from the pan; cool completely. Wrap and store overnight before slicing.

Before serving, prepare the Gingered Lemon Glaze. Drizzle the glaze over loaf.
Makes 1 loaf.

GINGERED LEMON GLAZE

In a small bowl, combine the powdered sugar and ground ginger. Stir in enough lemon juice to make a smooth and creamy glaze of drizzling consistency.

✦ TIP

Use soft, overripe bananas with skins that are starting to turn black. At this stage, the bananas are sweet and just right for baking.

Brandied Cherry Loaf

This is the quintessential quick bread. Made with dried cherries and golden raisins, it's moist and has a sweet brandy flavor with a subtle hint of orange—an absolutely exceptional bread. Spread it with cream cheese and serve it with chicken salad for summer luncheons.

2 cups all-purpose flour
2/3 cup packed light brown sugar
1/3 cup rolled oats
2 teaspoons baking powder
1 teaspoon ground cardamom or
   nutmeg
1/2 teaspoon salt
1/4 teaspoon baking soda
2/3 cup dried tart red cherries or
   cranberries

2/3 cup golden raisins
1/2 cup brandy
1/4 cup fresh orange juice
1 tablespoon freshly grated
   orange peel
2 eggs, lightly beaten
1/2 cup low-fat (1%) milk
1/2 cup vegetable oil
Cream cheese

Preheat the oven to 350°F (175°C). Grease an 8 x 4-inch loaf pan; set aside. In a large bowl, stir together the flour, brown sugar, oats, baking powder, cardamom or nutmeg, salt, and baking soda; set aside.

In a medium-size bowl, combine the cherries or cranberries, raisins, brandy, orange juice, and orange peel. Stir in the eggs, milk, and oil. Add to the flour mixture, stirring only until the dry ingredients are moistened.

Pour the batter into the prepared pan. Bake 55 to 60 minutes or until a wooden pick inserted off-center comes out clean.

Let stand in the pan on a wire rack 10 minutes. Remove from the pan; cool completely. Wrap and store overnight before slicing. Serve with cream cheese.

Makes 1 loaf.

+ TIP

Placing the loaf in a plastic bag once it is completely cooled and storing it overnight at room temperature allows the full flavors of the bread to develop.

Swiss–Wild Rice Muffins

"Cooking with wild rice is very special to me because I grew up in Minnesota, where every self-respecting cook has a favorite wild rice recipe," boasts Liz. "But I have another reason for loving wild rice. My dad was an engineering professor at the University of Minnesota, and he spent many years developing better ways to process the long, dark brown seed of the marsh grass (wild rice is not a rice at all!). As you might expect, we always had lots of wild rice at my house. In looking for new ways to use the rice, I developed these muffins."

1¾ cups all-purpose flour
⅓ cup sugar
2 teaspoons baking powder
⅛ teaspoon salt
⅛ teaspoon ground red (cayenne) pepper
1 cup cooked wild rice

1 cup (4 ounces) shredded Swiss cheese or Cheddar cheese
½ cup toasted chopped pecans
1 egg, lightly beaten
⅔ cup low-fat (1%) milk
¼ cup vegetable oil

Preheat the oven to 400°F (205°C). Grease 12 (2½-inch) muffin cups or line with paper liners; set aside.

In a medium-size bowl, combine the flour, sugar, baking powder, salt, and cayenne. Stir in the cooked wild rice, cheese, and pecans.

In a small bowl, combine the egg, milk, and oil. Add to the flour mixture, stirring only until the dry ingredients are moistened. (The batter should still be lumpy.)

Spoon the batter into the prepared muffin cups until about two-thirds full. Bake 20 to 25 minutes or until golden brown. Remove from the muffin cups. Serve warm.

Makes 12 muffins.

+ TIP

To cook wild rice, rinse 1 cup wild rice, lifting the rice with your fingers to clean thoroughly; drain. In a small saucepan, bring 2 cups water to a boil. Stir in the wild rice. Reduce heat, cover, and simmer, without stirring, 40 to 50 minutes or until the rice is tender. If needed, drain off the liquid. To store extra cooked rice, place it in a heavy plastic bag and refrigerate up to 1 week or freeze up to 2 months.

Makes 2¾ cups.

Gingered Fig and Oatmeal Muffins

Once you've tasted these impressive sugar-topped muffins made from an exquisite combination of figs, currants, orange peel, spicy ground ginger, and sweet crystallized ginger, you'll agree they're spectacular.

1 cup all-purpose flour
¾ cup rolled oats
½ cup whole-wheat flour
½ cup sugar
2 teaspoons baking powder
½ teaspoon ground ginger
⅛ teaspoon salt
⅔ cup chopped dried figs
⅓ cup currants or raisins
2 tablespoons chopped crystallized ginger

2 teaspoons freshly grated orange peel
1 egg, lightly beaten
¾ cup low-fat (1%) milk
¼ cup vegetable oil
2 tablespoons finely chopped crystallized ginger mixed with 1 tablespoon sugar, for topping

Preheat the oven to 400°F (205°C). Grease 12 (2½-inch) muffin cups or line with paper liners; set aside.

In a medium-size bowl, combine the all-purpose flour, oats, whole-wheat flour, the ½ cup sugar, the baking powder, ground ginger, and salt. Stir in the figs, currants or raisins, the 2 tablespoons crystallized ginger, and the orange peel.

In a small bowl, combine the egg, milk, and oil. Add to the flour mixture, stirring only until the dry ingredients are moistened. (The batter should still be lumpy.) Spoon the batter into the prepared muffin cups until each is about two-thirds full. Sprinkle the ginger-sugar topping over the muffins. Bake 16 to 18 minutes or until golden brown. Remove from the muffin cups. Serve warm or at room temperature.

Makes 12 muffins.

✦ TIP

The secret to avoiding crusty edges on homemade muffins is to grease the muffin cups on the bottoms and only halfway up the sides. The muffins will be nicely rounded without those unwanted rims.

Buttery Pineapple and Coconut Scones

Although tender and flaky like biscuits, golden, wedge-shaped scones are richer because they include eggs. The addition of candied pineapple, golden raisins, toasted coconut, anise seeds, and a dash of rum makes for very aromatic, sweet scones. Rosemary spreads a rum icing over the tops for an enticing finale.

2 cups all-purpose flour	½ cup pineapple juice
¼ cup packed light brown sugar	1 tablespoon rum
2 teaspoons baking powder	Low-fat (1%) milk
½ teaspoon anise seeds, crushed	Rum Icing (see below)
⅛ teaspoon salt	
⅓ cup unsalted butter	RUM ICING
½ cup chopped candied pineapple	½ cup sifted powdered sugar
⅓ cup golden raisins	1 tablespoon unsalted butter, melted
⅓ cup toasted flaked coconut	3 to 4 teaspoons rum
1 egg, lightly beaten	

Preheat the oven to 400°F (205°C). Grease a baking sheet; set aside. In a large bowl, combine the flour, brown sugar, baking powder, anise seeds, and salt. Using a pastry cutter or 2 knives, cut in the butter until the mixture resembles coarse crumbs. Stir in the candied pineapple, raisins, and coconut.

In a small bowl, combine the egg, pineapple juice, and rum. Add to the flour mixture, stirring only until the dry ingredients are moistened.

Turn out onto a lightly floured surface. Gently knead 6 to 8 strokes or only until the dough holds together. On the prepared baking sheet, pat the dough into a 7-inch circle. Cut into 12 wedges, but do not separate. Brush the wedges with milk.

Bake 14 to 16 minutes or until golden brown. Remove from the baking sheet. Cool on a wire rack 5 minutes.

While the scones are cooling, prepare the Rum Icing. Spread the icing over scones. Break the scones into wedges. Serve warm.

Makes 12 scones.

RUM ICING

In a small bowl, combine the powdered sugar and melted butter. Stir in enough rum to make a smooth and creamy icing of spreading consistency.

✦ TIP

Take care not to overknead the dough. Gently folding and pressing it for 6 to 8 strokes is enough to make the scones flaky.

Chèvre Cheese and Dried-Tomato Angel Biscuits

One bite is all it takes to figure out why this divine recipe is called "angel." As you eat these light-as-a-cloud yeast biscuits, you'll experience the lemony-tart flavor of chèvre cheese, the sweet-tasting accent of sun-dried tomatoes, and the distinctive tang of buttermilk. Serve them hot-from-the-oven with roasted poultry, hearty soups, or crisp salads. The biscuits are at their finest when eaten the same day they're baked.

⅓ cup sun-dried tomatoes (dry packed)	¾ teaspoon dried thyme leaves
1 (¼-ounce) package active dry yeast	½ teaspoon baking soda
2 tablespoons warm water (105 to 115°F; 40 to 45°C)	¼ teaspoon salt
	½ cup vegetable shortening
2½ cups all-purpose flour	½ cup (2 ounces) crumbled semisoft chèvre cheese (goat cheese)
1½ teaspoons baking powder	1 cup buttermilk

Preheat the oven to 450°F (230°C). In a small bowl, pour boiling water over the sun-dried tomatoes. Let stand 10 minutes; drain well. Finely chop the tomatoes; set aside.

In another small bowl, dissolve the yeast in warm water. Let stand 5 minutes. (The mixture will be very thick.)

In a large bowl, combine the flour, baking powder, thyme, baking soda, and salt. Using a pastry cutter or 2 knives, cut in the shortening until the mixture resembles coarse crumbs. Stir in the cheese and tomatoes; set aside. Add the buttermilk to the softened yeast, stirring until well combined. Add to the flour mixture, stirring only until the dry ingredients are moistened.

Turn out onto a lightly floured surface. Gently knead 6 to 8 strokes or only until the dough holds together. Roll out the dough until about ⅜ inch thick. Fold the dough in half. Using a round 2½-inch cutter, cut out the dough (dip the cutter into flour between cuts as needed to prevent sticking).

Place the biscuits on an ungreased baking sheet. Bake 10 to 12 minutes or until golden brown. Serve hot.

Makes 10 biscuits.

VARIATION

If you don't have any buttermilk, substitute soured milk. To make 1 cup soured milk, place 1 tablespoon lemon juice in a glass measuring cup. Add enough low-fat (1%) milk to measure 1 cup. Stir and let stand at room temperature 5 minutes.

✦ TIP

A trick for finely chopping the soaked, sun-dried tomatoes is to snip them with your kitchen scissors. The scissors will perform the job neatly and easily.

DISTINCTIVE DESSERTS

D o you dream about desserts? We do, and we've decided to make some of those dreams come true. We camped out in the kitchen and created the most breath-taking, luscious cakes, pies, ice creams, cobblers, puddings, shortcakes, cheesecakes, soufflés, and cookies we could conjure up. Take a look and see if your dream dessert is one of ours.

If cakes or tortes are what you crave, slice into Praline Upside-Down Cake, Almond Chocolate Torte with Espresso Buttercream, or Champagne Chiffon Cake with Strawberry-Champagne Sauce. When it's time to fill the cookie jar, choose everything from elegant Lemon and Caramel-Walnut Florentines to Italian-inspired Honey-Ginger Biscotti. During the dog days of summer, cool off with Frozen Vanilla Custard with Triple Berry Sauce, or with Strawberry and Orange Sherbet. And, when you're in the mood for something warm and comforting, enjoy White Chocolate Bread Pudding with Mango Sauce, Gingered Orange Soufflé with Kiwi Sauce, or Summer Pear, Plum, and Crystallized Ginger Cobbler. Finally, end that special dinner party with the likes of Poached Pears with Crème Anglaise Fluff, Chocolate Decadence, Dried Cherry–Sour Cream Pie, or Italian Ricotta Cheesecake with Amaretti-Almond Crust.

Have we tempted you enough? If so, don't just read about our desserts. Go ahead and splurge. Treat your family and friends to one of these remarkable sweet 'n' sassy masterpieces.

Pecan Torte with Black Raspberry Filling and Classic Buttercream

In the tradition of Austrian tortes, these tender layers are made with a mixture of ground nuts and crushed zwieback in place of flour. This combination gives the torte an enticing nutty flavor that blends magnificently with the black raspberry filling and lavish buttercream frosting.

6 eggs, separated
2½ cups coarsely chopped pecans
    or hazelnuts (filberts)
¾ cup finely crushed zwieback
1 tablespoon freshly grated
    orange peel

1 teaspoon ground cardamom
1 cup sugar
1 teaspoon cream of tartar
Classic Buttercream (page 218)
⅔ cup seedless black raspberry jam
Pecan halves, for garnish

In a large bowl, let the egg whites stand at room temperature 30 minutes. Lightly grease 3 (8-inch) round cake pans. Line the bottoms and sides with parchment paper or waxed paper; lightly grease the paper. Set the pans aside.

Place half of the coarsely chopped pecans or hazelnuts in a food processor or blender. Cover and process until the pecans are very finely ground but still dry (not oily). Transfer the ground pecans to a medium-size bowl. Repeat with the remaining pecans. Measure the ground pecans. Return 2 cups of the ground pecans to the medium-size bowl; reserve the remaining ground pecans for garnishing the torte. Stir the zwieback into the 2 cups ground pecans; set aside.

Preheat the oven to 350°F (175°C). In another medium-size bowl, beat the egg yolks, orange peel, and cardamom with an electric mixer at medium speed 6 minutes or until the egg yolks are very thick and light colored. Add ½ cup of the sugar, 1 tablespoon at a time, and continue beating until the sugar dissolves; set aside.

Wash the mixer beaters well in hot soapy water; dry thoroughly. Beat the egg whites with the electric mixer at medium to high speed until frothy. Add the cream of tartar and continue beating until soft peaks form. Add the remaining ½ cup sugar, 1 tablespoon at a time, and continue beating until the egg whites are stiff but not dry.

Gently fold about 1 cup of the beaten egg whites into the egg yolk mixture. Then, gently fold all of the egg yolk mixture into the remaining beaten egg whites until the mixture is an even light yellow color. Sprinkle about ⅓ of the zwieback mixture over the batter, then gently fold together. Repeat with the remaining zwieback mixture, ⅓ at a time.

Spread the batter in the prepared pans. Bake 18 to 20 minutes or until a wooden pick inserted off-center comes out clean. Immediately invert the cake layers onto wire racks. Cool the cake layers in the pans 10 minutes. (The cakes may fall slightly.) Remove the pans and peel off the paper. Cool the cake layers completely.

Meanwhile, prepare the Classic Buttercream.

To assemble the torte, place the first cake layer on a serving plate. Using an icing spatula or a wide knife, spread ⅓ cup of the jam over the top of the layer. Top with the second cake layer; spread the remaining ⅓ cup jam over the top. Top with the remaining cake layer.

Frost the side and top of the torte with the buttercream. Press the reserved ground pecans onto the side of the torte. Garnish the top outside edge of the torte with the pecan halves. Cover and refrigerate the torte until ready to serve (the torte is best served the day it's made).

Makes 16 servings.

◆ TIP

The consistency of the nuts for this torte is critical. Grind them very finely in a food processor or blender. They should be the consistency of coarse cornmeal, but should not be oily.

Almond Chocolate Torte with Espresso Buttercream

"This breathtaking dessert is the perfect choice for a special dinner party," recommends Sandra. *"The semisweet chocolate layers, almond filling, and coffee-flavored frosting make a heavenly combination. For a professional-looking finishing touch, I create a ribbed design in the frosting with a cake comb."*

9 eggs, separated
5 ounces semisweet chocolate
2 cups slivered almonds
⅓ cup dry bread crumbs
¾ cup (1½ sticks) plus ⅓ cup butter,
    at room temperature

⅔ cup sugar
4 tablespoons low-fat (1%) milk
1 teaspoon cream of tartar
Espresso Buttercream (page 218)
1 (7-ounce) package almond paste,
    room temperature

In a large bowl, let the egg whites stand at room temperature 30 minutes. Lightly grease 4 (8-inch) round cake pans. Line the bottoms and sides with parchment paper or waxed paper; lightly grease the paper. Set the pans aside.

In a small heavy saucepan, heat the chocolate over very low heat, stirring constantly, until the chocolate starts to melt. Remove from heat and stir until smooth. Set aside to cool.

Place half of the almonds in a food processor or blender. Cover and process until the almonds are very finely ground but still dry (not oily). Transfer the ground almonds to a small bowl. Repeat with the remaining almonds. Stir the bread crumbs into the ground almonds; set aside.

Preheat the oven to 350°F (175°C). In a medium-size bowl, beat the ¾ cup butter with an electric mixer at medium speed 1 minute or until softened. Add the sugar and beat until fluffy. Add the egg yolks, 3 at a time, beating at medium speed until smooth. Beat in the melted and cooled chocolate. Stir in the almond mixture and 2 tablespoons of the milk.

Wash the mixer beaters well in hot soapy water; dry thoroughly. Beat the egg whites with the electric mixer at medium to high speed until frothy. Add the cream of tartar and continue beating until the egg whites are stiff but not dry.

Gently fold about 1 cup of the beaten egg whites into the chocolate mixture. Then, gently fold all of the chocolate mixture into the remaining beaten egg whites until the mixture is an even light brown color.

Spread the batter in the prepared pans. Bake 18 to 20 minutes or until a wooden pick inserted off-center comes out clean. Immediately invert the cake layers onto wire racks. Cool the cake layers in the pans 10 minutes. (The cakes may fall slightly.) Remove the pans and peel off the paper. Cool the cake layers completely.

Meanwhile, prepare the Espresso Buttercream. For the almond filling, combine the almond paste, the ⅓ cup butter, and the remaining 2 tablespoons milk in a small bowl. With the electric mixer at medium speed, beat until smooth.

To assemble the torte, place the first cake layer on a serving plate. Using an icing spatula or a wide knife, spread ⅓ of the almond filling over the top of the layer. Top with the second cake layer; spread another ⅓ of the almond filling over the top. Top with the third cake layer; spread the remaining almond filling over the top. Top with the remaining cake layer.

Frost the side and top of the torte with the buttercream. Using a cake decorating comb, make straight or wavy lines in the buttercream. Cover and refrigerate the torte until ready to serve. (The torte is best served the day it's made.)

Makes 16 servings.

✦ TIP

You'll find a cake decorating comb in a kitchenware shop or gourmet food store.

Champagne Chiffon Cake with Strawberry-Champagne Sauce

Champagne adds a subtle tang to both the tender, light-as-air cake and the sophisticated fruit sauce. This appealing duo is a natural for your most elegant gatherings. For attractive slices, cut the cake with a sawing motion, using a serrated knife.

1¼ cups sifted cake flour
¾ cup sugar
1½ teaspoons baking powder
⅛ teaspoon salt
4 eggs, separated
⅓ cup extra-dry champagne
¼ cup vegetable oil
2 teaspoons pure vanilla extract
¼ teaspoon cream of tartar

STRAWBERRY-CHAMPAGNE SAUCE
½ cup sugar
2 tablespoons cornstarch
1¼ cups extra-dry champagne
1 cup mashed strawberries
½ teaspoon pure vanilla extract
2 cups sliced strawberries

Preheat the oven to 325°F (165°C). In a medium-size bowl, stir together the cake flour, sugar, baking powder, and salt. In a small bowl, combine the egg yolks, champagne, oil, and vanilla. Add to the flour mixture. Beat with an electric mixer at low speed just until combined. Beat at high speed 5 minutes.

Wash the mixer beaters well in hot soapy water; dry thoroughly. In a large bowl, beat the egg whites with the electric mixer at medium to high speed until frothy. Add the cream of tartar and continue beating until the egg whites are stiff but not dry. Slowly pour the egg yolk mixture over the beaten egg whites. Using a wooden spoon, gently fold together until the mixture is an even light yellow color. Gently spoon the mixture into an ungreased 10-inch tube pan.

Bake on the lowest rack of the oven 45 to 50 minutes or until the cake springs back when lightly touched on top and a wooden skewer inserted off-center comes out clean.

Immediately invert the cake (leave in the tube pan). Let stand at room temperature to cool completely. Run a narrow metal spatula around the edge of the pan and around the tube to loosen the cake. Invert and remove the cake from pan.

Meanwhile, prepare the Strawberry-Champagne Sauce.

To serve, slice the cake into wedges. Spoon a little of the sauce onto each dessert plate. Place a wedge of cake on top of the sauce, then spoon the remaining sauce over the cake.

Makes 12 servings.

STRAWBERRY-CHAMPAGNE SAUCE

In a medium-size saucepan, stir together the sugar and cornstarch. Stir in the champagne and the mashed strawberries. Cook over medium heat, stirring constantly, until the mixture thickens. Cook, stirring constantly, 2 minutes. Remove from heat. Stir in the vanilla.

Transfer to a medium-size bowl. Cover and refrigerate at least 2 hours or up to 1 day. Before serving, stir in the sliced strawberries.

Makes about 3¼ cups.

VARIATION

To use all-purpose flour, substitute 1 cup plus 1½ tablespoons all-purpose flour in place of the 1¼ cups cake flour.

Classic Buttercream

Making buttercream frosting with a sugar syrup is a classic French technique. It gives a satiny frosting that spreads on smoothly, pipes beautifully, and tastes incredible.

1 cup sugar
¼ cup water
6 egg yolks
1½ cups (3 sticks) unsalted butter,
    at room temperature

2 tablespoons kirsch or
    orange liqueur
1 teaspoon pure vanilla extract

In a medium-size heavy saucepan, combine the sugar and water. Bring to a boil over medium-high heat, stirring constantly with a wooden spoon to dissolve the sugar. (Avoid splashing the mixture onto the side of the pan.) Reduce heat to medium. If using a candy thermometer, carefully clip it to the side of the pan, making sure the bulb is immersed but not touching the bottom of the pan.

Cook, stirring occasionally, 4 to 6 minutes or until the mixture reaches 240°F (115°C) on candy thermometer (soft-ball stage). Remove from heat; remove the thermometer from saucepan.

In the top of a double boiler, beat the egg yolks with an electric mixer at high speed until the egg yolks are foamy. Continue beating while quickly pouring the hot sugar mixture into the egg yolks in a thin, steady stream.

Place the top of the double boiler over boiling water. Cook while beating at high speed 5 minutes. Transfer the mixture to a large bowl. Beat 5 minutes or until the mixture is cool.

Add the butter, 2 tablespoons at a time, while beating at medium speed 2 to 3 minutes or until the mixture becomes fluffy, scraping the side of the bowl frequently. Add the kirsch or orange liqueur and vanilla and beat until well combined. Cover and refrigerate 30 minutes or until the buttercream is stiff enough to spread.

Makes about 2½ cups.

VARIATION

Espresso Buttercream
Add 4 teaspoons instant espresso coffee powder to the sugar and water. Substitute 2 tablespoons amaretto for the 2 tablespoons kirsch or orange liqueur.

✦ TIP
If you don't have a candy thermometer, use the cold-water test to check for the soft-ball stage. Using a spoon, drop a small amount of the hot mixture into very cold (but not icy) water. Working in the water, use your fingers to form the mixture into a ball. Then, remove the ball from the water. If the ball immediately flattens and runs between your fingers, the mixture has reached the proper stage.

Dark Cocoa Buttermilk Cake with Cocoa Mascarpone Frosting

If you're a chocoholic, try a slice of this dynamite cake. The buttermilk gives it a pleasing tang, the cocoa a deep chocolate flavor, and the frosting a sweet, buttery richness. If you like, use chocolate leaves, shaved chocolate, or chocolate curls to dress up the top of the cake.

¾ cup unsweetened cocoa powder
⅔ cup boiling water
¾ cup buttermilk (see Tip, page 203)
2 teaspoons pure vanilla extract
2⅓ cups all-purpose flour
1½ teaspoons baking soda
⅛ teaspoon salt

¾ cup (1½ sticks) butter, at room temperature
¾ cup granulated sugar
¾ cup packed light brown sugar
2 eggs
Cocoa Mascarpone Frosting (page 220)

Preheat the oven to 350°F (175°C). Lightly grease 2 (9-inch) round cake pans. Line the bottoms and sides with parchment paper or waxed paper; lightly grease the paper. Lightly dust with flour; shake out the excess flour. Set the pans aside.

In a medium-size bowl, combine the cocoa powder and boiling water; stir until smooth. Cool slightly. Stir in the buttermilk and vanilla; set aside. In another medium-size bowl, stir together the 2⅓ cups flour, baking soda, and salt.

In a large bowl, beat the butter with an electric mixer at medium speed 1 minute or until softened. Add the granulated sugar and brown sugar and beat until light and fluffy, scraping the side of the bowl frequently. Add the eggs, one at a time, beating 1 minute after each addition. Using a wooden spoon, alternately stir in the flour mixture and buttermilk mixture, stirring after each addition until combined.

Spread the batter in the prepared pans. Bake 25 to 30 minutes or until a wooden pick inserted off-center comes out clean. Cool the cake layers in the pans on wire racks 10 minutes. Run a narrow metal spatula around the edges of the pans to loosen the cake layers. Invert the cake layers onto wire racks; remove the pans and peel off paper. Cool the cake layers completely.

Meanwhile, prepare the Cocoa Mascarpone Frosting.

To assemble the cake, place the first cake layer, upside down, on a serving plate. Using an icing spatula or a wide knife, frost the top of the layer with some of the frosting. Top with the second cake layer, right side up. Frost the side and top of the cake with the remaining frosting. Cover and refrigerate until ready to serve.

Makes 12 servings.

Cocoa Mascarpone Frosting

Creamy mascarpone cheese adds both richness and body to this marvelous frosting.

½ (8-ounce) tub mascarpone cheese
½ cup (1 stick) butter, at room
　　temperature
⅓ cup unsweetened cocoa powder

2 teaspoons pure vanilla extract
1 (16-ounce) box powdered sugar,
　　sifted (4¼ to 4½ cups)

In a large bowl, beat the mascarpone cheese, butter, cocoa powder, and vanilla with an electric mixer at medium speed until light and fluffy.

Slowly add 2 cups of the powdered sugar, beating until well combined. Slowly beat in enough of the remaining powdered sugar to make a smooth and creamy frosting of spreading consistency.

Makes about 2¼ cups frosting or enough to frost an 8- or 9-inch (2-layer) cake.

◆ TIP

If your cocoa powder is lumpy, sift it before beating it into the mascarpone cheese and butter.

Praline Upside-Down Cake

Combine a golden cake with a gooey caramel topper loaded with pecans, and what do you get? A great-tasting, gussied-up adaptation of pineapple upside-down cake.

7 tablespoons butter, at room temperature
⅓ cup plus ¼ cup packed light brown sugar
½ cup plus 2 tablespoons granulated sugar
½ cup plus 1 tablespoon half-and-half or whole milk
1 cup pecan halves
1¼ cups all-purpose flour
⅓ cup toasted ground pecans

1 teaspoon baking powder
¼ teaspoon baking soda
¼ teaspoon salt
¼ cup orange liqueur
1 egg
1 teaspoon pure vanilla extract

ORANGE WHIPPED CREAM
½ cup whipping cream
1 tablespoon orange liqueur
3 tablespoons sugar

Preheat the oven to 350°F (175°C). Place 3 tablespoons of the butter in a 9-inch round cake pan; place the pan in the oven until the butter is melted. Remove pan from oven. Stir in the ⅓ cup brown sugar, the 2 tablespoons granulated sugar, and the 1 tablespoon half-and-half or milk. Arrange the pecan halves evenly in the bottom of the pan; set aside.

In a large bowl, stir together the flour, the ¼ cup brown sugar, the ½ cup granulated sugar, the ⅓ cup ground pecans, the baking powder, baking soda, and salt. Add the ½ cup half-and-half or milk, the remaining 4 tablespoons butter, the orange liqueur, the egg, and vanilla.

Beat with an electric mixer at low speed until the dry ingredients are moistened. Beat at medium speed 1 minute. Carefully spoon the batter over the pecans in the prepared pan. Bake 30 to 35 minutes or until a wooden pick inserted off-center in the cake layer comes out clean. Cool in the pan on a wire rack 10 minutes.

Meanwhile, wash the mixer beaters well in hot soapy water; dry thoroughly. Prepare the Orange Whipped Cream.

Run a narrow metal spatula around the edge of the pan to loosen the cake. Invert the cake onto a serving plate; remove the pan. Serve the cake warm with the whipped cream.

Makes 8 servings.

ORANGE WHIPPED CREAM

In a chilled small bowl, combine the whipping cream and orange liqueur. Beat with the electric mixer at medium speed until the mixture starts to thicken. Gradually beat in the sugar. Continue beating until soft peaks form.

Makes about 1 cup.

Fresh Blueberry Cheesecake with
Spiced Streusel Topping

The fresh blueberries, buttery mascarpone cheese, and crunchy streusel topping make this cheese-cake unique. We think you'll enjoy every melt-in-your-mouth bite.

1 cup plus 2 tablespoons
   all-purpose flour
1¼ cups sugar
1 tablespoon freshly grated
   orange peel
⅓ cup butter
1 egg yolk, lightly beaten
3 (8-ounce) packages cream cheese,
   at room temperature
½ (8-ounce) tub mascarpone cheese
¼ cup low-fat (1%) milk
1 teaspoon ground cinnamon
1 teaspoon pure vanilla extract

3 eggs
2 cups blueberries
Spiced Streusel Topping (see below)

SPICED STREUSEL TOPPING
¼ cup all-purpose flour
¼ cup packed light brown sugar
¼ teaspoon ground cinnamon
⅛ teaspoon ground ginger
2 tablespoons butter
½ cup coarsely chopped walnuts or
   pecans

Preheat the oven to 375°F (190°C). For the crust, stir together the 1 cup flour, the ¼ cup sugar, and the orange peel in a medium-size bowl. Using a pastry cutter or 2 knives, cut in the butter until the mixture resembles coarse crumbs. Add the egg yolk. Using a fork, stir until the dry ingredients are moistened. (If needed, use your hands to help mix the dough.) Press a generous ⅓ of the dough onto the bottom of a 9-inch springform pan (with side removed). Cover the remaining dough; set aside.

Bake the crust 8 to 10 minutes or until golden brown. Cool on a wire rack. Butter the side of the springform pan; attach to the bottom. Press the remaining dough about 2 inches up the side of the springform pan; set aside.

For the filling, beat the cream cheese, the 1 cup sugar, the mascarpone cheese, milk, the remaining 2 tablespoons flour, cinnamon, and vanilla in a large bowl with an electric mixer at medium speed until well combined. Add the eggs and beat at low speed just until combined.

Pour half of the filling into the crust-lined pan. Sprinkle half of the blueberries on top of the filling in pan. Top with the remaining filling and the remaining blueberries. Place the springform pan in a large shallow baking pan. (The baking pan will catch any spills that may occur.) Bake 60 to 70 minutes or until 2 to 3 inches of the outside edge of the filling appear set when gently shaken.

Cool on a wire rack 15 minutes. Run a narrow metal spatula around the edge of the pan to loosen the crust. Cool 30 minutes. Carefully remove the side of the springform pan. Cool completely.

Meanwhile, prepare the Spiced Streusel Topping. Sprinkle the topping over the cheese-cake. Cover and refrigerate at least 6 hours or overnight.

To serve, set the cheesecake on a serving plate (do not remove the cheesecake from the bottom of the springform pan). Cut into wedges. To store any remaining cheesecake, cover and refrigerate up to 2 days.

Makes 12 servings.

SPICED STREUSEL TOPPING

In a medium-size bowl, stir together the flour, brown sugar, cinnamon, and ginger. Using a pastry cutter or 2 knives, cut in the butter until the mixture resembles coarse crumbs. Stir in the walnuts or pecans. Transfer the mixture to a pie pan. Bake in the 375°F (190°C) oven 10 to 12 minutes or until the walnuts are toasted and the topping is browned, stirring once. Cool completely. (The topping will become crisp as it cools.)

Makes about 1¼ cups.

✦ TIP

Be careful not to overbeat the filling or you will mix in too much air. The extra air will cause the filling to rise during baking, and then fall.

Chocolate Decadence

This marbled confection lives up to its name. It has a full-flavored chocolate-wafer crust and a filling made with white chocolate, unsweetened chocolate, and semisweet chocolate. It's outrageously delicious!

⅔ cup butter, melted
2¼ cups finely crushed chocolate wafers
2 tablespoons butter
2 (14-ounce) cans sweetened condensed milk
4 ounces white chocolate, coarsely chopped

8 ounces unsweetened chocolate, coarsely chopped
8 ounces semisweet chocolate, coarsely chopped
1 cup toasted coarsely chopped pecans
Whipped cream and raspberries, for garnish

Preheat the oven to 350°F (175°C). Lightly grease a 9-inch springform pan. For the crust, place the crushed chocolate wafers in a medium-size bowl and drizzle with the ⅔ cup melted butter. Using a fork, toss until the crumbs are coated with butter. Press the crumb mixture onto the bottom and about 2 inches up the side of the prepared pan; set aside.

In a small saucepan, melt 1 tablespoon of the butter over low heat. Stir in ½ cup of the sweetened condensed milk and the white chocolate. Cook, stirring frequently, until the white chocolate is melted. Remove from heat; set aside.

In a medium-size saucepan, melt the remaining 1 tablespoon butter over low heat. Stir in the remaining sweetened condensed milk, the unsweetened chocolate, and semisweet chocolate. Cook, stirring frequently, until the chocolate is melted. Stir in the pecans.

Pour the dark chocolate mixture into the crumb-lined pan. Using a tablespoon, carefully spoon the white chocolate mixture over the chocolate mixture in the pan, leaving space between spoonfuls of white chocolate mixture. Using a narrow metal spatula or the tip of a table knife, swirl the white chocolate mixture into the chocolate mixture, being careful not to disturb the crumb crust. Place the springform pan in a large shallow baking pan. (The baking pan will catch any spills that may occur.) Bake 30 to 35 minutes or until the edge is set but the chocolate appears moist in the center.

Cool on a wire rack 15 minutes. Run a narrow metal spatula around the edge of the pan to loosen the crust. Cool 30 minutes. Carefully remove the side of the springform pan. Cool completely. Cover and refrigerate until ready to serve.

To serve, set the dessert on a serving plate (do not remove the dessert from the bottom of the springform pan). Garnish the dessert with the whipped cream and raspberries. Cut into wedges. To store any remaining dessert, cover and refrigerate up to 2 days.

Makes 16 servings.

✦ TIP

A quick way to crush the wafers is to place them in a self-sealing plastic bag and break them up with a rolling pin.

Italian Ricotta Cheesecake with Amaretti-Almond Crust

"I've been intrigued by amaretti for a long time," explains Rosemary. "So, when I was looking for a new way to make cheesecake, I thought I'd crush some of these crisp cookies to put in the crust. The results were extraordinary! I've never tasted a cheesecake with such a great almond flavor."

1 cup finely crushed amaretti cookies
    (about 4²⁄₃ ounces) or
    dry macaroons
¾ cup very finely ground slivered
    almonds
¾ cup finely crushed zwieback
½ cup plus 2 tablespoons sugar
½ cup (1 stick) butter, melted
2 (15-ounce) containers ricotta
    cheese (about 3½ cups)

¼ cup amaretto
2 tablespoons all-purpose flour
1 teaspoon pure vanilla extract
3 eggs
½ cup golden raisins or miniature
    semisweet chocolate pieces
¼ cup finely chopped candied
    lemon peel
Edible flowers or fresh fruit,
    for garnish

Preheat the oven to 350°F (175°C). Lightly grease a 9-inch springform pan; set aside.

For the crust, stir together the crushed cookies, ground almonds, crushed zwieback, and the 2 tablespoons sugar in a medium-size bowl. Drizzle the melted butter over the mixture. Using a fork, toss until the crumbs are coated with butter. Reserve ¼ cup of the crumb mixture for garnishing the cheesecake. Press the remaining crumb mixture onto the bottom and about 2 inches up the side of the prepared pan; set aside.

For the filling, beat the ricotta cheese, the remaining ½ cup sugar, the amaretto, flour, and vanilla in a large bowl. Beat with an electric mixer at medium speed until well combined. Add the eggs and beat at low speed just until combined. Stir in the raisins or chocolate pieces and candied lemon peel. Pour the filling into the crust-lined pan.

Place the springform pan in a large shallow baking pan. (The baking pan will catch any spills that may occur.) Bake 50 to 60 minutes or until 2 to 3 inches of the outside edge of the filling appear set when gently shaken. Cool on a wire rack 15 minutes.

Run a narrow metal spatula around the edge of the pan to loosen the crust. Cool 30 minutes. Carefully remove the side of the springform pan. Cool completely. Sprinkle the reserved ¼ cup crumb mixture on top of the cheesecake. Cover and refrigerate at least 6 hours or overnight.

To serve, set the cheesecake on a serving plate (do not remove the cheesecake from the bottom of the springform pan). Garnish the bottom edge of the cheesecake with the edible flowers or fresh fruit. Cut into wedges. To store any remaining cheesecake, cover and refrigerate up to 2 days.

Makes 12 servings.

❧ TIP

Look for amaretti cookies in Italian specialty stores or gourmet food shops.

French Crunch Apple and Fig Pie

"*My daughter Kristin and I have experimented with lots of apples to find what we like best for pies. Our favorite pie is made with a combination of Granny Smith and Golden Delicious. This mix is so successful that Kristin won first place in the intermediate category at the Iowa State Fair with her two-crust apple pie,*" says Sharyl.

Butter Pastry for Single-Crust Pie
    (page 236)
5 cups peeled, cored, and thinly
    sliced pie apples
⅓ cup packed light brown sugar
1 to 2 tablespoons all-purpose flour,
    depending on juiciness of apples
½ teaspoon ground cinnamon
¼ teaspoon ground allspice
⅛ teaspoon ground nutmeg
1 cup chopped dried figs

PECAN-STREUSEL TOPPING
⅓ cup all-purpose flour
⅓ cup packed light brown sugar
⅛ teaspoon ground allspice
¼ cup (½ stick) cold butter
⅓ cup toasted chopped pecans or
    hazelnuts (filberts)

Preheat the oven to 375°F (190°C). Prepare the pastry and place in a 9-inch pie pan as directed in recipe; set aside.

In a large bowl, combine the apples, brown sugar, flour, cinnamon, allspice, and nutmeg. Toss gently to coat the apples.

Sprinkle the figs over the bottom of the pastry shell. Spoon the apple mixture over the figs. Prepare the Pecan-Streusel Topping. Sprinkle the topping over the apple mixture in the pastry shell.

Cover the edge of the pastry with 1-inch-wide strips of foil. Bake 25 minutes. Remove the foil strips. Bake 20 to 25 minutes or until the apples are tender and the topping is browned. If needed, cover the top of the pie loosely with foil the last 5 minutes to keep the topping from becoming too brown.

Makes 6 to 8 servings.

PECAN-STREUSEL TOPPING

In a medium-size bowl, stir together the flour, brown sugar, and allspice. Using a pastry cutter or 2 knives, cut in the butter until the mixture resembles coarse crumbs. Stir in the pecans or hazelnuts.

✦ TIP

The easiest way to chop figs is to snip them with kitchen scissors. Dip the blades into cold water often to keep the figs from sticking to the scissors.

Dried Cherry–Sour Cream Pie

Based on old-fashioned sour cream and raisin pie, this cherry-studded creation features a rich sour cream filling with plenty of citrus flavor as well as an orange-accented whipped cream topper.

Butter Pastry for Single-Crust Pie
   (page 236)
1 cup sugar
⅓ cup cornstarch
2½ cups whole milk
4 egg yolks, lightly beaten
1 tablespoon butter
1 teaspoon freshly grated orange peel
1 cup sour cream
1 cup dried tart red cherries

Whipped Cream Topping (see below)
¼ cup toasted slivered almonds,
   for garnish

WHIPPED CREAM TOPPING
1 cup whipping cream
2 tablespoons sifted powdered sugar
½ teaspoon freshly grated
   orange peel

Preheat the oven to 450°F (230°C). Prepare the pastry and place in a 9-inch pie pan as directed in recipe. Using a fork, generously prick the bottom and side of the pastry shell, being especially sure to prick where the bottom and side meet. Bake 11 to 13 minutes or until the pastry is golden brown and firm on the bottom and side. Cool in the pan on a wire rack.

Meanwhile, for the filling, stir together the sugar and cornstarch in a medium-size saucepan. Gradually stir in the milk. Cook over medium-high heat, stirring constantly, until the mixture thickens, about 5 minutes.

Gradually stir about 1 cup of the hot mixture into the egg yolks, then return yolks to the remaining hot mixture. Cook, stirring constantly, until bubbly. Cook, stirring constantly, 2 minutes. Remove from heat. Stir in the butter and orange peel. Let stand at room temperature 10 minutes to cool slightly.

Fold in the sour cream, then the dried cherries. Pour into the baked and cooled pastry shell. Cool on a wire rack 1 hour. Cover and refrigerate 4 to 6 hours.

To serve, prepare the Whipped Cream Topping. Spoon or pipe the topping onto the pie. Garnish with the toasted almonds.

Makes 6 to 8 servings.

WHIPPED CREAM TOPPING

In a chilled medium-size bowl, beat the whipping cream with an electric mixer at medium speed until the cream starts to thicken. Gradually beat in the powdered sugar. Continue beating until soft peaks form. Fold in the orange peel. Makes about 2 cups.

◆ TIP

For an extra-special look, decorate the edge of the pie shell with pastry cutouts. Instead of fluting the edge, trim the pastry to the edge of the pie pan. Roll out pastry scraps and use a knife or a small hors d'oeuvre cutter to cut out tiny decorative shapes, such as leaves, stars, or hearts. Then, brush the edge of the shell with water or milk and arrange the shapes around the edge. Gently press each shape to secure it in place.

Pear and Hazelnut Tart

A rich, yet easy, pat-in-the-pan pastry makes this company-special dessert one of our favorites. For a spectacular presentation, we serve wedges on individual dessert plates garnished with pansies.

Hazelnut Tart Pastry (see opposite)
4 firm-ripe pears
1 cup pear nectar or apple juice
2/3 cup sugar
1 tablespoon minced gingerroot
3/4 teaspoon pure vanilla extract
1/2 cup coarsely chopped hazelnuts
   (filberts)
1 tablespoon cornstarch
3 tablespoons cold water
1 tablespoon butter
Pansies or other edible flowers,
   for garnish

HAZELNUT TART PASTRY
1 cup hazelnuts (filberts)
1/4 cup packed light brown sugar
1 cup all-purpose flour
1/3 cup cold butter, cut into
   1-tablespoon-size pieces
1 egg yolk
2 tablespoons ice-cold water
1/2 teaspoon pure vanilla extract

Preheat the oven to 400°F (205°C). Prepare the Hazelnut Tart Pastry.

Lightly butter an 11-inch tart pan with a removable bottom. Using your fingers, firmly press the pastry dough evenly onto the bottom and up the sides of the prepared tart pan. Using a fork, prick the bottom and side of the pastry shell, being especially sure to prick where bottom and side meet. Bake 16 to 17 minutes or until the pastry is golden brown. Cool in the pan on a wire rack.

Meanwhile, peel, halve lengthwise, and core the pears. In a large skillet, combine the pear nectar or apple juice, sugar, gingerroot, and vanilla. Bring to a boil over medium heat; reduce heat. Carefully add the pear halves to the skillet, cover, and simmer 5 minutes or just until the pears are tender. (Test for doneness by inserting a wooden pick into the thickest part of a pear. The pears should still be slightly firm, but the wooden pick should penetrate easily.) Using a slotted spoon, transfer the pear halves, rounded side up, to a cutting board; set aside the nectar mixture in the skillet. Let the pear halves stand until cool enough to handle.

Cut each pear half crosswise, without cutting all the way through 1 side, into 8 slices. Keeping the pear halves intact, carefully transfer them to the baked and cooled pastry shell, arranging the pear halves with the narrow ends toward the center. Carefully pull apart the slices to fan the pear halves slightly. Sprinkle the 1/2 cup hazelnuts around the pear halves; set aside.

Bring the reserved nectar mixture to a boil over medium heat. Stir the cornstarch into the cold water until dissolved. Stir into the nectar mixture in skillet. Cook, stirring constantly, until the mixture thickens. Cook, stirring constantly, 2 minutes. Stir in the 1 tablespoon butter until melted. Remove from heat; let stand at room temperature 5 minutes to cool slightly. Spoon the nectar mixture over the pears and hazelnuts. Cover and refrigerate at least 2 hours or up to 1 day.

To serve, remove the side of the pan. Cut the tart into wedges, cutting between the pear halves. Garnish with the pansies or other edible flowers.

Makes 8 servings.

Hazelnut Tart Pastry

In a food processor, combine the hazelnuts and brown sugar. Cover and process until the nuts are very finely chopped.

In a medium-size bowl, combine the nut mixture and the flour. Using a pastry cutter or 2 knives, cut in the butter until the mixture resembles coarse crumbs. Make a well in the center. In a small bowl, combine the egg yolk, the ice water, and vanilla; add to the flour mixture. Using a fork, stir until the dry ingredients are moistened. Shape the dough into a ball.

✦ TIP

When choosing flowers to garnish foods, be sure to select edible blossoms that are free of chemical sprays. (Most floral-shop blossoms have been sprayed.) If you're a gardener, grow the flowers yourself. If not, you can find edible flowers in the produce section of larger supermarkets or restaurant- or produce-supply companies. Some common edible flowers are pansies, rose petals, marigolds, day lilies, geraniums, and chive blossoms.

Gingered Orange Soufflé with Kiwi Sauce

"To me a soufflé is the ultimate in elegant desserts," says Liz. "I especially like this light, nicely moist soufflé because its delicate orange and ginger flavor is exquisite with the fresh-tasting kiwi sauce."

¼ cup plus 2 tablespoons
   granulated sugar
5 eggs, separated
⅓ cup packed light brown sugar
3 tablespoons butter
¼ cup all-purpose flour
⅔ cup low-fat (1%) milk
⅔ cup fresh orange juice
2 tablespoons finely chopped
   crystallized ginger
2 teaspoons freshly grated
   orange peel

KIWI SAUCE
⅓ cup sugar
2 tablespoons cornstarch
1⅓ cups fresh orange juice
¼ teaspoon freshly grated
   orange peel
3 kiwi fruit, peeled, quartered
   lengthwise, and sliced
1 tablespoon butter

Preheat the oven to 400°F (205°C). Attach a foil collar to a 2-quart soufflé dish (see Tip, page 181). (The collar supports the soufflé as it puffs above the top of the dish during baking.) Generously butter the foil collar and the dish. Sprinkle the 2 tablespoons granulated sugar into the dish and swirl to coat the dish and the collar. Shake out the excess sugar.

In a medium-size bowl, beat the egg yolks and brown sugar with an electric mixer at medium speed 3 minutes; set aside.

In a medium-size saucepan, melt the butter over medium heat. Stir in the flour. Add the milk. Cook, stirring constantly, until the mixture thickens. Cook, stirring constantly, 1 minute. Remove from heat. Stir in the orange juice, crystallized ginger, and orange peel. Slowly stir the orange juice mixture into the egg yolk mixture.

Wash the mixer beaters well in hot soapy water; dry thoroughly. In a large bowl, beat the egg whites with the electric mixer at medium to high speed until frothy. Add the ¼ cup granulated sugar, 1 tablespoon at a time, and continue beating until the egg whites are stiff but not dry. Slowly pour the orange juice mixture over the beaten egg whites. Using a wooden spoon, gently fold together until the mixture is an even light yellow color. Gently spoon the mixture into the prepared soufflé dish.

Place the soufflé on the lowest rack of the oven. Reduce the oven temperature to 375°F (190°C). Bake 35 to 40 minutes or until a wooden skewer inserted off-center comes out clean.

While the soufflé is baking, prepare the Kiwi Sauce; cover and keep warm.

To serve, carefully remove the foil collar from the soufflé. Serve the soufflé immediately with the sauce.

Makes 8 servings.

KIWI SAUCE

In a small saucepan, stir together the sugar and cornstarch. Stir in the orange juice and orange peel. Cook over medium heat, stirring constantly, until the mixture thickens. Cook, stirring constantly, 2 minutes. Remove from heat. Stir in the kiwi fruit and the butter.

Makes about 2 cups.

✦ TIP

The way to get the most juice from oranges is to let them come to room temperature and roll each one under your palm before squeezing it.

Grand Marnier Butter Shortcakes with Berry Cream

Who says shortcake has to be round? Our square version is just as tender as any of the old-fashioned round ones. What's more, we've dressed it up with Grand Marnier liqueur and a thin layer of butter. Then, we've piled it high with both strawberries and blueberries and finished it off with a sumptuous raspberry cream topping.

Berry Cream (see opposite)
2 cups sliced strawberries
2 cups blueberries or blackberries
6 tablespoons granulated sugar
2 cups all-purpose flour
1 tablespoon baking powder
½ cup (1 stick) cold butter
1 egg, lightly beaten
¾ cup half-and-half or whole milk
2 teaspoons freshly grated
   orange peel
1½ teaspoons pure vanilla extract
½ cup finely chopped walnuts or
   pecans
1 egg white mixed with 1 tablespoon
   water, for glaze

1 tablespoon coarse sugar or
   granulated sugar
2 tablespoons Grand Marnier or
   other orange liqueur
2 tablespoons butter, at room
   temperature

BERRY CREAM
1½ cups fresh or thawed frozen
   unsweetened raspberries
6 tablespoons sugar
1 cup whipping cream
½ teaspoon pure vanilla extract

Preheat the oven to 450°F (230°C). Puree and strain the raspberry mixture for the Berry Cream. Cover and refrigerate while preparing the shortcake.

In a large bowl, toss together the strawberries, blueberries or blackberries, and 4 tablespoons of the granulated sugar; set aside. Lightly grease an 8-inch square baking pan; set aside.

For the shortcake, stir together the flour, remaining 2 tablespoons granulated sugar, and the baking powder in a medium-size bowl. Using a pastry cutter or 2 knives, cut in the ½ cup butter until the mixture resembles coarse crumbs. In a small bowl, combine the egg, half-and-half or whole milk, orange peel, and vanilla. Add to the flour mixture, stirring only until the dry ingredients are moistened. Stir in the walnuts or pecans.

Spread the dough in the prepared pan. Brush the top with the egg-white glaze; sprinkle with the 1 tablespoon coarse or granulated sugar. Bake 15 to 20 minutes or until a wooden pick inserted off-center comes out clean.

Cool in the pan on a wire rack 10 minutes. Remove from the pan. Meanwhile, beat the whipping cream mixture for the berry cream.

To serve, split the warm shortcake in half horizontally. Using 2 wide spatulas, carefully lift off the top layer. Place the bottom layer on a serving plate. Drizzle the Grand Marnier or other orange liqueur over the cut side of the bottom layer; spread with the 2 tablespoons butter.

Spoon about half of the fruit mixture over the bottom layer; carefully replace the top layer. Spoon the remaining fruit mixture over the top of the shortcake. Serve the shortcake warm with the whipped berry cream.

Makes 6 servings.

BERRY CREAM

In a food processor or blender, combine the raspberries and 4 tablespoons of the sugar. Cover and process until smooth. Set a sieve over a small bowl. Strain the raspberry mixture through the sieve; discard the seeds. Cover and refrigerate the raspberry mixture while preparing the shortcake.

Before serving, combine the whipping cream, the remaining 2 tablespoons sugar, and vanilla in a chilled medium-size bowl. Beat with an electric mixer at medium speed until soft peaks form. Add the chilled raspberry mixture. Continue beating until stiff peaks form.

Makes about 3 cups.

✦ TIP

Here's how to split the shortcake. Using a ruler to measure, insert 3 wooden picks on each side of the cake, halfway up the side. Then, with the wooden picks as a guide, slice the cake in half with a long-bladed serrated knife. Remove all of the wooden picks and lift off the top layer with 2 spatulas.

Butter Pastry for Single-Crust Pie

Making pastry is a balancing act. You have to measure the ingredients precisely. Too much flour or water will make the pastry tough. Extra shortening or butter will make it crumbly, not flaky.

1⅓ cups all-purpose flour
¼ teaspoon salt
¼ cup (½ stick) cold unsalted butter,
    cut into 1-tablespoon-size pieces

¼ cup vegetable shortening
4 to 5 tablespoons ice-cold water

In a medium-size bowl, stir together the flour and salt. Using a pastry cutter or 2 knives, cut in the butter and shortening until the mixture resembles coarse crumbs.

Sprinkle 1 tablespoon of the ice water over part of the flour mixture and toss together with a fork. Push the moistened mixture to one side of the bowl. Repeat, using enough of the remaining water, 1 tablespoon at a time, until all of the flour mixture is moistened. Form the dough into a ball. Wrap in plastic wrap and refrigerate 30 minutes before rolling.

Place the ball of dough on a lightly floured surface. Using the heel of your hand, flatten the ball of dough. Roll out the dough from the center to the edge into a 12-inch circle.

Line a 9-inch pie pan with the pastry. Trim the pastry to ½ inch beyond the edge of the pie pan. Fold under the extra pastry; flute the edge of the pastry. (To flute the pastry, press the dough with the thumb of one hand against the thumb and forefinger of the other hand.) Continue as directed in pie recipe.

Makes 1 (9-inch) pie crust.

⬥ TIP

To easily transfer the rolled-out pastry to the pie pan, lightly dust the top of the pastry circle with a little extra flour. Then, starting at the edge, carefully wrap the pastry around the rolling pin. Place the rolling pin on the rim of the pie pan. Then, unroll the pastry. Ease it into the pie pan without stretching it.

Summer Pear, Plum, and Crystallized Ginger Cobbler

"A cobbler, like this one, was my mother's signature dessert. We had both a pear and a plum tree in our backyard. Every summer, she made cobblers, and I would help. She was the first person to show me how to cut butter into flour using two table knives. I'd work on the butter and flour, while she got the fruit ready," reminisces Sandra.

⅓ cup all-purpose flour
¼ cup whole-wheat flour
¼ cup finely crushed graham
   crackers
2 tablespoons roasted and salted
   sunflower kernels
2 tablespoons light brown sugar
1½ teaspoons baking powder
¼ cup (½ stick) butter
⅔ cup apricot nectar or apple juice

¼ cup granulated sugar
1 tablespoon cornstarch
2 firm-ripe Bartlett pears, peeled,
   cored, and coarsely chopped
2 firm-ripe plums, pitted and sliced
1 tablespoon finely chopped
   crystallized ginger
¼ cup low-fat (1%) milk
Whipped cream or ice cream

Preheat the oven to 400°F (205°C). For the biscuit topping, stir together the all-purpose flour, whole-wheat flour, graham crackers, sunflower kernels, brown sugar, and baking powder in a medium-size bowl. Using a pastry cutter or 2 knives, cut in the butter until the mixture resembles coarse crumbs; set aside.

In a medium-size saucepan, stir together the apricot nectar or apple juice, granulated sugar, and cornstarch. Cook over medium heat, stirring constantly, until the mixture thickens. Cook, stirring constantly, 2 minutes. Stir in the pears, plums, and crystallized ginger. Cook, stirring occasionally, until bubbly. Reduce heat to low, cover, and keep hot.

Add the milk to the flour mixture, stirring only until the dry ingredients are moistened. Transfer the hot fruit mixture to a 1½-quart casserole dish. Immediately spoon the biscuit topping in 4 even mounds on top of the hot fruit mixture. Bake 18 to 20 minutes or until a wooden pick inserted off-center in a mound of biscuit topping comes out clean. Serve the cobbler warm with the whipped cream or ice cream.

Makes 4 servings.

✦ TIP

   The fruit mixture must be piping hot when you add the biscuit topping. This way, the topping will cook evenly and won't be doughy on the bottom.

Poached Pears with Crème Anglaise Fluff

Crème anglaise is a sauce we use frequently with fruits, cakes, soufflés, and even puddings. This rich, stirred custard is traditionally flavored with vanilla, but we've added raspberry liqueur to our version for a refreshingly fruity flavor that complements the pears. Then, we've folded in whipped cream for added body.

6 firm-ripe pears	1 cup half-and-half
4 cups water	3 tablespoons raspberry liqueur
2 cups sugar	1 teaspoon pure vanilla extract
1 teaspoon freshly grated lemon peel	½ cup whipping cream
2 egg yolks	

Peel the pears, leaving the stems intact. Inserting a long corer or a knife with a long thin blade into the blossom end of each pear, carefully core the pears.

To poach the pears, combine the water, 1½ cups of the sugar, and the lemon peel in a Dutch oven. Bring to a boil over high heat, stirring occasionally. Reduce heat to medium. Carefully stand the pears upright in the Dutch oven, cover, and simmer 15 to 20 minutes or just until the pears are tender. (Test for doneness by inserting a wooden pick or a small wooden skewer into the thickest part of a pear. The pear should still be slightly firm, but the wooden pick should penetrate easily.)

Using a slotted spoon, remove the pears from the Dutch oven and place them, standing upright, in a pie pan or shallow dish. Cover and refrigerate at least 2 hours or until chilled.

For the sauce, whisk the egg yolks in a medium-size heavy saucepan until mixed. Whisk in the remaining ½ cup sugar, 1 tablespoon at a time. In a small saucepan, heat the half-and-half over medium heat just until tiny bubbles form around the edge. Slowly stir the hot half-and-half into the egg yolk mixture. Cook over medium-low heat, stirring constantly with a wooden spoon, just until the mixture thickens enough to coat the wooden spoon. (The sauce should be thick enough to leave a smooth, creamy layer that clings to the surface of the wooden spoon.) Remove from heat.

Stir in the raspberry liqueur and vanilla. Pour into a small bowl and cover the surface with plastic wrap. Refrigerate at least 2 hours or until chilled.

To serve, beat the whipping cream in a chilled small bowl with an electric mixer at medium speed until soft peaks form. Gently fold the whipped cream into the chilled sauce. Place the pears on dessert plates. Spoon the sauce around the pears.

Makes 6 servings.

◆ TIP

If the pears you purchase are still firm, place the fruit in a paper bag, close the bag, and let the pears stand at room temperature for several days to ripen.

Poached Nectarine and Cherry Summer Compote

Come summertime, remember this spicy compote with its fresh-from-the-orchard flavor. With it, you can serve a satisfying dessert without turning on your oven.

1 cup water
⅓ cup sugar
4 inches stick cinnamon
2 teaspoons pure vanilla extract
3 firm-ripe nectarines, pitted and
   cut into eighths

2 cups fresh or thawed frozen pitted
   dark sweet cherries
Fresh mint sprigs, for garnish

In a medium-size saucepan, combine the water, sugar, stick cinnamon, and vanilla. Bring to a boil over high heat, stirring with a wooden spoon until the sugar is dissolved. Reduce heat and simmer 5 minutes.

Add the nectarines to the sugar mixture in the saucepan and return to a boil. Reduce heat, cover, and simmer 2 to 3 minutes or just until the nectarines are tender.

Transfer the nectarine mixture to a medium-size bowl. Stir in the fresh or frozen cherries. Cool slightly. Discard the stick cinnamon.

To serve, spoon the warm fruit mixture into dessert dishes. Garnish with the fresh mint. **Makes 4 to 6 servings.**

VARIATION

If you prefer, cover and refrigerate the fruit mixture at least 6 hours or overnight. Then, serve chilled.

Sweet Wine-Poached Figs à la Mode

The sweet, fruit flavor of the figs contrasts deliciously with the crisp texture and juiciness of the Asian pears in this sophisticated fruit sauce. Asian pears, also called Chinese or apple pears, are sold in Asian grocery stores and some supermarkets.

1¼ cups sweet white dessert wine
¼ cup cream sherry
2 tablespoons honey
1 tablespoon finely chopped
    crystallized ginger
1 teaspoon freshly grated lemon peel
1 (9-ounce) package dried Black
    Mission figs, halved lengthwise

2 medium-size Asian pears or tart
    apples, peeled and thinly sliced
    lengthwise
6 scoops French vanilla ice cream
1 tablespoon sliced almonds

In a medium-size saucepan, combine the white wine, cream sherry, honey, crystallized ginger, and lemon peel. Bring to a boil over high heat, stirring with a wooden spoon until the honey is dissolved. Reduce heat and simmer 5 minutes.

Add the figs to the wine mixture in the saucepan and return to a boil. Reduce heat, cover, and simmer 20 minutes. Stir in the Asian pears or apples. Cover and simmer 3 to 5 minutes longer or just until the pears are tender.

To serve, place the scoops of ice cream in dessert dishes. Spoon the warm fruit mixture over the ice cream. Sprinkle with the almonds.

Makes 6 servings.

VARIATION

If you prefer, replace the sweet dessert wine with ⅔ cup dry white wine, ½ cup water, and ⅓ cup sugar.

White Chocolate Bread Pudding with Mango Sauce

The mango sauce adds a tropical note to this glorious home-style pudding, made with white chocolate, half-and-half, and toasted French bread.

4 cups 1-inch cubes French bread
3 tablespoons butter, melted
6 egg yolks
1½ teaspoons pure vanilla extract
3 cups half-and-half
⅓ cup sugar
4 ounces white chocolate, coarsely
    chopped

MANGO SAUCE
2 ripe mangoes
⅓ cup sifted powdered sugar
1 tablespoon fresh orange juice
¼ teaspoon pure vanilla extract

Preheat the broiler. Arrange the bread cubes in a single layer on a large baking sheet. Drizzle the melted butter over the bread cubes; toss to coat the cubes. Broil 4 to 5 inches from the heat, stirring frequently, 3 to 4 minutes or until the bread cubes are golden brown. Set aside.

In a large bowl, use a wire whisk to beat together the egg yolks and vanilla; set aside. In a medium-size heavy saucepan, combine the half-and-half, sugar, and white chocolate. Cook over low heat, stirring frequently, until the white chocolate is melted. Using the whisk, gradually beat the white chocolate mixture into the egg yolk mixture. Stir in the toasted bread cubes. Let stand at room temperature 15 minutes.

Preheat the oven to 325°F (165°C). Pour the bread mixture into a 1½-quart casserole dish or soufflé dish. Bake 40 to 50 minutes or until a knife inserted off-center comes out clean. Cool on a wire rack 20 to 30 minutes.

Meanwhile, prepare the Mango Sauce. Serve the pudding warm with the sauce.

Makes 6 servings.

MANGO SAUCE

Peel, pit, and cut up the mangoes. In a food processor, combine the mangoes, powdered sugar, orange juice, and vanilla. Cover and process until smooth.

Makes about 1½ cups.

Buttery Chocolate Nut Cookies with Dark Chocolate Icing

These delicate cookies are rich and buttery with a wonderful pecan flavor. The chocolate glaze adds just the right note of bitter sweetness. To dress up the cookies, we imprinted them with a cookie stamp, but a flat-bottomed glass will work just as well.

2 ounces semisweet chocolate,
   coarsely chopped
1 cup (2 sticks) butter, at room
   temperature
½ cup sugar
2 egg yolks
½ teaspoon pure vanilla extract
2 cups all-purpose flour

¾ cup finely ground pecans
½ teaspoon baking powder

DARK CHOCOLATE ICING
⅓ cup whipping cream
2 teaspoons light corn syrup
3 ounces semisweet chocolate, finely
   chopped

In a small heavy saucepan, heat the chocolate over very low heat, stirring constantly, until the chocolate starts to melt. Remove from heat and stir until smooth. Set aside to cool.

In a large bowl, beat the butter with an electric mixer at medium speed 1 minute or until softened. Gradually beat in the sugar. Beat in the melted and cooled chocolate, the egg yolks, and vanilla. Stir in the flour, pecans, and baking powder. Cover and refrigerate 30 minutes.

Preheat the oven to 350°F (175°C). Shape the chilled dough into 1-inch balls. Place on ungreased baking sheets. Using a cookie stamp or a juice glass with a decorative bottom, press each ball until about ¼ inch thick.

Bake 10 to 12 minutes or until the edges of the cookies are firm. Quickly remove from baking sheet. Cool on a wire rack.

Prepare icing. Place waxed paper under wire rack for easy cleanup. Using a spoon, drizzle some of the icing over each cookie. Let the cookies stand on the wire racks until the icing is set.

Makes about 60 cookies.

DARK CHOCOLATE ICING

Combine the whipping cream and corn syrup in a small saucepan. Bring just to a boil over medium heat, stirring frequently. Reduce heat to low and cook, stirring frequently, 2 minutes. Remove from heat. Stir in the chocolate until the mixture is smooth.

✦ TIP

To grind the pecans use a nut grinder, coffee grinder, or food processor. If you plan to use an electric grinder or food processor, be sure to use quick on/off pulses so the nuts stay in tiny pieces rather than form a butter.

Lemon and Caramel-Walnut Florentines

Crisp and candylike, these butterscotch-flavored cookies are a little tricky to bake, but they're worth the extra care and attention. Be sure to bake only one sheet of cookies (about six) at a time.

⅓ cup butter
⅓ cup low-fat (1%) milk
¼ cup packed light brown sugar
2 tablespoons dark corn syrup
1 cup toasted chopped walnuts

⅓ cup finely chopped candied
  lemon peel
½ cup all-purpose flour
½ cup miniature semisweet
  chocolate pieces

Grease and flour a large baking sheet; set aside. (Be sure to grease and flour the baking sheet for each batch of cookies.) Preheat the oven to 350°F (175°C).

In a medium-size saucepan, combine the butter, milk, brown sugar, and dark corn syrup. Bring to a full boil, stirring occasionally. Remove from heat. Stir in the walnuts and candied lemon peel. Stir in the flour.

Drop the walnut mixture by slightly rounded tablespoons at least 3 inches apart onto the prepared baking sheet. Using the back of a spoon, spread each cookie into a 3-inch circle.

Bake 10 to 11 minutes or until the edges of the cookies are lightly browned. Quickly sprinkle each cookie with about 1 teaspoon of the chocolate pieces. Cool the cookies on the baking sheet 1 minute; carefully transfer to waxed paper. Using a narrow metal spatula, spread the chocolate pieces slightly. Cool the cookies completely.

Makes about 18 cookies.

⬥ TIP

Cool the cookies on the baking sheet only 1 minute or they may be difficult to remove. If they stick, return to the oven just long enough to heat slightly.

Honey-Ginger Biscotti

Rosemary grew up with biscotti. "When I went with my grandmother to her local Italian bakery, she would buy me a biscotti as a special treat. Then, I would take it home to enjoy with a large glass of milk," Rosemary remembers. "It was always an anise-flavored one. If fact, I didn't know biscotti came in other flavors or that they could be made from scratch until I started shopping and cooking for myself. Since then, I've tasted dozens of different biscotti, and this honey, pecan, and ginger version is a real winner."

½ cup (1 stick) butter
2 eggs
⅓ cup packed light brown sugar
⅓ cup honey
1 teaspoon pure vanilla extract
2½ cups all-purpose flour

2 teaspoons baking powder
2 teaspoons ground ginger
¾ cup toasted very finely chopped pecans
½ cup very finely chopped crystallized ginger

Preheat the oven to 325°F (165°C). In a large bowl, beat the butter with an electric mixer at medium speed until light and fluffy. Add the eggs, brown sugar, honey, and vanilla. Beat until smooth and creamy.

In a small bowl, stir together the flour, baking powder, and ground ginger. Add to the honey mixture and beat until combined. Stir in the pecans and crystallized ginger.

Lightly grease a baking sheet. Divide the dough in half. Shape each half into a log about 10 inches long and 1½ inches wide. Place the logs about 3 inches apart on the prepared baking sheet. Bake 35 minutes or until the logs are set and light brown on top. Cool the logs on the baking sheet 30 minutes.

Carefully cut the logs diagonally into ½-inch-thick slices. Place the slices, flat side down, on 2 lightly greased baking sheets. Bake 5 to 7 minutes or until the bottoms are light golden brown. Turn the slices over and bake 3 to 5 minutes or until the bottoms are light golden brown. Remove the biscotti to wire racks; cool completely.

To store the biscotti, place them in a tightly covered container at room temperature.
Makes about 30 biscotti.

✦ TIP
For best flavor and texture, be sure to make these twice-baked slices—and other cookies—with real butter.

Strawberry and Orange Sherbet

Sherbet, sorbet, ice—what's the difference? Over the years, these terms have become confused. This recipe is a classic sherbet because it includes both cream and fruit juice. Traditional sorbets and ices, however, are made only with fruit juice. No matter what you call it, this tantalizing refresher has a wonderful creamy texture that's similar to soft-serve ice cream.

1¼ cups sugar
1 envelope unflavored gelatin
4 cups fresh or frozen halved
   strawberries
2 cups fresh orange juice

2 teaspoons freshly grated
   orange peel
1 cup whipping cream
¼ cup orange liqueur

In a large saucepan, stir together the sugar and unflavored gelatin; set aside.

In a food processor, combine 2 cups of the strawberries and ¼ cup of the orange juice. Cover and process until smooth. Set a sieve over a small bowl. Strain the strawberry mixture through the sieve; discard the seeds. Stir the strawberry mixture into the sugar mixture. Repeat with the remaining 2 cups strawberries and another ¼ cup of the orange juice.

Stir the remaining 1½ cups orange juice and the orange peel into the sugar mixture in the saucepan. Cook over medium heat, stirring constantly, until the sugar and gelatin dissolve. Remove from heat; let stand at room temperature 15 minutes to cool slightly. Stir in the whipping cream and orange liqueur.

Pour into the freezer can of a 4- to 5-quart ice-cream freezer. Freeze and ripen according to the manufacturer's directions.

Makes 12 servings.

✦ TIP

To keep the orange peel from tasting bitter, grate only the orange part of the peel and avoid the white part.

Frozen Vanilla Custard with Triple Berry Sauce

"In my teens, long before I'd ever heard of 'frozen custard,' I created a recipe for cooked ice cream," recalls Sharyl. "What spurred me to experiment was that my dad was diagnosed as lactose intolerant and could no longer eat the uncooked homemade ice cream my family enjoyed. Over several months, I taste-tested my rich ice cream to perfection and it became a family favorite—all except for the time I scorched a batch and my ever-thrifty mother insisted we had to eat all of it before I could make another."

10 egg yolks
2 cups sugar
8 inches stick cinnamon, broken
   into pieces
2 whole nutmeg seeds, broken into
   pieces
4 cups half-and-half
3 cups whipping cream
3 tablespoons pure vanilla extract
Triple Berry Sauce (see opposite)
   (optional)

TRIPLE BERRY SAUCE
⅔ cup sugar
3 tablespoons cornstarch
3 cups cranberry juice cocktail
1 teaspoon pure vanilla extract
1½ cups fresh or thawed frozen
   raspberries
1½ cups fresh or thawed frozen
   blackberries

In a large saucepan, whisk the egg yolks until mixed. Whisk in the sugar, ¼ cup at a time; set aside. Place the broken cinnamon and nutmeg in the center of a 6-inch square of several layers of 100 percent cotton cheesecloth; bring the cheesecloth up around the spices. Using cotton string, tie the cheesecloth to form a spice bag.

In a medium-size saucepan, combine the spice bag, half-and-half, and 1 cup of the whipping cream. Cook over medium heat, stirring frequently, just until tiny bubbles form around the edge. Reduce heat to low and cook, stirring frequently, 10 minutes. Remove the spice bag; set aside.

Gradually stir the hot half-and-half mixture into the egg yolk mixture. Cook over medium-low heat, stirring constantly with a wooden spoon, just until the mixture thickens enough to coat the wooden spoon. (The mixture should be thick enough to leave a smooth, creamy layer that clings to the surface of the wooden spoon.) Remove from heat. Stir in the vanilla.

Pour into a large bowl; add the reserved spice bag. Cover the surface of the mixture with plastic wrap. Refrigerate at least 4 hours or until chilled. Discard the spice bag.

In a chilled large bowl, beat the remaining 2 cups whipping cream with an electric mixer at medium speed until soft peaks form. Gently fold the whipped cream into the chilled half-and-half mixture.

Spoon into the freezer can of a 4- to 5-quart ice-cream freezer. Freeze and ripen according to the manufacturer's directions.

Meanwhile, if desired, prepare the Triple Berry Sauce. Serve the sauce with the ice cream.
Makes 16 to 18 servings.

Triple Berry Sauce

In a medium-size saucepan, stir together the sugar and cornstarch. Stir in the cranberry juice cocktail. Cook over medium heat, stirring constantly, until the mixture thickens. Cook, stirring constantly, 2 minutes. Stir in the vanilla.

Pour into a medium-size bowl and cover the surface with plastic wrap. Refrigerate at least 2 hours or until chilled. Before serving, stir in the raspberries and blackberries.

Makes about 5 cups.

◆ TIP

Use the flat side of a meat mallet or the bottom of a heavy skillet to break the stick cinnamon and whole nutmeg into pieces.

MENUS TO CELEBRATE THE SEASONS

Preparing a dish that looks and tastes superb is one thing, but pulling off an exceptional menu can be quite another. To help you create pleasing combinations of full-flavored dishes, we've assembled some of our favorite recipes from throughout this book into sixteen glamorous, company-pleasing meals.

In putting our heads together to come up with the ideas, we discovered that many of our most successful meals combine ingredients that are in season, such as asparagus and morel mushrooms in spring or butternut squash and garden-ripe tomatoes in early fall. Also, our most memorable menus usually are prepared to celebrate specific events connected with the seasons, such as a spring graduation or a winter holiday open house. So we organized these meals the same way—by season and occasion.

When the warm breezes of spring and early vegetables from the garden put you in the mood to celebrate, host a champagne breakfast buffet or a family gathering for Mother's Day or Father's Day. As the summer sun climbs higher and farmers' markets sprout up everywhere, think about a casual barbecue or outdoor cocktail party. Come fall, take advantage of the cooler temperatures and the harvest crops to prepare everything from a Southwestern supper to a gourmet Thanksgiving dinner. And, in winter, warm hearts as well as please palates with a dazzling holiday dinner or a cozy griddle cake brunch.

Whenever you've penciled in hosting a party on your calendar, come back to these extraordinary menus. These imaginative ideas can help you plan a tantalizing feast to match no other.

Spring Menu 1

CONTINENTAL-STYLE CHAMPAGNE BREAKFAST
for 12

On a beautiful spring morning, what could be more fun than having family or friends over for a leisurely breakfast buffet. Start the celebration with a champagne toast in the form of mimosas. Just mix together equal parts of champagne and orange juice. Be sure to serve the mimosas icy cold, but not over ice.

   The homemade breads and fresh fruit compote can be made ahead, so you can serve twelve people with a minimum of fuss. To set up the buffet table, chill the cartons of yogurt in a very large decorative bowl filled with ice, arrange the breads on platters or in baskets, and place the fruit in an eye-catching glass bowl so guests can serve themselves. Then, except for occasionally replenishing bowls and platters, you can leave the kitchen behind and enjoy the party.

Mimosas (see above) and orange juice

Assorted fruit-flavored yogurt
Banana-Nut Gingerbread Loaf (page 204)
Brandied Cherry Loaf (page 205)
Butter-Almond Coffee Cake (page 202)
Gingered Fig and Oatmeal Muffins (page 207)
Fresh fruit bowl

Coffee or tea

Spring Menu 2

SPRINGTIME CELEBRATION
for 4

This inspired menu for four is the ultimate in formal elegance. It showcases morel mushrooms and rhubarb, two of spring's special gifts. You'll find the full-flavored mushroom, bell pepper, and sun-dried tomato sauce is an exquisite counterpoint for the succulent beef tenderloin.

Take a few moments to make this meal look as good as it tastes. For a beautiful presentation, give the steamed green beans a party flair by tying several beans together with a long strip of lemon peel, garnish the spinach salad with a few edible flowers, and scoop the sherbet into crystal goblets. Finally, set the table with your best dishes and glassware, and add a dramatic centerpiece of fresh lilies or tulips.

Crab claws and cocktail sauce
Fresh spinach salad

Iowa Beef Tenderloin Steaks with Morel, Ricotta, and Red Bell Pepper Sauce (page 114)
Wild rice
Steamed green beans
Red Wine

Strawberry and Orange Sherbet (page 245)
Sugar cookies
Coffee or tea

Spring Menu 3

FAMILY GATHERING
for 6

Sometimes simple foods are the most welcome. Take this delicious and satisfying menu for example. It features grilled lamb chops, creamed sugar snap peas, buttered new potatoes, and luscious shortcake with fresh berries. What a resplendent and glorious tribute to spring!

Turn this meal into a family affair. Make everything for the shortcake ahead. Then, when everyone arrives, let them help you put the rest of the dishes together. This way, all the fun and socializing will be in the kitchen, and you won't miss a minute of it.

Assorted cheeses and crackers

Lamb chops on the grill
Braised Springtime Peas and Pods in Crème Fraîche (page 78)
Buttered new potatoes
Garlic toast
Lemonade or iced tea

Grand Marnier Butter Shortcakes with Berry Cream (page 234)
Coffee or tea

Spring Menu 4

AFTER-WORK DINNER
for 4

When you're at work all day and everyone comes home famished, make it easy on yourself with a no-hassle meal. This carefree menu offers both impressive food and convenience, thanks to advance preparation and a little help from the deli and bakery.

Find some time the evening before to clean the asparagus and cook the fruit compote, then refrigerate them. On your way home from work, stop by the supermarket and pick up cole slaw from the delicatessen and a bag of bakery rolls.

Now, all that remains is oven-roasting the asparagus and sautéing the chicken breasts. For perfect timing, start cooking the chicken after the asparagus has baked about 15 minutes.

For four servings, you'll need 4 boneless skinless chicken breast halves (about 1 pound total). Rinse the chicken pieces and pat dry with paper towels. In a large skillet, heat 1 tablespoon cooking oil over medium-high heat. Add the chicken and cook 3 minutes on each side or until browned on both sides. There's nothing left to do but announce "Dinner is ready!"

Sautéed chicken breasts (see above)
Oven-Roasted Asparagus with Pine Nut Dressing (page 68)
Coleslaw
Whole-wheat dinner rolls
Iced tea

Poached Nectarine and Cherry Summer Compote (page 239)
Coffee or tea

Summer Menu 1

CARIBBEAN DINNER ON THE DECK
for 4

Break up the doldrums of a long, hot summer by hosting a Caribbean dinner party. This tempting menu has easy-to-follow recipes with plenty of flavor punch. Create a festive island atmosphere with patio torches and tablecloths with bold, colorful prints. To create a more authentic ambiance, play reggae as background music. The lively atmosphere and first-rate food will be a big hit with all your guests.

Start things off with a cool and refreshing tropical fruit appetizer. Papaya, mango, banana, carambola (star fruit), and pineapple are all good choices. Then, move on to a crisp salad, the lip smackin' ribs, and the pepper and cilantro–seasoned squash. Wind up the meal with a spectacular sundae bar that includes all the toppings.

To put the meal together, prepare the jerk seasoning the day before the party. Rub it on the ribs and place them in the refrigerator to marinate. About three hours before the festivities start, soak the hickory chunks and start grilling the ribs. Then, prepare the stuffed chayote, arrange the tropical fruit on ti leaves, and stir up the punch.

Assorted fresh tropical fruit (see above) with fruit yogurt for dipping
Rum punch

Tossed green salad

Smoked Jamaican Jerk Pork Ribs (page 130)
Spicy Stuffed Chayote (page 73)
Beer or lemonade

Make-your-own-sundae bar
Coffee or tea

Summer Menu 2

ALFRESCO COCKTAIL PARTY
for 12

When it comes to entertaining a large crowd, an outdoor cocktail party is ideal. Not only is it a fun way to entertain, it also gives everyone more room to spread out. This splendid menu of savory and sweet tidbits is especially suited for the occasion because all the food can be prepared in advance and served buffet style. Stage your gathering on a balcony, deck, or patio or in the backyard with the sunset as a backdrop. The breathtaking view, cool evening breeze, and wonderful food will go a long way toward ensuring everyone has a great time.

Start a day or two before the party and prepare all the food. Shortly before party time, arrange everything on a buffet table in a spot out of the main traffic area. Serve the beverages from a separate table to avoid congestion around the buffet table.

Caribbean Sweet Cheese and Papaya Dip with Fresh Fruit (page 13)
Mixed nuts
Salsa with tortilla chips
Roasted Red Pepper Dip with Crudités (page 7)
Breadsticks and assorted crackers
Crostini with Smoked Trout and Camembert (page 11)
Buttery Chocolate Nut Cookies with Dark Chocolate Icing (page 242)
Mixed drinks, wine spritzers, and soft drinks

Summer Menu 3

Star-Spangled Fourth of July
for 6

For surefire Fourth of July fun, select this menu for your backyard celebration. It's a brand-new flavor twist on the old-fashioned cookout. Besides the tantalizing Grilled Rib-Eye Steaks with Firecracker Barbecue Butter, the feast features the very best of summer ingredients—new potatoes in a walnut vinaigrette, a heaping platter of fresh fruits, and an impossible-to-refuse homemade vanilla ice cream crowned with a raspberry-and-blackberry sauce.

A day ahead, make and refrigerate the salad and the barbecue butter as well as the custard and sauce for the ice cream. The next morning, prepare the beans, vegetable dippers, and fruit platter. Then, freeze the ice cream. Once the fun begins, all that's left to do is grill the steaks.

Assorted chips and vegetable dippers
Dips and spreads

Grilled Rib Eye Steaks with Firecracker Barbecue Butter (page 121)
New Potato-Asparagus Salad with Walnut Vinaigrette (page 48)
Sicilian Fava Beans in Plum Tomato–Fennel Sauce (page 186)
Summer fruit platter
Assorted small dinner rolls
Beer and soft drinks

Frozen Vanilla Custard with Triple Berry Sauce (page 246)
Iced tea or coffee

Summer Menu 4

SUMMER'S LAST STAND
for 6

If you love to entertain, any reason to have a party—even the end of summer—is a good one. Celebrate in grand fashion with this exceptionally easy and mouth-watering meal. The intriguing entree is a whole fish baked on a ratatouille-style vegetable combination that features bell pepper, eggplant, tomatoes, zucchini, yellow summer squash, and herbs. This recipe is amazingly effortless and the results are extraordinarily delicious. End the meal with a spectacular flourish by serving the delicate poached pears with the incredible custard sauce.

To simplify the menu, prepare and chill the pears the day before and stop by the bakery or grocery store for the sourdough bread.

Tossed salad greens

Whole Baked Tilefish with Garden Fresh Ratatouille (page 145)
Crusty sourdough bread with butter curls
White wine or iced tea

Poached Pears with Crème Anglaise Fluff (page 238)
Coffee or tea

Autumn Menu 1

SIZZLING SOUTHWESTERN SUPPER
for 6

Enjoy this hearty southwestern ragoût of colorful vegetables on a chilly autumn day. Your guests will be intrigued by its tantalizing aroma as they walk in the door.

The morning of the party, bake the brownies. Also, make the salsa and tortilla chips. About two hours before supper, start cooking the stew. While the pork simmers, prepare the corn bread and get it in the oven. Next, chop the vegetables for the ragoût. This way it will be ready at about the same time as the corn bread. When your guests arrive, mix up sassy margaritas to wash down the spicy salsa and chips. For dessert, stir Kahlúa or another coffee-flavored liqueur into mugs of hot strong coffee. Top them with whipped cream and a sprinkling of ground cinnamon. Then, serve the café Kahlúa with a heaping plate of brownies. Olé!

Zesty Jicama Salsa with Crispy Tortilla Chips (page 2)
Margaritas

Butternut Squash and Pork Ragoût with Rich Blue Corn Bread (page 20)
Mexican beer

Brownies
Café Kahlúa (see above)

Autumn Menu 2

ITALIAN-STYLE VEGETARIAN DINNER
for 4

For a tantalizing meal that will have your guests showering you with compliments, try this satisfying vegetarian menu. From the first refreshing bite of salad to the last sensational sip of espresso, the memory of this sumptuous meal is one you and your guests will long treasure.

You'll find these elegant recipes are easy to prepare and allow you to do much of the work beforehand. Early in the day, scoop the *gelato* (a rich frozen custard ice cream) into dessert dishes and place them in the freezer. Then, prepare and chill the salad greens. About an hour before dinner, make the batter rolls. After the guests arrive, prepare the entree. Finally, sit back and savor the evening.

Tossed vegetable salad

Cheese Tortellini with Artichoke Hearts and Cannellini Beans (page 172)
Herbed Ricotta Batter Rolls with Pine Nuts (page 199)
Red wine

Gelato
Italian espresso

Autumn Menu 3

CANDLELIGHT GOURMET THANKSGIVING
for 4

Thanksgiving is more than just a holiday. It's the last festival of fall and what better way to make best friends feel very special than to invite them to a spectacular dinner party. Your reputation as a fabulous cook is assured when you serve this impressive pheasant with all the trimmings.

The menu for this sophisticated, sit-down dinner showcases an appealing array of flavors from the vermouth-accented soup, to the Italian-inspired pheasant, to the hazelnut-studded tart.

Make the tart well in advance and chill it thoroughly. Next, assemble the ingredients for the pheasant and the soup so they'll be ready to go as you start cooking. About an hour before serving, put the pheasant in the oven to bake and begin working on the sauce and the soup. Just before serving, stir the lobster, watercress, and saffron into the soup. For dessert, make a grand entrance by arranging the tart on an elegant platter and garnishing it with rose petals.

Lobster-in-the-Shell Watercress Soup (page 30)

Smoked Pheasant with Onion and Caper Sauce (page 110)
Linguine
Parsley-buttered baby carrots
Baguette
White wine and sparkling water

Pear and Hazelnut Tart (page 230)
Cappuccino

Autumn Menu 4

FISH FEAST FOR FRIENDS
for 6

A three-course dinner for six is a cinch with this very easy yet marvelous menu. It's a relaxed casual meal designed for a delightful evening of fine food and good friends.

Avoid hectic last-minute hassle by making the Honey and Sherry Yogurt Dressing and tearing the spinach the day before the party. The next day, go to your favorite delicatessen or supermarket and pick up the soup, dinner rolls, and dessert. Because there's only minor last-minute preparation, you're free to spend time with your guests.

Cheese soup
Breadsticks

Braised Shark Steaks with Chipotle Chile Sauce (page 149)
Fruit-Tossed Spinach Salad with Honey and Sherry Yogurt Dressing (page 44)
Rye dinner rolls
Dark beer

Chocolate cake

Winter Menu 1

GREAT BEGINNINGS AND GRAND FINALES
for 16

For the coldest months of the year, plan an appetizer and dessert buffet with a tableful of fabulous food accented by cozy ambiance and cheery hospitality. Whether you're hosting a December holiday open house, a New Year's Day celebration, or a Valentine's Day party, this magnificent menu and good friends are made for each other.

Although the list of foods may look formidable, if you start just a few days ahead, you can pull everything off without a hitch. By fixing one or two dishes at a time, you can make most of the food before the day of the party. This way, all that will be left to do is set the table, put out the food, and wait for your guests to ring the doorbell.

Brandied Gorgonzola Cheese Ball (page 3)
Apple slices and assorted crackers
Portobello Mushroom & Spinach Strudel (page 14)
Bourbon-Pecan Country Pâté (page 10)
Dark rye bread
Assorted cocktail nuts
Cooked shrimp and cocktail sauce
Mixed drinks and sparkling water

Chocolate Decadence (page 224)
Pecan Torte with Black Raspberry Filling and Classic Buttercream (page 212)
Lemon and Caramel-Walnut Florentines (page 243)
Dried apricots, dates, figs
Coffee or tea

Winter Menu 2

DAZZLING YULETIME DINNER
for 4

For a gloriously elegant meal, remember this enchanting chicken menu. Hearty and full of flavor, it's especially well suited for a cold winter evening. The star of the dinner is Four Cheese– and Chanterelle Mushroom–Stuffed Chicken. If you've never stuffed chicken breasts under the skin before, give it a try. It's easy and the gourmet-quality results are impressive.

For a sweet conclusion to the festivities, serve purchased pound cake with café Bénédictine. For each serving of this enticing coffee drink, simply stir 2 tablespoons of Bénédictine (a Cognac-based liqueur) and 2 tablespoons of half-and-half or light cream into a half-cup of strong coffee.

Fresh spinach salad

Four Cheese– and Chanterelle Mushroom–Stuffed Chicken (page 86)
Grand Marnier–Glazed Carrots and Spiced Grapes (page 71)
Crusty French dinner rolls
White wine

Chocolate pound cake with whipped cream
Café Bénédictine (see above)

Winter Menu 3

GRIDDLE CAKES BRUNCH
for 4

Treat family or friends to this appetizing brunch without having to rise at the crack of dawn to cook. With the help of these delightful make-ahead recipes, much of the preparation is done the evening before, freeing you to enjoy the brunch as if you were a guest.

Start by making and chilling the batter for the waffles. Next, assemble the apricot-walnut butter and refrigerate it. Then, prepare the Bloody Marys and fruit cups and let them stand in the refrigerator so the flavors have a chance to blend. For the fruit cups, combine winter fruits, such as oranges, grapefruit, and tangerines. Just before serving, slice in some banana.

Bloody Marys and tomato juice

Cracked-Wheat Yeast Waffles with Apricot-Walnut Butter (page 200)
Scrambled eggs with ham

Winter fruit cups
Coffee or tea

Winter Menu 4

'TIS THE SEASON
for 8

Razzle-dazzle your guests with this festive holiday party without spending days cooking. The keys to this exquisite dinner are preplanning and purchasing a bakery cheesecake and dinner rolls to round out the meal.

The day before the party, prepare the soup and assemble the potatoes. Refrigerate everything overnight. This way, the next day, you can serve the soup chilled, bake the potatoes along with the goose, and take just a few minutes to cook the broccoli.

About 3 hours before your guests arrive, put a 10- to 12-pound goose in a 350°F oven to roast for 3 to 3½ hours or until juices run clear and a leg moves easily in its socket. Add the potatoes to bake the last 30 minutes.

Roasted Eggplant and Tomato Soup (page 40)

Roast goose (see above)
Garlicky Potato, Fennel, and Carrot au Gratin (page 80)
Buttered broccoli spears
Assorted dinner rolls
Wine

Cheesecake
Coffee

Metric Conversion Charts

COMPARISON TO METRIC MEASURE				
When You Know	Symbol	Multiply By	To Find	Symbol
teaspoons	tsp	5.0	milliliters	ml
tablespoons	tbsp	15.0	milliliters	ml
fluid ounces	fl. oz.	30.0	milliliters	ml
cups	c	0.24	liters	1
pints	pt.	0.47	liters	1
quarts	qt.	0.95	liters	1
ounces	oz.	28.0	grams	g
pounds	lb.	0.45	kilograms	kg
Fahrenheit	F	5/9 (after subtracting 32)	Celsius	C

Fahrenheit to Celsius	
F	C
200–205	95
220–225	105
245–250	120
275	135
300–305	150
325–330	165
345–350	175
370–375	190
400–405	205
425–430	220
445–450	230
470–475	245
500	260

Liquid Measure to Liters		
1/4 cup	=	0.06 liters
1/2 cup	=	0.12 liters
3/4 cup	=	0.18 liters
1 cup	=	0.24 liters
1-1/4 cups	=	0.3 liters
1-1/2 cups	=	0.36 liters
2 cups	=	0.48 liters
2-1/2 cups	=	0.6 liters
3 cups	=	0.72 liters
3-1/2 cups	=	0.84 liters
4 cups	=	0.96 liters
4-1/2 cups	=	1.08 liters
5 cups	=	1.2 liters
5-1/2 cups	=	1.32 liters

Liquid Measure to Milliliters		
1/4 teaspoon	=	1.25 milliliters
1/2 teaspoon	=	2.5 milliliters
3/4 teaspoon	=	3.75 milliliters
1 teaspoon	=	5.0 milliliters
1-1/4 teaspoons	=	6.25 milliliters
1-1/2 teaspoons	=	7.5 milliliters
1-3/4 teaspoons	=	8.75 milliliters
2 teaspoons	=	10.0 milliliters
1 tablespoon	=	15.0 milliliters
2 tablespoons	=	30.0 milliliters

INDEX

About the Authors

(From left to right) Liz Woolever, Sharyl Heiken, Rosemary Hutchinson, and Sandra Granseth

Sandra Granseth, Sharyl Heiken, Rosemary Hutchinson, and Liz Woolever are professional home economists, food writers, and co-owners of Spectrum Communication Services, Inc., a food editorial service company established in 1992.

The four of them have extensive food backgrounds, including more than twenty years each as a food editor with Better Homes and Gardens® Book Group of Meredith Corporation. Plus, they have taught college food classes and adult education classes, appeared on radio and television, and conducted workshops and food demonstrations. They all live in Iowa—Sandra, Sharyl, and Liz in Des Moines and Rosemary in Ankeny.